the
homeschooler's guide

to

Portfolios
and Transcripts

the homeschooler's guide

to
Portfolios
and Transcripts

Loretta Heuer, M.Ed.

IDG Books Worldwide, Inc.
An International Data Group Company

Foster City, CA • Chicago, IL • Indianapolis, IN • New York, NY

First Edition

IDG Books Worldwide, Inc.
An International Data Group Company
919 E. Hillsdale Boulevard
Suite 400
Foster City, CA 94404

An Arco Book

For general information on IDG Books Worldwide's books in the U.S., please call our Consumer Customer Service department at 800-762-2974. For reseller information, including discounts and premium sales, please call our Reseller Customer Service department at 800-434-3422.

ISBN: 0-02-863738-0

Manufactured in the United States of America
10 9 8 7 6 5 4 3 2 1

Table of Contents

About the Author

Loretta Heuer, M.Ed., is a former classroom teacher who has homeschooled her two sons from preschool through high school. Long a user of portfolios and other alternative assessment techniques, Loretta has developed a variety of high school transcript models to describe non-traditional learning to employers and college admissions officers.

As part of her role as a home-based educator, Loretta has been the legislative liaison and electronic information coordinator for the Massachusetts Home Learning Association. She has written and spoken about the portfolio process for local, state, and national audiences, and has been a guest lecturer on home learning in graduate-level education courses. She has been a mathematics consultant to urban, suburban, and rural elementary schools, developing and implementing professional development programs and curriculum assessment projects.

Loretta's flexible approach to homeschooling is reflected in her sons' educational plans, which combined school coursework, structured home activities, and unschooling practices to best match each boy's needs. Her older son, Tad, recently received his Masters degree in public policy from Brown University and is doing postgraduate work at the London School of Economics. Jed, her younger son, has strong interests in the visual and performing arts and has attended both high school and college art courses in addition to his home education program. He was accepted to the advertising/graphics desgin program at Parsons, Pratt, and the School of Visual Arts.

Acknowledgments

With thanks to my sons, Tad and Jed, who were not only my students but also my co-learners and mentors and to my husband Bill, my partner in this lifestyle for over twenty years. To innovative educators Bev McCloskey and Pat Thatcher-Hill who spurred me on from the beginning; to Joe Schechtman who encouraged me to re-engineer high school transcripts; to Cafi Cohen who has supported college-bound homeschoolers through her writing, workshops, and website; and to Pat Farenga and Susannah Scheffer of *Growing Without Schooling* magazine/Holt Associates who have kept John Holt's vision of dynamic, eclectic learning alive and well.

Foreword

Are you are trying to organize a middle school portfolio? Are you struggling to create a high school transcript for your college application? Are you wondering how to handle a meeting with the principal to discuss the past year's work? Or, are you just starting out and wondering how you can best track and display your child's progress?

The Homeschooler's Guide to Portfolios and Transcripts has been designed by a practicing homeschooler to help you answer these kinds of questions. Throughout the book I will be sharing many of the techniques I developed for my own homeschooled sons, which are the same techniques I present at homeschool workshops now that my boys are grown.

USING TRANSCRIPTS AND PORTFOLIOS TO DISPLAY LEARNING

During the process of creating homeschool portfolios and transcripts, you will learn to answer questions not only for school officials, employers, and college admission officers. You will answer important questions for yourself. You will discover that portfolios and transcripts aren't dry documents that simply fulfill accountability requirements or verify learning. Instead they're powerful and dynamic tools that help you discover where you've been, what knowledge and skills you've acquired, where your interests have led you, and where you may be headed. *The Homeschooler's Guide to Transcripts and Portfolios* will show you how homeschoolers can create portfolios for their own personal use, in addition to those created for school officials or others outside the family.

Both portfolios and transcripts are used to display learning, but they *are* different. How are they different? And when do you use one rather than the other?

A portfolio is a collection of artifacts that has been selected from a larger body of work—a carefully designed sampler that is created for a specific reason, often for a specific reviewer. In essence, it is a portrait of you in a particular setting. A portfolio should contain enough items to answer the reviewer's questions, but it should not be overstuffed or cumbersome. Remember, the word "port"-folio indicates a *portable* collection.

A transcript on the other hand, is like a snapshot. It gives the reviewer a quick look at you, your skills, and your knowledge. It is usually presented through number or letter grades, or in clean, efficient prose. Often a transcript is part of a comprehensive portfolio, perhaps one designed for college admissions. At other times the transcript needs to stand alone as a single document. *The Homeschooler's Guide to Portfolios and Transcripts* will describe a variety of transcripts, help you select the type that best meets your needs, and show you how to format it for maximum effectiveness.

A homeschooler's first formal transcript is often created during adolescence, when employment or college is on the horizon. Many homeschooling families use portfolios throughout the primary and elementary years, however, to communicate with their local school. If you have young children, Chapter 5, "Presenting the Portfolio" will be especially valuable. It offers a complete toolkit to help you get ready for portfolio reviews with school administrators. It will also assist older students who will be presenting their portfolios during job or college interviews.

If you've been homeschooling for any length of time you have already started the portfolio and transcript process by keeping or archiving the artifacts of learning. Organizing all the formal and informal "stuff" of homeschooling into presentation pieces may seem like a daunting task, and this is where *The Homeschooler's Guide to Portfolios and Transcripts* can help. It will assist you in gathering your ideas and your artifacts, organizing them, writing about them, and presenting them with confidence. Throughout the book there will be exercises, samples, checklists, and other resources to guide you through the process step by step.

You may be starting the portfolio process late in the teen years and fear you haven't saved enough evidence or produced enough paperwork. Perhaps you are new to homeschooling and are concerned you are years behind in the process. Don't worry. There are strategies that will help you recall the past, discover documentation where you thought none existed, and even design courses retroactively from what you've already learned. Wherever you are on your homeschool timeline, now is the time to start mining your archives. Once unearthed, your artifacts will quickly begin to shape themselves into portfolios and transcripts.

WHO SHOULD USE THIS BOOK?

This book is designed so that it can be used by either the homeschooled adolescent, the homeschooling parent, or a designated mentor. Ideally, however, developing a homeschool portfolio or transcript is a team endeavor. In our home it was a family project, with each of us contributing ideas, artifacts and memories.

Creating portfolios and transcripts *with* my children has been one of the high points of my homeschool parenting. For me, the process was intensely personal, almost like looking through the baby book or a rediscovered photo album. For my sons, developing portfolios and transcripts made their learning visible and tangible. It allowed them to see in a dramatic and dynamic way the amazing growth that occurred while they had been homeschooling.

I wish you and your children this same pride and joy as you experiment with and learn from the portfolio/transcript process.

—Loretta Heuer, M.Ed.

CHAPTER 1

Evaluating, Documenting, and Communicating
Your Homeschool Experience

This is a book about discovering yourself, facilitating learning, and documenting your homeschool experience. You'll learn the steps you need to take when creating portfolios as alternatives to standardized tests. And you will learn to design a transcript from your homeschool experiences that will stand up in even the most high-stakes situations—such as college application. But you will also discover that portfolios are not just mechanisms for reporting learning. They are vehicles for self-evaluation and personal goal setting, both for the student and for the parent/mentor/educational facilitator.

 THE BASIC DEFINITION

A portfolio is . . .

- A portrait of you . . .
- As shown by a reflective selection of work . . .
- With a goal, a theme, and an intended audience.

It is not just a folder of unrelated best work for an anonymous reviewer.

DISCOVERING YOURSELF: PORTFOLIOS FOR THE STUDENT

When you create a portfolio for yourself, you reflect on six basic human questions:

- Who am I ?
- What do I need?
- What do I know?
- What am I able to do?
- What do I want to do?
- How have I changed?

The portfolio process enables you to look at the "stuff" of your life and learning with a fresh perspective. As you sift through all of the artifacts you've collected along the way and begin to select items to add to your portfolio, you will start to answer those six powerful questions in a tangible way. And when your learning is tangible, it becomes real to you.

Creating your portfolio and high school transcript will enable you to engage in self-assessment. It is an experience that will validate all that you have done during your homeschooling years. You will discover how much you have learned simply by doing the things you loved and pursuing a curriculum matched to your needs and goals. This self-discovery process will not only help chart a path for your future, but eventually it will also allow you to see homeschooling from a different angle—no longer as an adolescent, but as a young adult.

 YOUR PERSONAL PORTFOLIO

Your personal portfolio is for:

- At-home use

- Self-discovery

- Improvement of instruction

Personal portfolios have value even if never seen by anyone outside the home.

A tangible portfolio may be what you're after—you have meetings with the principal, a college admissions interview, etc.—but the portfolio process, the creation of the physical portfolio, brings valuable memories to the surface. As a young adult, the portfolio process offers a chance to reflect on what those memories—and your learning—mean to you today.

Homeschooling isn't idyllic. There are tough times as well as good ones. At some point during your adolescence you're probably going to question homeschooling. Am I really learning anything? Does homeschooling make sense? Is this all worth it? This is probably a signal that you need to make learning visible by creating a portfolio. A portfolio will help you see yourself, your skills, and your learning from another perspective. It will help you keep faith both in yourself and in homeschooling, giving you a badly needed boost when your confidence is low and you are plagued by doubts.

It is sometimes difficult to believe what your parents or mentors say about you—that you are talented and bright, that you are achieving great things—after all, they're your *parents!* They love you and care about you and want you to feel good about yourself, but are you really as great as they say you are?

Of course, the answer is, *Yes!* But sometimes it helps to have tangible evidence to battle those uneasy feelings. Creating a portfolio gives you evidence you can literally see and touch—reminders of how accomplished you have become by following your personalized path of learning. It is not simply a matter of parental pride. Creating a portfolio makes it clear that you have done wonderful and remarkable things!

PORTFOLIOS AS MIRRORS

Portfolios help us better understand ourselves. They act as mirrors that reflect our learning and growth.

Once you've created a portfolio, you can keep it private (as you would a journal) or share it with your family to celebrate what has happened during your homeschool years. Adolescence is a time to explore issues that are confusing and complex, and some parts of a self-discovery portfolio may reveal things that you are not ready to share with others. Other portfolios may best be kept private because they involve works in progress. For example, one of my sons keeps his song lyrics absolutely off-limits until they are polished enough to be recorded.

Some portfolios are of such a specialized nature that others in the family just wouldn't understand them. My other son became involved in historical reenactments and acquired a great deal of knowledge about Revolutionary War uniforms. I was glad he had a consuming interest, but I had no idea what he was talking about!

 PORTFOLIOS AS WINDOWS

Portfolios let others see what you know. They act as windows to your learning. They make:

- Your thinking visible
- Your ideas explicit

However private you may want to be, don't overlook the fact that your family has been an intimate part of your homeschooling career. Unfortunately, we live in a culture that assumes the teenage years to be a time of inevitable conflict with parents, a time to break away from family. But because of homeschooling, you are well positioned to challenge this stereotype, proving that adolescence can be a time not only to explore independence but to discover the rich resources of interdependence as well.

Of course, there's no reason to limit yourself to creating only *one* portfolio—either a personal portfolio or one to share. During your teenage years, you will probably develop several portfolios. Sometimes the audience will be yourself, sometimes it will be your family and those closest to you, and sometimes it will be those outside your immediate circle (school officials, employers, college admissions offices, etc.). Given that employers now are looking beyond grades on a transcript to tangible evidence of competency, you will probably need to create portfolios throughout your adult life. Homeschooling once again gives you early access to the way things are done in "the real world."

MOVING FROM PORTFOLIO TO TRANSCRIPT

You will probably use your portfolio (or portfolios) to assemble your homeschool transcript. In doing so, you will once again discover the breadth and depth of your learning. You will gain new insights, seeing how homeschooling has allowed you to pursue your interests and experience the world in a way few high school students are able to do. Creating a concise homeschool transcript is quite a challenge. Simply put, there has been so much learning going on during all those years that there is no way you can fit it all onto a half-sized sheet of paper the way that traditional high schools do. But portfolios that you create during adolescence can help simplify the transcript process and make it less overwhelming.

FACILITATING LEARNING: PORTFOLIOS FOR PARENTS AND MENTORS

One of the greatest gifts of homeschooling is getting to know our children very, very well. Still, even homeschooled children grow, change, and become puzzles, mysteries, challenges, strangers. *Who IS this child of mine?* In our struggle to be not only good parents but good homeschooling parents, we each entertain some share of self-doubt. We know that our children are terrific human beings, that they'll turn out fine, and that they're going to be well prepared for adulthood. Yet we still take deep breaths and try not to worry.

I found that my role as a homeschooling parent changed dramatically when my first son entered adolescence. The informal, impromptu learning experiences that had been the hallmark of his early learning no longer captured his interest. Working on projects as a family was no longer important. He wanted more structure in mathematics than I thought necessary. He wanted to read books, books, books and play music, music, music.

It was undoubtedly our most difficult adjustment period in over twenty years of homeschooling. Everything had been working so well. Now, nothing was working. Nothing was the way it had been. Why were we arguing? Why was I crying? What was going on here? *Who is this child of mine?* The answer, of course, was that he was himself. He was transforming into the fine, self-possessed young adult he would eventually become. But his needs were changing. He was developing his own homeschool philosophy, and I was being assigned a different role within it. We just didn't realize it at the time. Eventually, I came to the realization that I needed to become the home-schooling parent *he needed me to be,* not the one I had been, not the one I had expected to be.

How did I arrive at that realization? I worked my way through the portfolios we had kept in the past, looking for clues as to what worked and why, and what had changed and how. That is why portfolios are so valuable for us as parent-educators. When we review our children's portfolios, we give ourselves a bit of distance. At times we can get stuck and see only what is going awry. We get caught in overfocusing on the problem. Portfolios can provide us with a wide-angle lens so that we can see the situation from a more objective perspective.

PORTFOLIOS TO BOOST SELF-CONFIDENCE

When your confidence is at a low, portfolios can reassure you that your children have indeed learned something! Portfolios can counter that depressing feeling we all have occasionally, that maybe "they" are right and that homeschooling—especially unschooling—isn't *really* education after all. A portfolio can restore your faith in homeschooling and in your children's ability to learn. In short, a portfolio can prove that "they" are wrong!

To admit that some days I get discouraged is very difficult for me. Frustration and discouragement are perfectly normal reactions, but not very comfortable ones. For homeschoolers, our home is our workplace, and we are very much like other home-based workers. It is sometimes difficult to get peer feedback and encouragement when we most need it. Even though I enjoyed a great deal of support as a homeschooling parent, there were moments when I needed to see and touch evidence of a job well done. On days like that, portfolios held visible, tangible proof that I was competent at my job. They reminded me that:

- I *am* a capable and caring teacher/mentor/facilitator/coach.

- I *do* have good observation skills.

- I *am* a good diagnostician.

- I *do* see patterns in my children's learning.

- I *have* discerned their learning styles.

- I *do* try to meet their unique needs.

- I *do* attempt different strategies until something "clicks."

- I *do* get out of the way of my children and let them learn from their own mistakes.

Because we are watching our children learn on a daily basis, it is often difficult to notice their growth. Sure, sometimes there are dramatic quantum leaps in our children's learning, but usually growth is more subtle. As homeschoolers, we can be so close to what is happening that we may fail to notice the small, incremental changes that occur unless we have a yardstick to measure progress. Just as a yearly checkup at the pediatrician's office makes us aware of how much our children have grown physically, reviewing a portfolio shows how learning has progressed over time.

When our children were young, our pediatrician had us on the lookout for "developmental milestones." These were all the "firsts": first time turning over, first step, first word, etc. Portfolios are a repository for those learning "firsts," which we sometimes recognize only in retrospect. Homeschoolers usually don't separate learning activities from real-life ones, and because of this, experiences that were developmental learning milestones can often be overlooked. In developing a portfolio, one of the steps in the process is to look through the archives of items we've saved. At that time we often realize that something casually stored away is indeed a treasure that marks a milestone event in our child's growth. Discovering these items is cause for celebration, which is another reason for creating portfolios. Portfolios help us celebrate our lives as homeschoolers!

PORTFOLIOS TO ENHANCE INSTRUCTION

As homeschooling parents, we know that our job is not limited to instruction. In fact, as our children enter their teenage years we tend to wean them from direct or didactic instruction (if that was ever our style) and act more as our children's facilitator of learning. This radical redefinition of what it means to be a teacher is easy for us to understand. It means helping our sons and daughters find resources other than ourselves, both in our homes and beyond, that will develop their interests and passions. In addition, we want them to learn the knowledge and skills needed in order to become competent young adults.

For parents, the same six basic questions apply, but we ask them in a slightly different form:

- Who is this child of mine?

- How has he changed during adolescence?

- What does he need from me *now?*

- What does he know?

- What is he able to do?

- What does he want to do with his life?

Sometimes our adolescent children want us to be actively involved with their learning as their instructor, academic coach, or guidance counselor. This is when portfolios can work for you just as they do for traditional educators—as a powerful tool to help provide better instruction. Portfolios can help you to be a wise and sophisticated diagnostician. They help you discern what is happening in your children's intellectual lives and point out new ways to help them.

A portfolio used as a diagnostic tool allows you to see the fullest possible picture of your child as a learner. Portfolios will not only give you access to the products of past learning activities, but they will also remind you of your child's earlier interests. Luckily, when faced with a decision about learning, homeschoolers can use *all* the information they've acquired throughout the child's lifetime. A homeschool portfolio kept for diagnostic purposes should show not only work of high achievement to remind you (and your child) how competent he or she is, but also work that indicates struggle and even weakness. Because these types of portfolios are kept for the private use of the family, even problematic work samples can be saved without apprehension.

 SNAPSHOT OR ALBUM?

A test and its grade is like an isolated snapshot. A portfolio, however, can show progress over time, like a series of photographs in an album.

At some point, a diagnostic portfolio becomes a prescriptive one. You may think to yourself, *I can see what is wrong. Now, what do I do to give my child the help he needs? More of the same? Clarity in explanation? Something completely different?* A prescriptive portfolio will help you review the past in order to remember which strategies worked and which didn't. As you probe the question, *Why didn't he understand?*, a prescriptive portfolio also suggests new strategies to try, making you more sensitive to your child's unique learning style.

One of my sons has always been an artistic youngster with a strong visual learning style. Although he actually enjoyed studying geometry, algebra was not coming easily for him. I noticed, while reviewing work samples in his geometry portfolio, that many of the problems had algebraic equations accompanying them. He had understood algebra when it was linked to geometric figures. Why was he having difficulty with it now? Could he learn new algebraic principles more easily by pairing them with geometric examples? The answer was yes! His portfolio held the all clues I needed in order to facilitate his learning . . . and to restore both his self-confidence and my own.

Finally, creating, maintaining, and utilizing portfolios made my sons better, more thoughtful observers of their own work. It caused them to be more accepting and appreciative of their personal learning style and it required them to engage in honest, reflective self-assessment. This, of course, is more than just an academic skill. It is a hallmark of the mature adults we expect our children to become. And for a homeschooling parent, *that* is the job well done!

 A HOMESCHOOL PRACTITIONER PORTFOLIO

Classroom teachers create portfolios to chronicle their own professional growth. Consider developing a homeschool practitioner portfolio to show how you as a parent have grown and changed because you homeschooled.

PORTFOLIOS FOR THOSE OUTSIDE THE FAMILY

The third reason for constructing a portfolio or transcript is to document and communicate homeschool achievements to those outside the family. This may be because you need to—or because you want to.

The issue of needs versus wants is a familiar one to any family. A homeschooling family must distinguish between situations when you *need* to give school officials information in order to fulfill legal requirements and when you *want* to share your success stories with employers, college admissions officers, writers, and the media.

It is important to realize that these portfolios have a very different purpose from those created for self-discovery or facilitation of learning. These portfolios are primarily for evaluation. They may be used to evaluate your child's abilities, your skills as a teacher, your family's homeschool program, or homeschooling itself.

Because of this, homeschoolers need to be cautious about the information they choose to share by means of a portfolio. I am certainly not an advocate of using standardized tests to assess homeschoolers, but test scores do provide a degree of distance between your family and the school. A portfolio, on the other hand, is a window to your child's mind and heart.

 YOUR DOCUMENTATION PORTFOLIO

Your documentation portfolio is for:

- Use outside the home

- Communication with others

- Accountability to school officials

A documentation portfolio is designed for the person who reviews it.

CREATING AND SHARING PORTFOLIOS BECAUSE YOU NEED TO

Some homeschoolers may need to create portfolios in order to fulfill the requirements of state homeschooling law. It is imperative that you know what your state's legal requirements are. Do not rely on school officials to interpret the law for you. Read the actual text of the law yourself. See what it says about evaluation of homeschoolers. What options do you have? More important, what does it *not* say about assessment?

Portfolios Required by Law

State departments of education and local school districts create policies and procedures that should be aligned with state law. However, in many cases what are presented to homeschoolers as statutory requirements are really departmental interpretations and local regulations. Often local regulations are designed by administrative staff members who do not have an understanding of homeschooling practices and who are not familiar with the fine points of their state's homeschooling law. Because of this, districts often ask homeschoolers to provide far more information than is legally required. In some districts, for example, you may be asked to present documentation to school officials on a semester or annual basis, but legal research may show that this is simply local administrative procedure.

 A WIDENING CIRCLE, A NARROWING OF INFORMATION

Your personal portfolio should be filled with rich, detailed information about yourself. That information becomes progressively more streamlined as you share it with family, teachers, mentors, private institutions, and government agencies.

A good guiding principle is to give schools the minimum amount of information required by law. There are assuredly legal reasons for keeping a portfolio for school administrators as simple and basic as possible, but there are educational reasons, as well. School administrators deal primarily with institutional details, not educational theory and practice. They usually do not engage in dialogue and discussion with individual students unless there is a behavioral problem. Most would admit they are not equipped to assess student learning in some of the courses taught in their own building—such as trigonometry or world literature. Furthermore, it is unlikely that administrators have had professional development and training in alternative assessment techniques. Remember those six existential questions we explored earlier? For most public school administrators, they are usually replaced with two pragmatic ones:

- What documentation does he or she have?

- Does the documentation show progress since the last review?

Design a portfolio that answers these two questions efficiently and you protect your homeschooling freedom. However, if homeschoolers give schools more information than required, it is cause for concern in several areas.

Extra information can impact our children's privacy. We would hope that information about our children's achievements, whether in portfolio or standardized test format would be kept confidential by the school. However, school records may be shared by staff members. They may be available to a variety of governmental agencies. Information may be considered out of context and have implications for our children's educational future or employability. All items and information must be carefully considered before inclusion in a portfolio, and as will be explained later in Chapter 5, "Presenting the Portfolio," ownership of portfolio items must be clarified by the parents.

In addition, offering information beyond the minimum that is required can set a precedent for other homeschooling families . . .and for ourselves in the future. A school may assume that if one family presents copious information, all homeschooling families in the district should henceforth offer the same amount. And in following years they may expect them to submit even more! As will be discussed later in Chapter 3, a portfolio is a judicious selection. We wisely choose the minimum number of artifacts needed to fulfill legal requirements and communicate effectively. No more, no less.

 ACCOUNTABILITY PORTFOLIOS

Who is being held accountable? Is the school using a portfolio to assess the student? Or is the portfolio being used to evaluate the parent, teacher, or homeschool program? Make sure you know what your school has the legal right to assess!

Private Schools and Outside Consultants

Perhaps the school you are dealing with is not a public institution, but a homeschool-friendly private one. Most correspondence schools have their own evaluation systems, for instance, so you can anticipate that they will tell you how to configure a portfolio to meet their requirements. So will an umbrella school, which acts as an interface between you and your school system. As they help you accumulate course credits toward a diploma, they will be reviewing your son or daughter's portfolio.

Rather than dealing with private schools, other families may have portfolios reviewed by either an educator in private practice that they have hired as a consultant or a friend or acquaintance who has expertise in the content area of the portfolio. A native speaker, for example, might review a Spanish language and culture portfolio and write an evaluation. This assessment could then be used as documentation for a college admissions portfolio, a high school transcript, or as a prerequisite if your child wanted to take courses at a nearby college or university.

Portfolios in the Courtroom

Finally, a portfolio that documents homeschool learning can be required not only by state law, but by the court system. This might occur in a divorce settlement and/or custody dispute, in a care and protection case brought by the state department of social services, or in a case where homeschooling itself was being investigated and challenged. In these situations, it is crucial to confer with both an attorney and an educator experienced in portfolio assessment. You want your portfolio to make the strongest case possible and, by doing so, protect both your freedom to homeschool as well as that of other families.

SHARING PORTFOLIOS AND TRANSCRIPTS BECAUSE YOU WANT TO

Perhaps you are submitting material for college admission. Maybe you are engaged in a job search and have an interview with a prospective employer. Or, perhaps you're being interviewed by a reporter who is writing a feature on homeschooling. In each of these situations, you want to impress a specific audience, one that may have had only limited prior experience with homeschoolers. In each case, a portfolio can help explain more about you, your learning, and your homeschool experience.

EMPLOYABILITY PORTFOLIOS

Create an employability portfolio to:

- Set career goals

- Assess your job skills

- Present yourself as a candidate for employment

These are the showcase portfolios. You need to show yourself off in the most attractive light possible, and a portfolio can present, through artifacts, many achievements that might sound boastful in words. Better still, your portfolio can go beyond showcasing these achievements. It can demonstrate to colleges or employers that your homeschool experience will have added value for them.

High-stakes portfolios, with college and career opportunities riding on them, will probably include a transcript of your adolescent homeschool experiences. If the reviewers are acting as gatekeepers between you and your goal, it is essential that you create a portfolio or transcript that will meet their specifications in order for it to be effective. Your portfolio, even if it doesn't contain a diploma as evidence of high school graduation, can still provide answers to the questions that colleges and employers ask. The persons reviewing your portfolio and transcript package will be considering those six basic questions, this time phrased as:

- Who is this young person?

- What is his or her interest in our school or organization?

- What does this person know?

- What is he or she able to do?

- What does this person want to do with his or her life?

- Are we a good match for each other?

In creating a portfolio for these audiences, the last question, that of "the good match," needs to be uppermost in your mind. During the selection process, you have many artifacts that display a great deal of information and evidence, but that doesn't mean that you need to share everything! The items that paint a portrait of you as a promising candidate for this particular school or job are the ones you should use to build your portfolio. Whether you want to go to an Ivy League university or an art school, or to be employed as a landscape designer or a legislative intern, the rule is the same: Give them what they need so they can say yes.

 When asked to produce artifacts to demonstrate or verify learning, make sure they are in a format and a language familiar to those reviewing the materials.

WHEN SHOULD YOU START DEVELOPING PORTFOLIOS AND TRANSCRIPTS?

Relax. You have already taken the first step of the portfolio and transcript process just by keeping or archiving the "stuff" of your homeschooling life. The second step, selecting the most appropriate items or artifacts from your archives to create a portfolio, or compacting all that information into a transcript, is discussed in detail later in the book.

 FROM PORTFOLIOS TO TRANSCRIPT

Creating a transcript is heavy-duty memory work. Your early adolescent portfolios will make the job easier.

GETTING AN EARLY START

Although transcripts, which tend to be cumulative documents, are usually assembled toward the end of the homeschool experience, they often emerge quite naturally from portfolios that you already created in earlier years. Ideally, you should begin creating portfolios as early as possible. You may be six years away from college admissions. Or, your school district may not require a portfolio. Start anyway! The reasons are simple:

- Portfolios are not primarily for "them"; they're for you! You create portfolios primarily for self-discovery and facilitation of learning, not accountability and verification of learning.

- By starting early, you get more practice in creating portfolios. When you need to create a high-stakes portfolio, it will not be your first attempt. An initial portfolio is usually bursting at the seams—full of wonderful artifacts that provide a great deal of extraneous information. Later portfolios tend to become leaner, more focused, and more sophisticated in presentation.

- Homeschooling parents wear many hats and fulfill many roles. Portfolios that help you reflect on your role as a facilitator of learning will have payoffs throughout adolescence. By developing portfolios in the middle school years, you can make your role as a teacher or mentor easier later on.

- I consider homeschooling parents to be professionals, experts in their field. Most homeschoolers read widely about alternative education, attend conferences and workshops, and belong to support groups. Portfolios are another tool, in fact probably the most personalized one, in a homeschooler's professional development program, offering a process and a format for reflecting on your growth as an alternative educator.

- Your initial attempts at creating portfolios probably will be based on the suggestions and examples in this book. However, you will soon move beyond the step-by step suggestions given here. Your later portfolios will be more personalized, not only in content, but in format. You will develop an instinct for how a few carefully selected artifacts can create a richly detailed portrait, and you will know which presentation method is most suitable to show off those items to their best advantage.

- Finally, portfolios are organizational devices not just for learning, but for homes! When you start to create portfolios, you will begin to sort though all the piles and milk crates that tend to clutter a homeschool household. There are treasures hidden among all that "stuff." Portfolio building helps you discover those gems and provides you with a place for their safekeeping.

GETTING A LATE START

Luckily, most homeschoolers are masters of what is called "just-in-time learning." We can pull off amazing feats and accelerate the learning curve. While it is preferable to start the portfolio process early, you can still create an effective transcript and high-stakes portfolio in a short amount of time.

Those getting an early start can afford to browse through this book, experimenting with a variety of approaches to portfolio and transcript development. You, on the other hand, will need to be more focused. It is critical that you research and investigate your audience as thoroughly as possible so that you will not spend precious time developing a portfolio or transcript that is off target. Again, your goal is to give the reviewers precisely the information that they need, request, or require.

If time is of the essence, you may feel that you should just slap together a portfolio with whatever looks good and is easily accessible. Resist that urge! I strongly encourage you to set aside time to try at least four of the memory activities suggested in Chapter 4, "Creating Your Portfolio." Their goal is to help you recall exemplary activities and artifacts that have been forgotten. I guarantee that you have more available than you think you do!

 IMAGE IS IMPORTANT

Your portfolio's first impression is important. It should be full of wonderful stuff, not stuffed full!

I also suggest that you pay special attention to the physical appearance of your portfolio and transcript and that you allot time for basic aesthetics. You may be scurrying to pull all your materials together, but the finished product should never have a hasty, slapdash look. In cases when you will not be meeting with the reviewers, your portfolio will serve as your proxy. You want it to make a powerful and polished presentation on your behalf.

C H A P T E R 2

Assessment
Basics

This chapter will introduce you to nonstandardized assessments and reporting tools. It will give you direct experience with and a working vocabulary for:

- Why alternative assessment works for homeschoolers

- What a portfolio is and isn't

- The portfolio process

- Transcripts

- Performance assessments

- Rubrics and scoring devices

- Reviews and interviews

- Technology and portfolios

ALTERNATIVE ASSESSMENT WORKS FOR HOMESCHOOLERS

For homeschoolers, alternative assessments aren't alternative at all. They're the norm! We observe our children. We listen to them. We sit with them as they struggle. We get feedback from them over lunch. We help them proofread what they've written. We ask for their opinions . . .and make them defend their ideas to our satisfaction. This is all in a day's work, part of our normal lives—without conscious thought that we've been busily "assessing learning."

If we do it so effortlessly, why do we need to delve into the subject? Well, even though we do it well, we can learn to do it better. Homeschooled teenagers can become better at critiquing their own work, and they can learn more about themselves in the process. Improving their everyday assessment skills can also help them participate more fully when developing the high-stakes assessments related to college admissions or employment. For parents, learning about alternative assessment will show us techniques we can use to become better, more reflective mentors of our children.

For me, discovering more about these types of assessment has built my confidence. As I learned about various assessment formats, I realized that I had been using them intuitively all along! On

HOW CAN YOU EVALUATE LEARNING?

If you want to know whether a student understands electric circuits, you can have him or her:

- Take a paper-and-pencil test on circuitry

- Draw a diagram of different types of circuits

- Design and conduct an experiment with batteries and bulbs

- Engage you in dialogue about the subject

- Write directions for others

- Diagnose why the computer's new printer isn't properly installed

days when I felt inundated by the latest news on state achievement tests or heard talk-show hosts and political leaders touting high accountability through standardized tests, it felt good to be validated for the wise and sophisticated assessments I had been making in an alternative manner.

Learning a vocabulary for alternative assessments equips homeschoolers to communicate more effectively with traditional educators. When we learn their words we begin to speak their language. And when we use their language to frame the things we do at home, we increase their comfort level and encourage them to relax about our alternative route to the same goal: creating competent young adults. This is not just true for your local school officials. College admissions personnel and employers rely on a school-oriented vocabulary when speaking of student achievement, too.

Remember that accountability is incredibly important for public school officials. Even though our children are not bound by the same agenda as that of the public school, administrators tend to look at homeschoolers with an eye toward assessment, too. They feel it is part of their job. By giving officials only what is legally required and by identifying contemporary methods of assessment as part of our program, we let them know that we are aware of both the legal and the educational issues surrounding assessment. In short, when it comes to assessment we know our stuff and are not to be trifled with. For this reason, I included in Appendix D, "Print and Internet Resources," a list of articles appearing in periodicals to which your Superintendent probably subscribes. I have found it helpful to copy and/or cite such articles (or indicate the relevant website) when speaking with administrators. This helps remind them that their forward-thinking peers are also encouraging the use of leading-edge authentic assessments—that it isn't simply a homeschool phenomenon.

AUTHENTIC ASSESSMENT

I've used the term "authentic assessment" several times. What does it mean? Authentic assessment is assessment that is embedded in the learning tasks themselves—not separate from them. It doesn't interfere with learning or interrupt it. Rather, authentic assessment enhances learning, fine-tunes it, celebrates it! In fact, as I mentioned before, these assessment strategies that we homeschoolers use are the same ones that contemporary education researchers agree that all schools ought to adopt. However, when a principal wants his or her staff to use nonstandardized assessments or when a teacher wants to use portfolios in her classroom, they inevitably run into problems. Why does authentic assessment seem so aligned with what we do and so difficult for schools?

A MINI-GLOSSARY

- **Alternative Assessment:** Evaluation of learning via performances, products, projects, logs, journals, portfolios, etc., rather than via traditional paper-and-pencil or standardized tests.

- **Performance-Based Assessment:** Evaluation of learning by watching a student apply knowledge while he or she performs a task, usually one that has been constructed by the teacher.

- **Authentic Assessment:** Evaluation of the student's applying knowledge in a real-world context.

- **Embedded Assessment:** Evaluation so fully integrated with the project or task that learning and assessment occur simultaneously.

- *There are storage problems.* Where can you house all the items twenty-four students produce each year? We homeschoolers have the physical space, our actual houses—or apartments—where we are able to "house" all that evidence of learning.

- *Schools have time-management issues.* How can teachers find time to review all the work that their students produce, much less use alternative assessment strategies to evaluate them? Homeschoolers deal with time management, too, but we have a greater degree of flexibility in time and in space. We can engage our children in dialogue about a book they are reading, get feedback from them, and then assess the sophistication of their understanding—all while doing errands at ten in the morning.

- *Teachers need written assignments.* Of course, homeschoolers enjoy small class size which allows us to assess information from verbal feedback. Unlike classroom teachers, we don't need frequent written assignments from our students to assure us that they are completing assignments or showing progress. Progress is evident in our students' answers to our questions, the level of their discourse, even the "Aha!" of comprehension evident on their faces.

- *Alternative assessment means change, and change in American education takes time.* Trying to get a single school, much less a whole district, to do things differently is a major three- to five-year plan for most school systems. Adopting a new textbook or report card procedure requires committees, study groups, and a task force. Changing something less tangible such as assessment practices can be extraordinarily difficult. Homeschoolers, on the other hand, can quickly and efficiently implement change whenever we need to do so.

  In addition, change can be disconcerting. Teachers need to develop a sense of ownership over new assessment practices before they feel comfortable using them in their classroom. We homeschoolers, however, find these practices easy to incorporate into the way we are already doing things.

- *Finally, change is risky, and not just for school personnel.* The average citizen sees high standardized test scores as evidence of good schools and a good return on his or her tax dollar. When schools begin to use new instruments for assessment, there is often a public outcry. Portfolios and performances may be just too complicated and too different. But we homeschoolers have embraced change and are already using different models of learning and assessment. We have looked at our education options, considered the risk-benefit ratio for each, and decided to do things differently than the general public.

UNDERSTANDING WHAT A PORTFOLIO DOES

Before I discuss the portfolio definition, I would like you to create a mini-portfolio by doing the following brief visualization. You'll need a pen or pencil to record your responses.

EXERCISE 1: Creating a Mini-Portfolio

- Go to somewhere in your home that is reflective of who you are, a place that has the "stuff" of your life in it. If that isn't possible, visualize yourself being there.

- Sit down and make yourself comfortable. If you are not physically in your chosen space, do this exercise with your eyes closed.

- Look around. Your eyes will linger on something. Write its name next to #1 below.

- Turn to another direction, and you eyes will notice something else. Write this down as #2. Look around and you'll see a third item, #3. And a fourth, #4.

- Perhaps you feel that something or someone that ought to be included is missing. This can be #5.

- Beneath the name of each item, note why you chose it and what it reveals.

Item #1

_____

Why I chose it:

_____

What it shows about me:

_____

_____

Item #2

_____

Why I chose it:

_____

What it shows about me:

_____

_____

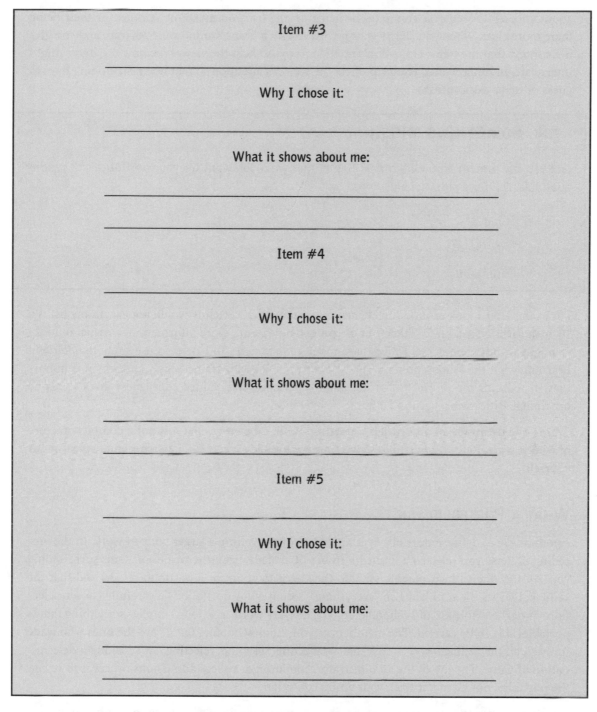

Item #3

_____

Why I chose it:

_____

What it shows about me:

_____

_____

Item #4

_____

Why I chose it:

_____

What it shows about me:

_____

_____

Item #5

_____

Why I chose it:

_____

What it shows about me:

_____

_____

Congratulations! You have just developed a sample portfolio!

Your list is a miniature but revealing picture of who you are, the artifacts that surround you, the things that interest you, the items that are important to you, and perhaps a person you'd like to be with. This specific combination of things tells me something about you. If I were to arrange your five items together and take a picture of them, I would have a photograph that shared a great deal of personal information about you.

More important, by telling me why you have included an item and how it relates to you, you have made me better able to understand what it represents and what you are trying to communicate about yourself. When you annotate the items on the list, you make the reasons for their being there more clear. When you clarify your intent, you set a frame around your portrait, and you give it a context that the items alone don't provide. You also help the viewer see how the items might interrelate. In other words, you help direct the viewer's attention so that he or she doesn't have to guess or make assumptions.

 SOMETHING MISSING?

Did you list something for item #5? Sometimes what you want for your portfolio isn't readily available. In those situations you need to:

- Find it

- Acquire it

- Create it

For example, if I look around my kitchen one artifact that certainly would appear on my list is a 10-inch carbon steel knife. Taken out of context, not having more information, a casual onlooker might wonder about me. Knives have many *connotations,* so I need to use some *annotations*! Learning what the knife represents (that I am a professionally trained chef) and why it is important (it reminds me of creative professional experiences and valued colleagues) gives someone unfamiliar with my background a frame of reference.

This is one definition of a portfolio: a portrait. Realize, however, that it is not a complete picture of who you are. Rather, a portfolio shows only the limited aspects you have chosen to reveal about yourself.

WHAT A PORTFOLIO ISN'T

Another way to define a portfolio is as a *selection* of items from a larger body of work. In the preceding exercise you selected a limited number of artifacts from the wealth of items surrounding you. All too often I hear parents say that they need to go in for a portfolio review and that the principal wants them to bring in "everything." Not at all! A portfolio is a carefully chosen selection—not the whole kit and caboodle. In fact, the very word "portfolio" implies something that is portable, able to be carried. The members of your homeschooling family are the ones who wade through all the artifacts you've collected—reflecting, selecting, rejecting, and making a determination of value. The job of the administrator, employer, or college admissions officer is to *review* the portfolio, not extract it from your entire collection.

Another common misconception is that a portfolio is a showcase of only your best work. Sometimes it is, but most likely you'll use other criteria to build a portfolio. Many times a

---

 HOW MANY ARTIFACTS?

A portfolio should not be rated on the number of artifacts you put into it. Selectivity is more important than quantity.

portfolio shows a single work in various stages of construction, from rough beginnings to polished end result. This type of portfolio, a *progress* folio, displays growth and change over time. This would be especially appropriate for a work in progress such as a writing sampler including first, intermediate, and final drafts. A *process* folio, on the other hand, shows the sequence of steps a project goes through from its inception to its completion. You might organize your material this way if you were documenting a theatrical production from auditions through final performance. Just be aware that there are a number of portfolio types, which will be discussed at length in later chapters. For now, however, it bears repeating: A portfolio is a *portrait* of you as shown by a *reflective selection* of work with a *goal,* a *theme,* and an intended *audience.* It is not just a folder of unrelated pieces of your best work for some anonymous reviewer.

 THREE TYPES OF PORTFOLIOS

Portfolios serve a variety of functions. They can show:

- **Product:** What I Have Achieved

- **Process:** How I Learn

- **Progress:** How Far I Have Come

THE PORTFOLIO PROCESS

Portfolios can mean serious business with long-range implications. All the more reason for homeschoolers to become comfortable with them! Yes, a college admissions portfolio can be created in a well-orchestrated, one-month campaign. But it would be wiser if this type of high-stakes portfolio wasn't your first. A homeschooling family can experiment with portfolios in a nonthreatening manner early in adolescence, practicing the process and acquiring skills and sophistication along the way. Moreover, because a portfolio is not just a product but also a process, you will learn something about yourself and your approaches to life and learning. While I may learn more about you from the content of your portfolio, you will learn more about yourself by reflecting on how you assembled it.

When you create a portfolio for self-discovery, you go through a three-step sequence:

- Collect

- Select

- Reflect

In order to familiarize yourself with the portfolio process and demystify it, try your hand at creating a nonacademic portfolio first. The following two exercises will help you explore the portfolio process in an informal way. When you read through Exercise 2, it will sound like play. But homeschoolers know that relaxed, playful situations can produce powerful learning. Nonacademic portfolios teach us to trust the incidental learning that happens simply by living a fruitful, interesting, and playful life. We live in a school-based culture, and these personal portfolios are powerful reminders that much of our important learning goes beyond areas that traditional educators label "academic." And remember, a personal, nonacademic portfolio can be an important self-discovery tool not only for adolescents but for adults in the family, as well. Because of this, I urge parents to complete the next two activities for themselves before doing it with their children.

EXERCISE 2: Collage Portfolio (Collect and Select)

The instructions for this activity are deliberately open-ended.

1. Collect materials:

   - poster board

   - scissors

   - glue sticks

   - magazines

   - catalogs

   - small artifacts

   - a glue gun

2. Paste stuff from the magazines and catalogs onto the poster board.

3. Glue objects onto the poster board, too.

Resist the urge to give directions! Instead, observe the process as well as the emerging product. When finished, go on to Exercise 3.

In parent workshops, everyone's collage portfolio, the end *product*, looks different. What is most important to notice, however, is that each person uses a different approach in the *process* of creating his or her collage. That is because we all work differently—which is one of the reasons we homeschool! That is, to honor our child's individual learning style and approach to the world. When you engage in this project and create what appears to be a simple collage, you are revealing much about yourself. Your personality type, your organizational behavior, and your visual-spatial style all are evident. In workshops, some participants use only pictures, while others cut out phrases and paste them neatly below their pictures to serve as captions. Some carefully cut everything into rectangles and paste them in orderly arrays while others rip and overlap. One woman ripped out a full-page photo of a flamenco dancer in a flaming-red dress and pasted it right in the middle of her poster board. Then she arranged smaller pictures in a border around the edge. Another folded her display into three parts so it could stand up on the table. What process did *you* go through?

EXERCISE 3: Collage Portfolio (Reflecting on Product and Process)

You just created a collage portfolio. What did you learn as you observed the *process*? Did you or your child:

- Use the whole piece of poster board, just as it came from the store?
- Fold it?
- Cut it?
- Use scissors to cut pictures from magazines and catalogs?
- Rip pictures out?
- Paste down whole pictures?
- Cut out specific parts of pictures to paste down?
- Include words or phrases?
- Glue on many three-dimensional objects?
- Lay out the items in a particular format?
- Arrange things in what appears to be a haphazard way?
- Overlap things?
- Paste things so they go beyond the edge?
- Cut everything out first, then arrange everything before pasting?
- Paste each item as soon as it was cut?
- Finish in an hour?
- Complete the project over several days?

What did you learn as you observed the finished *product*? Did you see:

- A particular theme?
- An eclectic mix?
- Connections?
- Contradictions?
- Surprises?
- Humor?
- Someone you recognized?
- Aspects of yourself or your child that you hadn't seen before?

Let's take the collect-select-reflect sequence and see how it has played out in these two exercises:

- **Collect.** Your stack of catalogs and magazines was your master collection for this activity. The fact that you chose to save these particular periodicals means that you were already collecting images and thoughts that you felt had some value. This happens in the portfolio process, too. You will collect things in which you have some level of interest, not always knowing how they will be used in the future. You build your collection with an eye toward its potential use.

- **Select.** As you thumbed through your magazines and catalogs, it probably was evident that some of them appeared to be more useful for this project than others. You selected certain ones from the stack and put the others aside. Browsing through the ones that grabbed your attention, you engaged in more selection by ripping or cutting out the words and pictures that mirrored your interests. You may have created a pile of these cutouts to sort through again, this time selecting only those that you wanted to use for the collage. This select, sort, sort again process happens when creating a portfolio. Since there are usually far too many artifacts to go into one portfolio, you will need to become increasingly selective about what you decide to include.

- **Reflect.** You probably had a rationale for each item's inclusion in your collage. However, once the final collage is complete, you can view the project as a whole—rather than just the sum of its individual parts. Your thoughts and interests have been made visible, perhaps in new and illuminating ways. Even the manner in which you chose to arrange items may indicate themes and connections you hadn't perceived before. And because the task was so open-ended, you might have discovered something about your learning style and how you instinctively approach a task. This is what happens when you create a portfolio, too. Your thoughts and thinking processes become evident to both your viewers and yourself.

THE TRANSCRIPT DEFINED

I have always found the concept of a high school or college transcript a bit ironic. In the judicial system a trial transcript contains every single word that was spoken; an academic transcript, however, is pared down to the bare-bones minimum: the name of each course and the grade that was given. If we consider a portfolio to be a portrait, then a transcript is a snapshot. It gives the reviewer a quick look at you, your skills, and your knowledge. Another way of thinking about transcripts is that they are really just grown-up report cards. They usually are written in the shorthand of number or letter grades. Additionally, while portfolios can be developed for either personal use or for review by those outside the family, transcripts are usually created specifically for those outside the homeschool community.

 PORTFOLIOS VS. TRANSCRIPTS

Portfolios describe learning.

Transcripts summarize it.

While homeschoolers might consider creating portfolios throughout the primary and elementary years, they usually delay designing a formal transcript until late in adolescence when employment or college is on the horizon. Again, while a last-minute transcript can be cobbled together to meet a college application deadline, you will be better off experimenting with various transcript formats earlier in the teenage years. This way you will have time to discover which transcript style matches your family's homeschooling philosophy while being most likely to advance your child's college or career goals. The different types of transcripts will be described in detail in Chapter 7, "Transcript Basics."

Homeschoolers use transcripts in much the same way that schooled students do. Transcripts, like diplomas, are portable credentials. When my son was sixteen, someone asked him why, as a homeschooler, he wanted a high school diploma. He responded, "Look, you know me and what I can do, and I *still* have to explain to you how homeschooling made me qualified. What about people who *don't* know me?" I could hear the edge of frustration in his voice. Let's be honest: Of course, he didn't *need* a diploma. He was capable, qualified, mature, and no piece of paper was going to make him more or less so. But sometimes a teenager just wants to move the process along and avoid getting bogged down in explaining, describing, or defending homeschooling or alternative assessment to those who are wary, hostile, or simply uninformed. You choose your battles, and in these instances a portable credential such as a transcript or a diploma can be useful.

On the other hand, many employers and colleges are justifiably suspicious of transcripts. They know that all schools' grading systems and transcripts are not created equal, and that an A– in algebra in one school may be a C+ in another. This is where homeschoolers' transcripts can shine. We are not limited only to letters and numbers. Sure, we can create quantitative transcripts with grades of A through F, but we also can create concise *qualitative* transcripts that tell colleges and employers what they want to know: what this young person knows and can do.

Sometimes the transcript needs to stand alone as a single document. This might be the case if you are asked to staple a copy of your transcript to a job application. In other situations, your transcript will be supported by other documentation, such as when it is included as one component of a comprehensive college admissions packet. In either case, it is important to have some sort of transcript available because its absence will surely be noticed.

So, how does a homeschooler acquire a transcript? Some homeschooling families use curriculum that has a grading component built into the program. Certain materials even come with a form that should be filled out to show course completion and then filed securely away. Other families work with correspondence schools or umbrella schools. If they routinely submit work to the school for grading, they should receive a copy of the school transcript, which then becomes part of the student's permanent record and is held in the school's files. Still other homeschooled adolescents take courses in training workshops or adult education programs. In these cases, a certificate of completion may be available, but remember, the school rarely grades the student or keeps a record of participation after the course is over. Finally, homeschoolers taking college coursework as nonmatriculated students will be starting their formal postsecondary transcript. This, of course, is kept on file at the college and will be asked for whenever the student applies to any institution of higher learning. All this paperwork can be thought of as part of your high school transcript. But because homeschoolers are not limited to institutionally granted grades, our transcripts can be far richer and more dynamic.

Because much of our homeschooling is not limited to courses or classes, we need to use alternative reporting tools to adequately describe the homeschool experience to others. Letter grades simply cannot do it justice. Alternative transcripts can be especially important for unschoolers who haven't acquired a paper trail. Or for describing powerful learning experiences where no obvious credential is granted. Or for knowledge that doesn't fit neatly into the English, Math, Science, and Social Studies framework. In these instances we go back to the definition of a transcript: a snapshot of what you learned during adolescence. Later, in Chapter 8, "Creating Your Transcript," you will discover more about how you can edit your complex knowledge down to snapshots—course descriptions in a format familiar to employers and educators. To get a feel for the process, try your hand at Exercise 4.

 UNSCHOOLING

For the purposes of this book, "unschooling" refers to learning that is dynamically structured rather than arranged into scheduled courses and classes. Unschoolers prefer to use a wide variety of real-life resources rather than commercially prepared educational materials.

Exercise 4: Create-A-Course

Do you live in New England? During the past few years have you visited Walden Pond, Concord, Salem, and Longfellow's Wayside Inn? Have you read Thoreau's *Walden,* an essay by Emerson, *The Scarlet Letter,* several of Hawthorne's short stories, and a selection of Longfellow's narrative poetry? Do you know the meaning of the word "transcendentalism"? Have you discussed your reading with others? Found master websites where you can read scholarly interpretations of these authors' works? Looked at student essays on *The Scarlet Letter* on the Internet that ranged from extraordinary to downright awful?

If so, you are well positioned to describe your experience in a short paragraph of about a hundred words:

> **19th-Century New England Writers: A Survey of Literary Forms.** Content included the essays and poetry of Ralph Waldo Emerson and Henry David Thoreau, the poetry of William Cullen Bryant, Henry Wadsworth Longfellow, and Emily Dickinson, and the short stories and novels of Nathaniel Hawthorne. Herman Melville's Civil War poetry was read, as was his novella *Billy Budd.* Readings were supplemented by literary analysis of each author, filmed renditions of major works, photographs and illustrations, and visits to each author's home. Connections between authors were explored, as were the literary movement known as transcendentalism and the political role of New England writers in the years preceding the Civil War.

Far more interesting than "10th Grade English," yes?

Now it's your turn. Think of a group of related experiences that you could "bundle" into a package of learning. Give it a title and write a one-paragraph course description that will interest and intrigue the reader.

By working through this transcript exercise, you will start to translate your alternative education into the language of traditional educators. Most important, you will learn how to construct your own learning. This means that you will reflect on *all* the learning of your teenage years, see connections, and then put it into some sort of meaningful order. When others see it on paper, it will look like a transcript. You, however, will know that the act of shaping your adolescent experiences into a coherent whole is evidence of true adult learning.

 THE TRANSCRIPT PROCESS

- Recognize your learning.

- Document it.

- Format it for your audience.

PERFORMANCE ASSESSMENTS

Assessment should be linked to instruction. For a student who is studying mathematics from a textbook, multiple-choice tests may be an appropriate way to assess learning. Indeed, a sampling of these tests should probably be included in the child's math portfolio. But what constitutes appropriate assessment for a student who learns in nontextbook ways? The answer is performance assessments.

When you assess a performance you observe the task being done and then rate the skill level of the performer. An audition would be a performance assessment, and so would a film critic's review.

 SHOW WHAT YOU KNOW

In a performance task, actions speak louder than words . . .or at least louder than the words on a paper-and-pencil test.

To adolescents, of course, the ultimate performance assessment is their driver's road test: Perform a series of criteria-referenced tasks, meet the reviewer's standard, and earn your driver's license. This type of performance assessment is termed *summative*. It sums up what the student has learned, usually at the end of a unit or grading period, and the performance stands alone.

On the other hand, some performance assessments are *formative*. This means that the student's proficiency is not only evaluated, but that the information discovered during the assessment is used as feedback to help the student improve. This would be similar to a distance runner's getting feedback on his performance from his coach in order to improve his time.

Performance evaluations of this type, the formative kind, are probably the mainstay of our homeschooling assessment toolkit. We watch our children when they are busy doing a multitude of tasks, listen to their questions and ideas, informally assess their skills and understanding, discern what they need to do next, and then adjust the curriculum or our manner of teaching in order to better meet their needs. If you did Exercise 3, "Collage Portfolio (Reflecting on Product and Process)," earlier in this chapter, you were directed to observe the ongoing process. I hope you saw something new and illuminating in the way your child approached and completed the task.

Perhaps the questionnaire that accompanied the exercise helped alert you to potential information that could be used in the future. If so, you engaged in formative assessment.

> **TWO TYPES OF ASSESSMENT**
>
> • **Formative:** Occurs during the learning process so adjustments can be made to improve learning.
>
> • **Summative:** Occurs after the learning process, often to report learning.

Of course, not every performance needs to be assessed. For example, you can watch a film the way a critic would with a certain degree of intensity—analyzing the acting, the directing, the editing, even the costumes and music. But you can also watch a film in a more relaxed manner, primarily for entertainment value. Similarly, you do not want to wring the joy and mystery out of your children's learning by living in a constant state of heightened, hovering awareness! Usually, it is enough to simply witness their performances, without formally evaluating them. Remember: The goal of authentic assessment is to improve learning, not to interrupt or interfere with it. But sometimes, especially as you build portfolios or transcripts for those outside your home, you will need to assess and document your children's learning. In these circumstances, performance assessments may be just what homeschoolers need.

The Value of Performance Assessments

In a school setting, performances and performance assessments are consciously constructed so as to simulate the real world. The goal is to design a task that is similar to the way life is lived beyond school walls, and then to see if the student can complete it. This is critical for homeschoolers to remember, for homeschoolers do not need to simulate or model the real world—we are immersed in it. The irony here, of course, is that good schools are struggling to imitate *our* life experiences!

> **THE TEACHER'S ROLE**
>
> **Test-Based Instruction:** Teach toward the test.
>
> **Performance-Based Instruction:** Teach toward the task.

Performances are considered novel and leading-edge because schools traditionally have engaged in *test-based instruction*. Teachers taught toward a test that would supposedly assess knowledge. Teachers "covered the material," which was then regurgitated by the student. However, in *performance-based instruction* the goal is not just for students to know the material, but for them to *apply* the content skillfully in solving multifaceted problems. Thus, by observing a student perform a task, an evaluator can assess both specific knowledge *and* the application of that knowledge in a realistic setting. In fact, the ultimate goal would be that the student knows the content so well that he or she can apply it not only in teacher-constructed performance assessments but also in situations beyond the classroom.

A performance is a dynamic way to demonstrate that knowledge has been acquired and in-depth learning has occurred. While a test is an out-of-context assessment tool, a performance assessment provides the student with a meaningful context in which to display learning. Again, the road test is a good example. Unlike the written test for a learner's permit, the road test asks the student driver to demonstrate his or her skills at the wheel of the car. But in order for the context to be meaningful, novice drivers need to demonstrate their skills not on a closed track but in traffic on public streets and roads.

Another characteristic of performances is that they mix content and skills. For example, in a performance that demonstrates your knowledge of how cloud formations predict the next day's weather, you don't write short answers or fill in bubbles. Instead, you develop a research project, determine what variables you need to consider, design a record-keeping device using your computer's calendar creator, enter daily information in your log, take photographs of clouds with a digital camera, use your data to compare one day's clouds with the next day's weather, and then finally present your findings in a display that links graphics and text to show the interesting connections you discovered. Did you notice all the designing, computing, recording, comparing, contrasting, analyzing, visualizing, organizing, and communicating skills that went into the project? Skills were practiced in context. And if new skills needed to be learned—for example, using a digital camera and downloading pictures to use in the presentation—you learned them in context, too. There was no whining, "When will I ever have to *use* this?"

Good performances involve a number of variables. This complexity is precisely what makes performances so valuable. Whether or not it is singled out for formal assessment, a performance is an exercise using complex higher-order thinking and problem-solving skills. Both take time, and time is a precious commodity in schools. We homeschoolers, on the other hand, not only have more time to spend on these types of activities, we can schedule them flexibly, at any time of the day, year-round.

 HOW HARD SHOULD IT BE?

Whether consciously designed or naturally occurring, every performance task will present a certain level of difficulty for the student. The three basic levels are:

- **Recreational Level:** too easy

- **Frustration Level:** too hard

- **Challenge or Growth Level:** just right

A test in which all the right answers are predetermined is termed *closed-ended*, whereas an assessment that invites individualized responses is typically described as *open-ended*. Because performances are open-ended, they allow for surprises in approach and execution—presenting a student's knowledge in ways the teacher might not have anticipated. In fact, at the secondary school level a student's research-based knowledge on a topic may surpass that of the teacher or parent. In a good performance, the student shares material that informs the adults, and in doing so blurs the line between teacher and learner.

USING PERFORMANCES IN CREATING PORTFOLIOS AND TRANSCRIPTS

Most homeschooling families, even those who use packaged curricula, do not literally do school-at-home—duplicating the routines, schedules, and assignments of their local district. Because of this, informal open-ended performances, rather than closed-ended written work, is the norm. In essence, we tend to collect experiences rather than paperwork.

If portfolios are being used for self-discovery or to better facilitate learning, then utilizing the formative aspects of performance assessments is incredibly powerful. As you become a more skillful observer you are better able to offer individualized feedback to your child. Rather than being general in your praise ("Nice job!"), or in your encouragement ("You can do it!"), or in your suggestions for improvement ("Try harder!"), you will become more specific. You will be able to find specific ways to adjust the program, offer specific suggestions on how to improve an oral presentation, or note specific areas of mathematical misunderstanding to review.

If you are developing portfolios or transcripts primarily for review by others outside your family, realize that you don't have the same paper trail that schools provide their students. *The raw data you need to build your homeschool documentation lies in remembering performances of the past and being attentive to those that are happening right now.*

Browse through Appendix B, "The Discovery Process." The worksheets there will help jog your memory, find old photos, inventory your attic, and record your day trips. These are the stuff transcripts and portfolios are made of, and this book has been designed to assist you in your search. The worksheets will do more, however, than just remind you of the things you've already saved. They will alert you to other artifacts and information you should start to collect.

RUBRICS

Rubrics are the tools we use to make judgements when faced with a number of competing or interrelated variables. Movie critics, restaurant reviewers, and figure skating judges all rely on rubrics in their work. Actually, everyone uses rubrics; they're part of our common sense.

USING RUBRICS TO IMPROVE HOMESCHOOL LEARNING

In educational terminology, "rubric" means a scoring system that is used to judge a student's performance. Even if we homeschoolers do not use formal rubrics, thinking in rubrics is important for us.

Rubrics allow students to engage in self-evaluation. One of the characteristics of mature learners is their ability to judge their own work. Because rubrics are shared with students, there is no hidden agenda. A clear rubric shows students *specific* ways to improve their work. Equally important in the rubric process is the use of samples that indicate gradations of quality. What does a well-organized project look like? What constitutes poor craftsmanship? By giving our children the opportunity to examine models that show the full range of quality, we can help them determine where they are, what they can aspire to, and what they need to avoid. Once students know which criteria are important and what constitutes quality, they can critique their own work, be proud of their successes, and begin to correct areas that need improvement.

Look at the following example. This is a rubric that describes how I helped my son edit an essay. There are many criteria for good writing, but on this occasion we decided to work with four aspects: titling, first and final paragraphs, paragraph sequence, and sentence construction. These were our criteria. In a first draft, most of these criteria were at stages of underdevelopment. That's what first drafts are for! But, because I was specific, my son knew where he should focus his attention (the criteria) and what would constitute improvement (the gradations of quality).

Example 1: A Rubric for Writing				
Criteria	**Excellent**	**Acceptable**	**Not So Hot**	**Starting from Scratch**
Title	Title piques the reader's curiosity by using unique vocabulary	Title is based on the vocabulary of essay's content	Title reiterates name of book or assignment	No Title
First and Final Paragraphs	Strong engagement, and sense of closure	Avoids the template, but doesn't grab the reader	Flat, template-like beginning and close	Not distinguishable from other paragraphs
Paragraph Sequence	Uses text to effect seamless transition from one paragraph to the next	Transition achieved, but by overuse of transitional words	Paragraphs ordered, but no sense of transition	No logical sequence to paragraphs, disjointed
Sentence Construction	Variety of sentence forms used to achieve balance	Complex sentences, but inflated prose	Declarative and compound sentences	Short declarative sentences, choppy texture

Because I was working with my son and offering feedback, this was a formative use of the rubric. If he had turned in his essay to a teacher who was using this same rubric to rate his work, the rubric would have been used in a summative manner.

In addition, when students are active participants in the evaluation process they begin to take ownership of it. In doing so they learn how to utilize parent or instructor feedback rather than becoming dependent *on* it. Furthermore, the question, *Who is my teacher?*, is one that homeschoolers need to answer many times during adolescence. A rubric can help homeschooled teenagers evaluate when they can learn on their own, and when it is time to seek outside instruction.

 RUBRICS FOR SELF-EVALUATION

Rubrics are for students, too! Rubrics give students the feedback they need to:

- Assess the quality of their work

- Set new learning goals

- Ask for the assistance necessary to meet those goals

USING RUBRICS TO VALIDATE HOMESCHOOL LEARNING

Thinking in rubrics is also important for homeschoolers when they are displaying student achievement to those outside the family. Rubrics can help students determine which work they include in a portfolio and why. When you consider each artifact, rubrics help frame the question in terms of criteria (*Is this what they want?*) and quality (*How good is it?*).

Because so much of what we do as homeschoolers is not quantifiable by grades or test scores, it is often difficult to communicate to administrators, employers, or college admissions officials about our children's achievements. Rubrics give both parents and students a vocabulary with which to reflect on and discuss student performance and growth.

 OPEN ASSESSMENT

There ought to be no secrets in authentic assessment. The criteria and indicators of quality should be clear to the student, not left to speculation.

The work we do as homeschoolers is deeply embedded in our lives. Because of this, it is often difficult to pin down our work for others to review and evaluate. Although we engage in rigorous learning and have powerful experiences, we usually have little discernable documentation to show for our efforts. In schools, where student performance occurs in view of the public, teachers still struggle with the central question regarding performance assessment: *How do I turn my observations into credible documentation?* For homeschoolers, student performance is often a private affair, so we find it even more challenging to document learning. Further, it is discouraging when, having given our children opportunities for mature self-reflection, their assessments are considered "soft" or suspect.

How can you deal with the credibility issue? The answer is twofold:

- Make it public.

- Convert the *quality* that you can see into a *quantity* that can be communicated.

Rubrics can help do both. When you share your evaluation criteria with those outside the family, you are going public—letting the interested parties know that you do have standards and precisely what those standards are. In effect, you let others know the rules of the game. Second, by using a rubric in a scoring grid format (see the sample rubric, "A Rubric for Writing," above) you can demonstrate how a particular product or performance was rated on a scale from exemplary to poor. This quality-to-quantity conversion is one way to maintain the integrity of your homeschooling practices and avoid standardization, while helping administrators, employers, and college officials see and value your children's achievements.

REVIEWS AND INTERVIEWS

There are portfolio reviews and interviews that you *want* to do; there are also those that you *need* to do to fulfill legal requirements.

In order to get the job you want or get into the college of your choice, you will be submitting documentation. In most cases, your portfolio, transcript, or college admissions packet will be reviewed without your being present. You submit your materials, and then you wait. At other times, you will attend an interview where you can present supporting documentation in person and discuss it with the interviewer.

Art students, for example, are familiar with both scenarios. If interested in a nearby school, they can schedule an interview where their portfolio of original works is formally reviewed as part of the application process. If they are applying to schools at a distance from their home, they will need to submit a portfolio of slides representing their best work along with their application. In both of these cases, the student receives a *summative* evaluation. On the other hand, if students are not ready to submit their portfolios "cold" and are still looking for feedback on what to add, what to delete, and which pieces are strongest, they can attend a National Portfolio Day program in their area. On National Portfolio Days admissions representatives from art schools across the country review student portfolios, make suggestions on how to strengthen them, and evaluate the chances of being accepted. These are *formative* evaluations that students can use to improve their chance of admission.

 WHO MIGHT INTERVIEW ME?

You might show your portfolio to:

- Local school administrators

- College admissions officials

- Prospective employers

- Members of the media

When you are not physically present to speak for yourself, your materials have to stand in for you. As your alter ego, they need to be absolutely clear—clear to the point of what is called *transparency*. The reviewer should never pick up an artifact and say, *What is this doing here?* While techniques to improve transparency will be addressed in Chapters 4, "Creating Your Portfolio," 8, "Creating Your Transcript," and 9, "Preparing for College Admissions," it is critical to keep this concept in mind from the very beginning as you start to collect, organize, date, and annotate artifacts. Memories fade. How well I know the sinking feeling of looking at a piece of work and thinking, *When did he do this?* or *Why did we save this?* If an item's relevance isn't clear to me, the parent, it surely will be useless to an outside reviewer. Worse, its lack of clarity will make a portfolio (and the student it represents) look unfocused and disorganized.

If you bring your portfolio to an interview, you will have a bit of leeway. In speaking to the interviewer, you will be able to add informal bits of information that flesh out the rationale for an artifact's inclusion. However, remember that you will most likely need to leave the portfolio with the reviewer. It probably will then be seen by an admissions committee or other staff members who were not present at your interview. Once again, this should make a case for clarity.

Realize, too, that whenever you are interviewed you will be asked about things in your background that are not evident from your portfolio's contents. In these situations, the portfolio is not only adding credibility to *you,* you are adding believability to *it*. Remember: Your portfolio is a portrait. The interviewer should see a striking resemblance between the portfolio on his desk and the person sitting across from him. Admissions officials interview hundreds of students each year.

They are professionals who will notice any lack of correspondence between what you say and what your portfolio says about you. Keep yourself and your mirror image in alignment.

 KNOW YOUR AUDIENCE

Before you walk in to your interview try to find out these three things:

- The organization's mission statement
- The title of the person chairing the interview
- Something about the reviewer's background

Perhaps you are submitting a portfolio because you need to, because you are fulfilling a legal requirement for homeschooling in your state. If so, you need to think long and hard not only about what you will include in the portfolio, which will be subject to review, but about what you will say if you choose (or are required) to be interviewed by school personnel. In addition, you may need to decide if only the parents will attend the interview or if it will be a family affair. Knowledge of the law, caution, and careful preparation are essential in these circumstances. Because this is a situation where your freedom to homeschool with minimal restriction may be at stake, it is more fully discussed in Chapter 5, "Presenting the Portfolio."

TECHNOLOGY AND PORTFOLIOS

When thinking about creating portfolios and transcripts, it is important to consider the relationship you and your family have with technology. Different families use technologies in different ways. And, of course, most homeschooling families utilize technologies differently than schools do. In our family, even when using low-tech resources we have always followed an integrated approach, combining a variety of texts and materials when learning about a given subject. At any given time, we might have four math texts open and ten poetry anthologies bookmarked and ready for use. By the same token, as homeschool computer users we have tended to integrate individual software components rather than buy single-use packages. This way, we can utilize the products that we already own (and are comfortable with), and build on them to create what we need. Similarly, your family will need to look at the technologies you have at your disposal and decide how to utilize them into the portfolio and transcript process.

 THE ESSENTIAL QUESTION

How can I use technology to better manage student work?

The use of technologies to build portfolios and transcripts is more fully addressed in Chapter 6, "Using Technology in Portfolios." However, it is important to keep technology options in mind when reading all the remaining chapters. We still need to remember the basic portfolio-building questions (*What do I have? How good is it? Who is my audience? How can I show what I know?*) even when utilizing technologies. However, the basic question of *what* to save becomes altered if we have access to technologies that permit us to archive voice, movement, and interactivity.

Nowadays it is necessary to think beyond the file folder and the milk crate when collecting and inventorying "stuff." But technology is more than just a storage device. When using technology to build portfolios, we really need to think in the plural form of the word: *technologies.* For example, when my older son was applying to college in the mid-1990s, a technology-based portfolio meant having his word-processing files on diskette instead of on paper. For my second son, it meant a website with audio clips and still photos taken with a digital camera.

We have seen that the portfolio process requires reflection and selection. In the same way, even if you have a variety of technologies available to you, you still need to reflect on your needs before selecting a tool. While you don't want to limit yourself to thinking in only one or two technologies, you also need to practice discernment. Because technologies can play a variety of roles in the portfolio process, you want to maximize their usefulness. This means deciding when the use of a particular technology is appropriate, and when other less-virtual options are better.

Because new products are continually coming to market, it is impossible to offer software recommendations that will be useful when you begin to create a digital portfolio. However, it is important to realize that the companies developing digital portfolio products are designing them for use in schools. Manufacturers are creating these software packages to meet the needs of classroom teachers and school districts. Because their specifications are different from ours as homeschoolers, most educational portfolio products will have built-in features and limitations that homeschoolers will neither need nor want. In our house, we make a distinction between using educational technology and using technology for education. We rarely buy a product that the manufacturer advertises as "educational" unless it is truly extraordinary. Instead, our rule of thumb has always been to purchase the most powerful real-world software we can afford and then use it for educational applications.

 COMPUTER CONCERNS

If you create a portfolio on diskette you need to think about:

- **Compatibility:** Consider both the hardware and software at the reviewer's end.
- **Memory:** It fills up quickly once you include pictures and sound.
- **Security:** Reviewers may be forbidden to use diskettes from outside sources because of viruses.

To address all of these issues, you can put your portfolio on a website instead.

Does the use of technologies to build transcripts and portfolios sounds intriguing to you? If so, you may want to skip ahead to Chapter 6, "Using Technology in Portfolios," to begin learning more about the subject.

CHAPTER 3

Portfolio
Basics

A portfolio is a carefully chosen collection of items that tells a story about you. When you develop a portfolio, you tell your story not only through words, but also through images and artifacts, each of which has its own role to play. As the portfolio designer you have a great deal of control over how you tell the story—but you must decide which of your many stories you want to tell. It is important to understand that not all portfolios are stories about end results and achievement. Your portfolio may be about your progress over time or your struggle to learn.

 WHO IS THE STORYTELLER?

A portfolio tells the student's story. Parents may start the tale during the middle school years, but by the end of adolescence the student should be telling it.

Personal portfolios are richly detailed. They tell us much about ourselves and jog our memories to help us reflect. In most cases, a documentation portfolio for your school department will be quite different from the personal and introspective ones created for use within the family. While portfolios for school use still can be dynamic and engaging, they should contain only those artifacts that are necessary to be in compliance with state homeschooling laws. These portfolios should be accurate, descriptive, and treated as high-stakes assessments since they may relate to your continued ability to homeschool with minimum oversight.

 WHO OR WHAT ARE THEY EVALUATING?

Make sure you know what is being assessed when those outside the home look at your portfolio. Is it . . .

- The student?
- The program?
- The parents?

The time will come when your personal portfolios and your accountability ones will merge for use in job searches or the college application process. These hybrid portfolios will demonstrate to prospective employers and college officials how capable, accomplished, and mature you are and how complex, rich, and interdisciplinary your homeschooling experience has been. This chapter will discuss concerns about portfolios, setting goals for your portfolio, choosing the portfolio type that's right for you, and storing records and artifacts.

TIMING YOUR PORTFOLIO

Formal portfolios may be required annually or on a semester basis by your school district throughout your entire homeschooling career. Employability portfolios aimed at landing a job or an internship might be created throughout the teenage years, and college application portfolios occur toward the end of adolescence. Exit portfolios and exhibitions are suitable as a culminating activity and rite of passage for homeschoolers who are finishing their high school experience and are ready to move to another level or dimension of learning. Also, creating annual or end-of-semester portfolios is a good way to build review, reflection, and goal-setting into your schedule. Finally, a portfolio can help round out and put closure on a thematic unit you have been studying.

In addition to these more programmed times, there are a host of occasions when creating a portfolio might be in order. For instance, portfolios are an excellent way to consolidate materials and memories after returning from a trip or after attending a number of events that share a common theme—such as concerts, reenactments, or festivals. Portfolios can be done seasonally, perhaps with reflections on the changes that you notice in yourself. They can be created when you are "stuck" and want to assess how homeschooling is working. They can act as a break in routine. Instead of structuring time for learning the way you have been, experiment with portfolio-making as a learning strategy. Portfolios can also be used to celebrate the completion of a project. You can even get the urge to create a portfolio from the artifacts you discover while cleaning the garage or sorting through drawers.

I know it goes against the rule of creating a portfolio for a specific audience, but it pays to create a basic portfolio to have on hand should you be asked to bring one to an interview on short notice. In such instances, you can add to your generic portfolio a few extra artifacts tailored to meet the needs of your audience. And, of course, creating that generic portfolio gives you one more chance to collect, select, and reflect.

Whether you decide to create a portfolio for inner direction or because of external circumstances, BEGIN! And begin SOON! Your early portfolio attempts will probably go by the book, this book. But, like most homeschoolers, you will soon leave the text behind and develop new hybrids that better suit your needs and personality. These more personalized portfolios created later in adolescence will have more authenticity than your earlier template-based ones.

OVERCOMING PORTFOLIO CHALLENGES

For homeschoolers, the portfolio process can and should be an ongoing, integral part of life. But this doesn't mean you'll feel comfortable jumping right into portfolio creation. I've found that the following concerns surface frequently when the time comes to formulate a portfolio.

DECISION-MAKING ISSUES

Homeschooling is a family affair, and one of the benefits of homeschooling is watching our children grow into thoughtful, independent thinkers. Portfolios can help them on the route to adulthood by providing opportunities to reflect, self-assess, and make decisions. Thus, when it comes to portfolio development, it only makes sense that our children have major input in the decision-making process. One might argue that a student's work products are his or her own, not the teacher's (or when it comes to homeschooling, the parents'). But when you consider that homeschool parents are both parents and primary educational facilitators, these issues are not always so easily resolved on the home front. Three key questions tend to surface:

- Who decides what goes into the portfolio?

- What is the parents' role in the portfolio process?

- How can family members collaborate?

Let us remember that regardless of curriculum content or the manner in which our children learn, homeschooling focuses on the individual. It recognizes each child's unique academic needs, learning styles, personalities, gifts, and talents. During adolescence these same children are also discovering, exploring, and giving voice to their feelings, thoughts, and strongly held convictions. They are taking personal ownership of their learning, and our roles as parent-educators change with their increasing independence.

Student Input

It is helpful to remember that if portfolios are about reflection, then it is the student who has the insight about his or her work. Pieces that you might consider to be of lesser quality may have great personal significance for your child or may have been the result of tremendous effort. If you are looking only for achievement-oriented pieces, ones that seem to meet the standards for "best work," you might not give these other uniquely qualified pieces proper attention. Ask your child why he or she wants to include the piece. Does the disputed piece have the following attributes?:

- Credibility

- Clarity

- Quality

- Purpose

More about these guidelines will be discussed later in this and the following chapter; focusing on these four criteria and having your child evaluate how well an artifact meets them is a helpful way to step out of what teenagers may perceive as a power struggle. My sons have had some odd, bordering on the bizarre, items in their portfolios—like the postcard of Ella Fitzgerald in a red dress or the list of Shakespeare's insults. But they could always give me a sound rationale for an item's inclusion. The key here is not to dismiss an artifact out of hand, but rather to discuss with your son or daughter why he or she feels its presence is appropriate and important.

Family Collaboration

All in all, most decisions about the portfolio's contents will be made through shared decision-making. When a student engages in the portfolio process collaboratively with his or her parents, it is almost like a mini-review. This is because conversation can be grounded in the artifacts, and if rubrics (even informal ones) are used there is a shared vocabulary for offering feedback. This is one of the ways families can circumvent the role confusion that occurs when a teen is unsure if Mom or Dad is responding to his or her work as a parent or as an educational facilitator. In fact, portfolios can serve as a conversational bridge between student and parent just as they would between student and outside reviewer. Remember that issues surrounding decision making may surface again and again during adolescence, becoming more intense during the college application process. If you learn to resolve them amicably throughout the teenage years, however, you will be better able to help your child develop a high-stakes portfolio in the stress-filled environment that surrounds the preparation of his or her college admissions packet.

When Parents Must Be Involved

It is often easy for parents to let go of decision making when it involves personal growth discovery portfolios, but they still may expect to participate in the development of high-stakes portfolios presented outside the home. This is especially true when a family's freedom to homeschool with minimal supervision is contingent upon a favorable portfolio review by a school administrator. In this case, the selection of artifacts is more of a family-centered pragmatic decision than a student-centered personal one. In a less dramatic example, there have been samples of my sons' writing that I thought were extraordinarily good but which were on topics that I considered either too personal or too controversial for a local school portfolio review. In these instances, I felt I was exercising wise and appropriate parental decision making by having those pieces removed from the portfolios before submission.

Portfolio reviews for legal oversight are more about assessing program and parent competency than for evaluating student performance. The portfolio should be thought of as program-centered even though the products in it are composed of the student's work. Under these circumstances, when parents are asked to take responsibility for the program described by the portfolio's contents, they need to be the decision-makers.

 PROGRAM ASSESSMENT

Program assessment is different from the verification of student achievement. Some school administrators mistakenly attempt to evaluate homeschool programs based on state-mandated or classroom-based:

- Curriculum

- Methods

- Types of assessment

Portfolios can show school districts that progress is occurring even when homeschool programs differ from those of the school.

TIME ISSUES

Because a portfolio takes time and energy to assemble, families need to ask if the benefits are worth the effort. The portfolio process should not be a burden to your homeschooling. The last steps in the process—the actual assembling of the portfolio—take time, care, and precision. But, the collecting and record-keeping steps should be an integral part of your life. Be realistic. Save, store, and inventory on an ongoing basis, but spend time and effort creating only a few well-developed portfolios each year.

 TIME WELL SPENT

From personal to pragmatic here are some reasons why you might decide it is worth your time to create portfolios:

- To answer major questions about yourself
- To learn to self-evaluate your academic work
- To focus on your accomplishments
- To perceive the interdisciplinary nature of your learning
- To show that you can put your knowledge into practice
- To document your homeschool high school experience
- To complement or substitute for standardized methods of assessment

Remember that creating portfolios is a skill that gets better with practice. Starting early in adolescence means that you can become more discerning in your selectivity, becoming better attuned to which items best meet the standards of purpose, credibility, clarity, and quality.

A WARINESS ABOUT ASSESSMENT

When it comes to education, everyone—schooled and homeschooled alike—struggles with the word "assessment" because nobody likes to be judged. Those who homeschool with a set curriculum and use standardized tests for evaluation often worry about how their children's test scores may be used. Those who homeschool more flexibly struggle with the very idea of reducing something as personal as learning down to a test score.

But homeschoolers must remember that formal assessment is not always a requirement—we can assess our children's learning in authentic, alternative ways. Parents and students can work together to develop rubrics, which are mutually-agreed upon criteria to describe quality work. These standards would be considered internal to the homeschool, as opposed to the external standards that are created by state governments and education organizations. Rubrics are developed by human beings. As a homeschooling parent, you can look to external guidelines as a basis for content, scope, and sequence, but you (and your child) still need to create the evaluation standards that match what is happening in the home.

ASSESSMENT IS NOT ALL BAD!

Too often assessment has been used to label, reward, and punish. But homeschoolers can use assessment to accomplish the following:

- To describe learning

- To set goals

- To provide direction

When assessment is used to give feedback, it is described as "formative." It suggests alternative strategies and points to new goals, helping answer the question, *What do I want to do next?* The difficulty comes when colleges or employers want to compare the homeschooled adolescent's knowledge, skills, and maturity to that of his high-school-age peers. This would be a "summative" assessment. Given that homeschooling is primarily a student-centered and individualized process, outsiders may wonder what basis there is for comparison. This is when you need to make your homeschool standards and your reflective assessments public. If you want others to recognize the quality of your work, you need a way to help them understand who you are, what you know, what you can do, and what your homeschool program has been like. The reflective self-assessments that you write as part of the portfolio process do precisely that.

Of course, not every portfolio and every artifact needs to be assessed with a written rubric detailing multiple criteria. Nor do all reflective observations need to be written. To do so would sap the energy and joy out of learning. Assessment has its place in the learning process, and it should know its place! Assessment is not the goal of learning but a means to it. It not valuable in isolation, but only as it contributes to the daily, ongoing discovery process we call learning

RESISTANCE TO CHANGE

Instituting a new type of documentation and assessment system means a change in the way you have been doing things. As with most changes there probably will be a burst of enthusiasm at the start, followed by a feeling that you have bitten off more than you can chew. That is when discouragement and resistance usually set in. This sequence of events is predictable and perfectly normal, but the key to successful portfolio-building is to move through the resistance, continuing to save, archive, and informally reflect until your confidence returns.

 OVERWHELMED AT THE THOUGHT OF CREATING A PORTFOLIO?

At first you may feel overwhelmed, assuming you have nothing to show for all of your time spent homeschooling. Then you may become immobilized by the huge quantity of artifacts you discover. Both feelings are perfectly normal!

NOT KNOWING WHAT TO DO

You have a great deal of freedom to design a portfolio just the way you like. Because of this, you may be asking, "But how am I supposed to *do* this?" The answer is to relax and realize that you are already doing something far more complex and open-ended by homeschooling your children. Portfolios are simply a management system for what you are currently doing. There is no one right way to create a portfolio, just as there is no one right way to homeschool. This chapter and the next will get you started, as will the worksheets and wordlists in Appendix B, "The Discovery Process." The best advice is to start slowly. Do the exercises in Chapter 2, "Assessment Basics," and create a five-item portfolio complete with annotations and cover sheet using the suggestions here. If your family has a website, try creating that same five-item portfolio online. These are experiments. Use the guidelines you'll find here to discover what works for you and your family.

ISSUES OF OWNERSHIP

If your children are resistant to the idea of creating a portfolio, it may be an issue of ownership—the impression that this is Mom's idea, not theirs. The paradox, of course, is that the reason for creating portfolios is to help teenagers become more reflective owners of their learning and to give them more opportunities to self-assess and make decisions. I always suggest that parents create a portfolio of their own. This not only familiarizes you with the process, but lets your child see you go through it as an adult learner who is trying something new, struggling to figure it out and willing to share any discoveries.

VULNERABILITY

There may be another source of resistance for your children. Portfolios are powerful tools for self-discovery, demanding honest self-evaluation. Furthermore, portfolios and the artifacts they contain alert parents to their children's feelings, values, thought processes, and inner struggles. Teenagers may feel that they are learning far too much about themselves, or that in working collaboratively with their parents they will reveal too much about who they are and what they think. Respecting a child's privacy while trying to facilitate learning is something all parents of homeschooled adolescents wrestle with. It can become more intense around a project as self-revealing as a portfolio. Again, this issue tends to resurface and be resolved several times throughout adolescence. Keep trying. It is a wonderful feeling when your young adult feels comfortable sharing his or her newly defined identity with you.

CHOOSING AN ASSESSMENT STYLE

Finally, how does the portfolio process fit your child? Some teenagers prefer a more traditional approach to record-keeping and assessment. For them, numbers and scores seem to be a sensible way to measure learning. Others can't be bothered reflecting on their life and learning no matter how many opportunities you provide. Still others consider organizing a portfolio too time consuming. If, after a good-faith effort at trying this approach, it is clear that the portfolio process is causing a disruption of life and learning, *move on*. Homeschooling is an eighteen-year learning experiment. Portfolios can be the ideal way to collect, assess, and reflect on learning. They can be a catalyst to help parents and adolescents connect, collaborate, and build stronger, more trusting relationships. But, as with any learning tool, they only work if they match your child's personality and learning style.

CREATING A QUALITY PORTFOLIO

Your collection can become a portfolio once you have determined a goal, decided on a theme, and gotten to know your audience. But what makes a *good* portfolio? Before you start planning your portfolio, take a look at the criteria and indicators of quality in the following rubric. This rubric is a flexible instrument designed to assess any type of portfolio. You will probably find it necessary to return to it during the portfolio process to help assess how your portfolio is progressing. Remember that the purpose of this rubric is to give you an opportunity to self-assess by offering you feedback that can improve your work.

Evaluating a Portfolio			
Criteria	Excellent	Good	Poor
Alignment with Audience Expectations	Excellent understanding of audience criteria; all criteria met	General understanding of audience criteria; most criteria met	Does not understand what the audience wants; criteria not met
Credibility	Documentation supported by dates, sources, credentials, reliable references	Documentation is included but sources less reliable	No documentation or sources not reliable
Clarity	Each artifact annotated or self-explanatory; comments make each artifact's inclusion clear to the point of transparency	Most artifacts annotated or rationale for their inclusion is clear; comments are informative but somewhat lacking in clarity	No annotations or annotations confusingly written; rationale for inclusion of artifacts not evident
Quality of Artifacts	Quality of all artifacts is superior	Quality of most artifacts is adequate to good	Quality of most artifacts is inadequate to marginal
Depth	Exceeds or extends requirements; shows creativity in higher-level thinking and reasoning skills	Meets requirements; shows higher-level thinking and reasoning skills but lacks originality	Does not meet minimum requirements; thinking is shallow and confused
Reflections and Self-Assessment	Thoughtful, perceptive, insightful comments on both parts and whole; good understanding of indictors of quality and strengths and weaknesses relative to them; good sense of direction about steps to be taken toward future learning goals.	Comments are thoughtful and insightful about content but less so about self as learner; general understanding of indicators of quality and strengths or weaknesses relative to them; has learning goals but not plans to achieve them	Comments lack reflection or are bland and generic; not aware of indicators of quality or strengths and weaknesses relative to them; lack of future learning goals

continues

Evaluating a Portfolio (cont.)			
Criteria	**Excellent**	**Good**	**Poor**
Unity	Goal and thematic focus is strongly evident throughout; all parts contribute to whole; nothing is extraneous	Goal stated; theme evident from and supported by artifacts; some duplication or extraneous material	Goal unclear; theme is either lacking or too broad; materials stand alone and do not create unity
Variety	Dynamic: Uses a wide variety of media, color, texture, etc.	Generic: Uses several media, some color, graphics, etc.	Bland: Relies on only one or two media
Presentation: Appearance, Mechanics, Format	Neat; organized; proofread; in requested format	Generally organized; some mechanical errors; format somewhat confusing	Sloppy; disorganized; many errors; not in requested format
Completeness	All relevant artifacts and complementary materials present and interrelated	One or two missing components or unrelated artifacts	Several artifacts or components missing, unrelated, and/or unfinished

Notice that there are only three levels of quality listed: excellent, good, and poor. More gradations of quality can be added, and in certain high-stakes portfolio reviews. Other criteria could be included. For example, the criteria list for a progress portfolio would include criteria to assess change over time whereas a showcase portfolio would score high achievement.

Note, too, that this rubric rates the portfolio as a whole, not the individual artifacts in it. While mention is made of the artifacts' overall quality, they are not being scored individually. To do so would require another rubric which would involve criteria and quality indicators pertinent to the materials and subject matter. Thus, the artifacts in an astronomy portfolio would be assessed by different criteria than those in a poetry portfolio.

WHO IS YOUR AUDIENCE AND WHAT DO THEY EXPECT?

It is crucial that you know something about the person or group who will review your portfolio. I cannot stress it enough: Research your reviewers! Second, discover all you can about their criteria and standards of quality. If you don't know their criteria, you will be spinning your wheels trying to guess what they want and how good it needs to be.

When you create portfolios for yourself, you have your own goals and standards of quality. You can put in whatever you want so long as you are able to see a relationship of that particular item to the portfolio as a whole. Add a table of contents, write several reflective paragraphs about the learning your portfolio represents, and your personal portfolio is complete.

Once you begin designing a portfolio for another audience, however, there is a monumental difference even though the basic sequence is the same. These are essentially *client-based* portfolios, designed to meet the needs and expectations of someone you wish to impress. In order to design a client-based portfolio you need to ask two essential questions: *Who is my audience?* and *What will they be looking for?* This subject is treated more fully in Chapter 5, "Presenting the Portfolio," but because you need to determine your audience before organizing your portfolio, it needs to be addressed briefly here.

KNOW YOUR REVIEWER

Some organizations make it very clear as to what they want to see in your portfolio, actually giving you a list of the artifacts they expect you to submit. Rhode Island School of Design, for example, requires a drawing of a bicycle done in pencil on white paper that measures 16" × 20". Since this is one of their admissions criteria, if you are serious about applying to RISD you draw a bicycle according to their specifications.

But most times you will need to do your homework in order to determine your audience and discover their expectations. Begin by asking if your audience is a single person, a committee, or a large group. A government official or your mentor? Someone who knows you well or someone who has never met you? Is it your parents? Will your portfolio be on view in a public place and have an audience of passersby?

Once you determine who your audience *is,* you want to know more about what that person or group *does.* For clues, look at the *U.S. Department of Labor's Dictionary of Occupational Titles* in Appendix C, "Helpful Words and Terms." How would your portfolio differ if it were to be reviewed by a volunteer coordinator, an organic farmer, or a research chemist? You need to anticipate their expectations. What sort of outlook might your reviewer have? School officials, for example, are not all alike. A building principal will have a different job and therefore a different perspective on education than a director of curriculum. Check out the list of personal traits in Appendix C. Do you think the reviewer will be looking for you to demonstrate potential as a team player or the ability to work on your own? Show evidence of creative problem-solving or a willingness to follow directions? Which aspects of yourself will you showcase?

 THE DOT LIST

The U.S. Department of Labor's Dictionary of Occupational Titles (DOT) organizes jobs into three major categories based on the amount of worker interaction with:

- Data

- People

- Things

KNOW YOUR REVIEWER'S CRITERIA

In addition to knowing who your reviewer is and what his or her outlook may be, you also need to discover what criteria will be used to evaluate your portfolio. If you don't know the criteria, you are left to guess what to do and hope for the best. This lack of direction is frustrating and wastes your time and energy. Whenever possible *ask the reviewer* what he or she wants to be included and what the judging criteria will be. The more you know about the criteria, the better you can build your portfolio's contents toward it. For example, when an art school previews portfolios, it often tells students that they need to do more observational drawings or that they should include background and context in their self-portraits. If a student gets reviewer feedback beforehand, he or she can submit a portfolio that is better aligned with the school's criteria.

 GUESSING GAMES

Don't know the criteria? You'll end up:

- Playing it safe

- Hedging your bets

- Spinning your wheels

- Going around in circles

- Second-guessing

In addition, when you create a portfolio that will be evaluated by persons outside the family, you are always wise to assume that they are relatively unfamiliar with homeschooling. You need to respect their level of understanding and meet them halfway. Avoid homeschool jargon and describe the significance of artifacts in language they understand.

 HOW DO I KNOW IF I MET THEIR CRITERIA?

You get their feedback! In the high-stakes assessment of college admissions, for example, your feedback is the acceptance letter. Of course, the same portfolio sent to two different schools may result in acceptance from one but not the other. Knowing and working the criteria is not a guarantee. It is simply a strategy to optimize your chance of success.

It is important that you learn to assess your portfolios because formally or informally they will be assessed by others when you share them. Admittedly, most portfolios will not come under scrutiny, but to prepare for the ones that will you should become comfortable giving them a critical eye and discerning where you can make improvements. This is one more skill that will evolve over time and another reason to begin the portfolio process early and not wait until college application time approaches.

PORTFOLIO PROTOTYPES

Your goal determines the type of portfolio you create. If your goal is too broad, your portfolio will lack a clear organizing structure and its artifacts will appear to be isolated entities that do not contribute to the unity of the portfolio as a whole. Even worse, if you have two conflicting purposes, your portfolio will be disjointed and at odds with itself. If my goal is to showcase my best writing

I cannot include experiments and drafts no matter how much affection I have for them. On the other hand, if my goal were to show my effort and perseverance in polishing a piece, then it would be appropriate to include less finished work

Because there are many kinds of portfolios, you need to select the type that best fits your goal. To help you create that good match, I'll briefly cover more than a dozen different portfolio prototypes along with a description of when it is most suitable to use each.

 Once you . . .

- Are clear about your goal

- Choose an appropriate prototype

- Decide on a topic for the contents

. . . your portfolio will actually begin to organize itself.

Product-Oriented Portfolios

Product-oriented portfolios require that you submit specific artifacts that have been determined by the person or organization who will review your portfolio. Creating one of these portfolios is like filling in the blanks. The reviewers tell you what they want, and you include each artifact on the list. Usually there is a "no omissions, no substitutions" rule for these portfolios. If you do not send exactly what is required, your portfolio will be penalized. Product-oriented portfolios are often used to screen a large applicant pool. They require you to follow instructions exactly, and candidates with incomplete or irregular portfolios will rarely make the cut.

The drawback to product-oriented portfolios is that you may not be able submit your best work if it differs from the specific items listed. Or, perhaps one of the artifacts isn't in your inventory or it isn't easily accessible, and there is not enough time for you to create it or acquire it. Or, perhaps you have samples of everything required but feel your work isn't of high enough quality.

Competency- or Trait-Oriented Portfolios

The key phrase written into the instructions for these portfolios is "evidence that shows . . . ." You are still required to submit a set group of artifacts, but you are given much more leeway in the selection process. Rather than asking for a specific product, such as an essay on leadership, you will be asked for evidence (of your choice) that shows you have the skills or traits the reviewers desire. In this case, you have a number of options and can select whichever artifact you believe demonstrates your leadership best.

In a competency- or trait-oriented portfolio the reviewers are looking for intangibles in an individual's personality rather than specified products he or she has available or can create quickly. The drawback here is that you will not know what other respondents are placing in their portfolios. However, if you have quality evidence you should send it along. This type of portfolio may also be used when there is a large applicant pool and comparisons need to be made between your portfolio and those of others.

SHOWCASE PORTFOLIOS

Showcase portfolios allow you to show off your achievements. They are the type that usually comes to mind when we hear the word "portfolio." These are the "best work" portfolios that you submit to school systems to show how well you are doing. They are also the ones a graphic designer might create in order to show clients samples of his or her highest quality work. These are created to impress the audience, and the payoff (unimpeded homeschooling, college admissions, a job offer) is usually a big one. Because of the high stakes involved, this is not a place to display your lesser-quality work or work that is ambiguous.

In showcase portfolios credibility and clarity are paramount, as is presentation. Remember that your portfolio represents you, and as such you want to make sure a showcase portfolio does what it says: shows you off in style. This is the last place you want to appear disorganized or sloppy.

Showcase portfolios may be eclectic and include your best work samples in a number of areas. In fact, it may be important for you to show a range of content and/or styles in your work. This would be typical in an end of the year school review where best work from several subject areas was to be submitted. However, even showcase portfolios are usually built around a theme. Academically, for example, you might showcase your best work in mathematics. If you are looking to be employed at a florist's shop, your portfolio might be an album containing photographs of your most artistic flower arrangements. While schools, colleges, and employers may have additional ways of assessing you, a thoughtful, well-designed showcase portfolio can impress the reviewer, give you an edge, and close the deal.

SPOTLIGHT PORTFOLIOS

Spotlight portfolios shine a spotlight on you at one particular moment. Rather than looking at a continuum of work to perceive your progress or growth, a spotlight portfolio looks at several aspects of yourself all at once. This is similar to a report card, where the goal is to see an overview of many subject or skill areas at the end of a marking period. Indeed, they can be used as an academic benchmark from which future growth can be measured. Do not be put off by the school-based analogy, however. Spotlight portfolios can be used for more than academics. They can be especially effective when used as the basis for personal discovery portfolios. You may want to create a spotlight portfolio to take inventory of your physical, intellectual, social, emotional, and spiritual self on a personal benchmark date—perhaps your eighteenth (or fiftieth!) birthday. Spotlight portfolios are a good place to face the unevenness in our skills and knowledge, to notice areas which we would like to develop more purposefully.

DISCIPLINE-BASED PORTFOLIOS

Discipline-based portfolios take one subject and look at it over a specified period of time. Because most high schools are organized around the academic disciplines, this type of portfolio probably is the one most familiar to school administrators. A student might have a math or writing portfolio that chronicles a year's worth of work. Homeschoolers can create discipline-based portfolios from their work folders, too, by selecting representative artifacts that show both curriculum content and achievement through work samples. A year's worth of work may be culled to twelve or fewer pieces, one for each segment of the curriculum. The term "discipline-based" should be interpreted broadly. Because homeschoolers have the freedom to create their own curricula, our discipline-based portfolios will have different focuses than those of schooled students. Nutrition, jazz, Latin, ceramics: Any subject can be studied in some degree of depth over the course of a semester or year.

THEMATIC PORTFOLIOS

Thematic portfolios are ones that demonstrate an interdisciplinary approach to learning. Rather than focusing on one discipline in isolation, a thematic portfolio will show how one overarching content theme—for example, Elizabethan England—can be studied from multiple entry points: Shakespeare's plays, history and politics, religion, the Black Plague, clothing design, etc. This method, which is called *thematic unit studies,* is frequently used by homeschoolers since they are not constrained by the subject area boundaries of the traditional school. The portfolios that result from thematic unit studies can document learning in a dynamic and vibrant way. However, the artifacts in a thematic portfolio need to be well annotated so that the reviewer understands the relevance and connectedness of items from a variety of disciplines.

SKILL-BASED PORTFOLIOS

Skill-based portfolios are also interdisciplinary, but unlike thematic portfolios they do not focus on content. For example, a "writing across the curriculum" portfolio designed to display written communication skills would show writing samples for a variety of content in literature, science, mathematics, the social sciences, and the arts.

Most times, skills need to be demonstrated, and this means including dynamic multimedia artifacts. A video might be necessary to show your using tools or technology, leading a group or chairing a meeting. These records of performance can be especially important when the skill, such as public speaking, does not result in a tangible product.

Skill-based portfolios can be utilized at many points in the learning process. While still a novice, you can use them to get feedback and create a benchmark from which to chart progress. Once you have achieved mastery, you can develop a skill-based portfolio to highlight your expertise.

 SHOW ME WHAT YOU CAN DO

Your portfolio can demonstrate both general and specific skills:

- Communication
- Problem-solving
- Oral presentation
- Leadership
- Musical ability
- Manual ability
- Mechanical ability

DIAGNOSTIC PORTFOLIOS

Diagnostic portfolios are in many ways the opposite of the showcase portfolio. They usually hold samples of problematic work so that the parent, mentor, or instructor can work with the student to discern patterns of confusion, prescribe a change of curriculum, or suggest alternative modes of learning. When the student participates in both the creation and the review of a diagnostic portfolio, he or she engages in error analysis in order to clarify the kind of mistakes he or she is making so as to avoid them in the future. Diagnostic portfolios need to be reviewed and used with both honesty and sensitivity, and the student needs to trust that the material will be used for constructive feedback. One positive and powerful aspect of diagnostic portfolios is that they actually chronicle a success story of problems analyzed and overcome through joint effort. The reflective writing that a student does for a diagnostic portfolio can be very powerful and introspective since it focuses on his or her strengths, weaknesses, academic goal-setting, and growth as a learner.

PROGRESS PORTFOLIOS

Progress portfolios show growth over time in one specific area. This is the opposite of the spotlight approach, which looks at many different aspects of yourself at one specific moment. By taking a chronological approach, you are able to see how you used to think, what your former skill levels were, and what kind of work you had been able to do. Reviewing similar work samples from each of the past five months, or the past five years, should indicate the way you have changed. In writing your reflections you should note the strategies that made you more knowledgeable and skillful, areas where you finally developed mastery, and places where you are not pleased at the extent of your growth. This knowledge about your progress and productivity can help you set goals and suggest strategies and tactics for achieving them.

Progress portfolios can help homeschoolers in another important way, also. Adolescence is a time of great change, yet growth in learning is often subtle and gradual. For homeschoolers, where informal evaluation is usually the norm, ongoing daily assessment may not alert us to changes that have occurred. A progress portfolio can demonstrate that, despite what we may think, enormous growth and change *has* been taking place.

PROJECT PORTFOLIOS

Project portfolios track the stages of a project's development, showing how it moves from start to finish. They are especially well suited to community service activities, dramatic productions, and agricultural projects. Project portfolios may describe either an individual project or participation in a group activity. They have an activity-oriented tone and are ideal vehicles for color, graphics, and multimedia presentations that show you in action. Your intended audience may well be the general public, since project portfolios are often displayed at a library, town hall, or civic center. When developing a project portfolio make sure that you save artifacts from each step along the way since it may be difficult to locate materials once the project or production is over. If you were part of a group, cast, or ensemble, your portfolio should indicate the extent and level of your participation. When writing your reflections for a project portfolio think of how you would answer the question, "But what did you *learn* doing that?" Your answers should alert you to the deep and powerful learning that can occur when you are fully engaged in a project.

RESEARCH-BASED PORTFOLIOS

Research-based portfolios allow homeschoolers to delve into a subject that interests them, study-ing it intensively in a way that is all but impossible for students who need to be in school most of the day. Homeschoolers have flexible time in which to collect data through interviews, observa-tion, library research, and exploration of web-based resources. They are also not bound by the conventional school calendar and, therefore, can engage in field research either locally or at con-siderable distance from their home. Furthermore, good research entails more than collecting data. It also involves mulling over one's data, observing patterns, drawing inferences, and coming to conclusions. All these things take time, and homeschoolers have the luxury of time to think about what their data mean.

When developing a research portfolio, include artifacts that show both the depth of study and the breadth of resources used. Your portfolio also should include a report that synthesizes your data and comes to an integrated conclusion. Your reflective comments should address not only what you learned about the subject of your research, but what you discovered about the research process itself. A research-based portfolio can be powerful and credible evidence to a college or university that you are not only capable of doing independent study at a sophisticated level, but that you have already have done so.

LEARNER REFLECTION PORTFOLIOS

Learner reflection portfolios create a profile of who you are as a learner. Homeschooling might be thought of as an experimental process for which the goal is discovering how you learn best. Because homeschooling encourages individualized approaches to learning, adolescents are able to discover their personal learning style (auditory, visual, kinesthetic) and preferred learning dimen-sion (verbal-linguistic, logical-mathematical, musical, spatial, bodily-kinesthetic, interpersonal, intrapersonal). In light of this self-knowledge, they can approach learning in ways that differ sig-nificantly from classroom-based instruction. In addition, homeschooling provides a safe and ideal vehicle for taking risks, exploring options, relying on intuition, and learning from mistakes.

Because of these factors, homeschoolers can develop a rich repertoire of learning strategies that allows them to learn deeply and efficiently. Samples in a learner reflection portfolio might include work that came easily, evidence of failure, struggle and eventual success, experimental work, work that you were unable to complete, work that that you absolutely loved creating, work for which you hated the process. Documenting the learning-about-learning process is especially suitable for late adolescence when students can look through past work to discover evidence of how learning occurred. While all portfolios should include reflective commentary, this particular portfolio is about reflection itself. As such, it is a valuable way not only to increase self-knowledge but also to share this information with college admissions officials when they ask how homeschooling has prepared you for learning at the post-secondary level.

EXIT PORTFOLIOS AND EXHIBITIONS

Exit portfolios and exhibitions demonstrate that the student has matured to the point of putting closure on the family-centered aspect of the homeschool experience. Exit portfolios and their accompanying exhibitions are part of the graduation requirements in certain high schools; thus, they might be considered as homeschool graduation portfolios. These portfolios are presented to the community—more specifically, the community that will hold the student to the graduation standards set by the family.

The public nature of exit portfolios and exhibitions attests to the fact that the student is ready to assume adult responsibility for his or her learning, most likely beyond the home. The premise is similar to that of a research portfolio (to study a narrow, defined subject in depth) but with three major twists: presenting the portfolio to a community of reviewers outside the family; making a formal oral presentation on the subject to the reviewers, family, and friends; and standing for questions much the same as one needs to do for a thesis presentation. This type of portfolio plus review demands that the student demonstrate the ability to explain a complex project succinctly and to respond to rigorous questioning. In short, to respond as a mature young adult.

COLLEGE APPLICATION PORTFOLIOS

College application portfolios are comprehensive packages that contain a sampling of all the portfolios discussed so far. In fact, one way to assemble a college application portfolio is to develop several other types of portfolios during your teenage years and then extract from them your best work, project pieces, items that show progress over time, evidence of yourself as a researcher, and a profile of who you are as a learner. Other items can answer questions about your homeschool program, while highlights from your exit portfolio will show the standards required by your family for graduation. The college, of course, will have its own required submissions. These need to be treated as artifacts for a product-oriented portfolio, and as such, you will need to prepare each item to the school's specifications. Applying to a college is a complex process, and it is dealt with in detail in Chapter 9, "Preparing for College Admissions."

FOCUSING YOUR PORTFOLIO

Now that you have reviewed the different portfolio options, you may have a pretty good idea of your portfolio's theme and the content you want to tell about. My advice? Whatever your topic is, narrow it some more! Narrowing your focus is important. You simply cannot explore every facet of a topic in a dozen artifacts! Trying to do so will give your portfolio a scattered, unfocused look. You are looking for unity and coherence, and you will achieve it by keeping close to your focus. This does not mean that your portfolio needs to be dull. The variety of artifacts you select should be of diverse media, colors, and shapes, be of two and three dimensions, include graphs to illuminate text, and so on. But all should be related to the theme and be consistent with both your goal and the type of portfolio you have decided to create.

 FOLLOW YOUR INTERESTS

How do you decide what your portfolio will be about? Begin with a current interest! You probably have a stockpile of artifacts ready to organize.

The way the portfolio process was presented in this chapter was as a sequence: Determine a goal, select a portfolio type, decide on a theme, and choose your artifacts. It was a very analytic approach. Of course, people vary in their way of organizing tasks. If you perceive a pattern in a group of artifacts, you can use a synthetic approach—going from parts (the artifacts) to a whole (the goal). This method is how museums, for example, organize gallery shows—taking paintings that share a common theme from their inventory, and then hanging them in fresh and innovative combinations. This method works well if you already have a collection of artifacts and start to see new patterns and connections as you look through them.

PLANNING YOUR ARTIFACTS

RECORD-KEEPING

Your records, both information and artifacts, are the material from which your portfolios are built. Every family (and every individual within the family!) has a preferred timeframe for keeping records. Think for a moment of how you organize your records for income tax purposes. Do you enter purchases and mileage in a daily log, keep folders of paperwork, or do you scurry around trying to reconstruct events using receipts and the refrigerator calendar? Is your approach to homeschool record-keeping similar? While there is no one right way to keep homeschool records, you still want the process to be efficient and non-intrusive. The idea is to use what works for your family, but with an eye toward how you might adapt your current record-keeping style to make collection and retrieval of information and artifacts more efficient when you begin to assemble portfolios.

Most families have some sort of informal daily recording system. It can be as simple as a daily planner or a to-do list. However, these types of record-keeping systems note what you intend to do, not what actually happened. Most homeschoolers are open to serendipitous opportunities, and unschooling families may not have a concrete plan or schedule in mind as they begin the day. This is when a journal, diary, or log, written in the evening, can serve to document what transpired during the day. If you keep a personal calendar or a plan book, enhance its usefulness by making it function as a log book. When you enter tomorrow's schedule, take note of what actually happened today.

 PLANNED SPONTANEITY

Schedule a weekly session to record all those spontaneous homeschool activities that are just too easy to forget.

Entering personal and family activities on a weekly planning chart or monthly calendar is something most busy families do. While all of life is educational, much of what is recorded on a calendar is information of a general or functional nature, usually entered in advance, before the activity occurs. If you gather for a family meeting on a weekly basis, you may want to keep a second calendar, one for what actually occurs. It is usually easy to reconstruct a week's worth of activities if all family members have input. Naturally, if there are several children in the family, each will have his or her own calendar to fill in.

Even though not bound by the school calendar, many homeschoolers find it sensible to write a quarterly or semester narrative. There are so many things that go on in a homeschool household and memories fade so quickly that it is difficult to reconstruct a year-long stretch. Furthermore, nuances that might have been remembered if recorded earlier are often forgotten by year's end.

Thus, because they lack immediacy, annual narratives tend to sound flat. It may help to determine specific benchmark dates for writing your narratives and work toward them, rather than promising to write something up "in the spring" or "when things are less busy."

Ongoing record-keeping occurs as we go about the business of organizing our affairs. We pick up photos at the drugstore, bring home a concert program, rip out a magazine article, and then put them away when we tidy the house . . .or get around to it! You probably remember to put the date on items that look like traditional schoolwork, but what about those maps, brochures, photos, surveys, magazine clippings . . .all the non-traditional artifacts you collect? Homeschooling is so crammed full of interesting and dynamic activities that we tend to lose track of which year we did what. A date-as-you-go mindset will serve you well when you start to assemble your portfolio. The date will help you organize materials sequentially, add a context, remember other activities that occurred at about the same time, and act as a baseline or reference from which to note progress.

One word of caution, however: Since many homeschoolers do not organize learning around the traditional school year calendar and do not think of education in terms of "courses," you will want to date artifacts primarily for your own reference. If you organize material for a transcript thematically, you will often be using activities and experiences that happened during several "school years." Administrators who are most familiar with learning organized into semesters can find it puzzling that you built a "course" in oceanography, for example, from experiences that happened over a four-year span. As homeschoolers we tend to focus on the fact that learning occurred, not *when* it happened. Yes, a date can add credibility to an artifact, but I still have found it wise to add those dates either in pencil or with sticky notes.

How Much to Save

In a brainstorming session, many ideas are generated but judgment on their usefulness is delayed until the session is over. Most will eventually be discarded, but one never knows during the brainstorming process which idea will generate another one that is better, more productive, and more worthwhile. I feel the same way about saving artifacts and storing information. I never know until after the fact which items or information my children viewed as important to their learning. Because of this, I developed the following three rules:

- If you talked about it, save it.

- If it looks interesting, save it.

- If you can't get another one, save it.

The list of artifacts in Appendix B, "The Discovery Process," looks comprehensive. But what about all the things that are *not* listed, the items that are personally meaningful to your particular child? Make sure you save them, too, even if they seem unimportant to you at the time.

Where to Save It All

You know that the information is here somewhere, but where? You know exactly where that guidebook is, but it's such a chore to extricate it from where you stored it away. What about the items you don't even remember you have? Or the ones right before your eyes that you don't notice anymore? Simply put, where can you store all the artifacts you want to save, and how can you locate them when you need them?

Should you install a shelf system in the basement? Move everything to the guest room? Vow never to have another yard sale for fear of selling a potential portfolio artifact? Of course not! Unless it's awkwardly stored away or inaccessible (in which case, retrieve it and store it more efficiently) leave stuff where it is. The secret is to treat your artifacts the same way a museum deals with the items in its collection: inventory them!

Realize that your artifacts are already archived throughout your household. What you need to do now is note their locations. The "Household Archives" worksheets in Appendix B, "The Discovery Process," can help. They will create a comprehensive inventory of homeschool artifacts that you have stored away. Furthermore, they will help you discover not only where you tucked away things, but where you stored information. Information can be turned into artifacts, but only if you know where it is housed. The "Household Archives" worksheets will help you mine your hiding places, calendar, checkbook, and computer for the information you need.

As you start to acquire more artifacts, you probably will purchase storage components from an office supply store. In our household, hanging file folders in milk crates have proved to be more useful than traditional filing cabinets. Using colored folders or sticky dots (blue for literature, purple for Shakespeare, green for anything to do with money and finance) has proved to be a flexible way to encode both two- and three-dimensional items for reference. Of course, we never have enough book shelves, so we developed a computer database for books that we boxed, labeled, and stored in the attic.

If there is one piece of advice I could give (and I built it into the "Household Archives" worksheets for your convenience) it would be to label every container that you use for storage. When you come back from your vacation, go ahead, throw all your Everglades and NASA Space Center information into a box. Don't worry about organizing it now, but *label the box!* It is fairly simple to retrieve information once it's labeled but nearly impossible to find if it sits in an anonymous box on a basement shelf.

TWO INVARIABLE RULES

Regardless of your family's archival habits, do two things on a consistent basis:

- Date the artifact.

- Label the box.

TURNING YOUR RECORDS INTO ARTIFACTS AND INFORMATION

As you get ready to develop your portfolio, you will return to your records and mine two things from them: artifacts and information. But what kind of artifacts and information should you collect?

ARTIFACTS

A homeschooler's definition of artifacts goes beyond the paper products thought of as school work. Once you open the definition of credible documentation to include the floor plan of the National Gallery of Art, a Spanish language cookbook, and a video store receipt for two different versions of *Richard III,* you begin to realize that your entire home is a veritable treasure trove of homeschool products. In fact, think beyond your living space to your attic, basement, garage, vacation cottage, and even relatives' homes. Your extended family has memories and mementos to share: videos, photographs, maybe even letters or thank-you notes your child wrote. Never feel that you don't have enough "stuff" to show that learning has been going on!

Remember, too, that there are artifacts around us in plain sight that we just don't see. They are such familiar parts of our everyday lives that we forget that they are homeschool artifacts. It is easy to overlook the *Walden* T-shirt my son wears or Mozart's *Clarinet Concerto in A* playing in the background. These describe our family's homeschool experience, but they are simple everyday items or experiences easily taken for granted. Once you begin to develop transcripts and portfolios, however, you need to be alert to these all-too-familiar evidences of homeschool life.

Check the list, "Artifacts & Evidence," in Appendix B for a list of artifacts you might consider saving. It includes two- and three-dimensional items as well as virtual ones. They range from traditional academic evidence such as science diagrams to mentor's business cards, ticket stubs, tools, and ethnic artifacts. When you glance through the list, give each word the broadest possible definition.

 COLLECTIBLES

Homeschool artifacts are spread throughout your household. You need to know three things:

- What you have

- Where it is

- How to retrieve it exactly when you need it

> ## THREE KINDS OF ARCHIVES
>
> Homeschoolers archive:
>
> - Artifacts
>
> - Information
>
> - Memories
>
> Use the worksheets in Appendix B, "The Discovery Process," to take an inventory of all you've filed away.

INFORMATION

Information can be invisible. Because of this, it is difficult to retrieve quickly unless we are certain where it is filed. Think again about your financial records. How would you approach searching for information if you were audited by the IRS? Where could you find evidence to support your deductions? You would probably start with calendars, checkbook registers, auto logs, and dated receipts. Well, calendars, registers, logs, and receipts can provide information to homeschoolers, too. They might remind us of a course audited, books taken out of the library, or a museum visit with our homeschool group. Once we have those reminders, finding supporting evidence becomes easier. Indeed, sometimes the receipt or log alone is evidence enough.

Often you can use information to create artifacts. You can reconstruct projects and events in which you participated but for which you have no tangible product as evidence. You might, for example, take information about community service hours and construct a calendar showing your participation. You could create a spreadsheet to display information on a fund-raiser you helped organize, or design a graph to show the results of a survey you took. Organizational software can be used to create charts that describe in a visual way the sequence of events you went through to complete a project.

WHAT IF SOMETHING IS MISSING?

As you build your collection, you will begin to notice that you lack certain types of artifacts and have very few of others. If you find that you need something for your portfolio that isn't in your inventory, create the item especially for portfolio use. Art students do this all the time. It is simply a matter of knowing the reviewer's criteria and making sure you fulfill it. If you have very few artifacts to represent a particular area of learning in which you have been involved, it may mean that much of your work has been done orally, through travel, or by using technology. Think of how you might translate those experiences into credible products that display what you know and can do. On the other hand, a lack of artifacts may indicate that you haven't done a great deal of work in a particular subject. If you don't see much evidence of learning, you may want to reflect on how important the subject is to you and how this information and self-knowledge can help you set new goals and direct your future learning.

Managing information and materials is only one aspect of homeschooling. It is not the goal and should not become an end unto itself. Creating portfolios should enhance and support learning. Yes, an efficient system of storage and retrieval can make the process easier, but preoccupation with materials and information management is counterproductive. My threefold advice about the subject is the same as it is for homeschooling: Take a pragmatic approach, do what works for your family, and enjoy your time together.

PORTFOLIO PLANNING WORKSHEET

The following worksheet, which is also found in Appendix B, will help you begin a sample portfolio. Decide on a theme, something fun and personal. It can be anything that interests you: Gregorian chant, photojournalism, Teddy Roosevelt, Thai food, whatever! Then, fill in the blanks with ten items that seem like potential portfolio artifacts. Try to assess each item's quality, too. Finally, add a note about context, why you think each item deserves to be included.

Portfolio Planner

Theme: _____

Type of Portfolio: _____

Your Audience: _____

Their Criteria: _____

Artifacts:

1. _____

    Quality: _____ Context: _____

2. _____

    Quality: _____ Context: _____

3. _____

    Quality: _____ Context: _____

4. _____

    Quality: _____ Context: _____

5. _____

    Quality: _____ Context: _____

6. _____

    Quality: _____ Context: _____

7. _____

    Quality: _____ Context: _____

8. _____

    Quality: _____ Context: _____

9. _____

    Quality: _____ Context: _____

10. _____

    Quality: _____ Context: _____

11. _____

    Quality: _____ Context: _____

12. _____

    Quality: _____ Context: _____

C H A P T E R   4

Creating Your Portfolio

So far you've collected, archived, and inventoried materials. You've changed your definition of portfolio artifacts from "simple paperwork" to "lively and dynamic items that reflect homeschool learning." You've gone through the list of portfolio types and thought about which one best suits your needs. You've even completed a planning sheet that lists your intended audience, the theme of your portfolio's contents, and a preliminary list of artifacts. Now you're ready to move to the next phase of the portfolio process: select, reflect, and assemble.

 WHERE DO I BEGIN?

If you filled out a preliminary planning sheet, you already know what you're looking for. Start to retrieve those items now!

WHAT DOES A PORTFOLIO LOOK LIKE?

The following items will go into your portfolio, usually in this order from front to back:

- Cover letter
- Title page
- Table of contents
- Narrative summary
- Reflections
- Artifacts
- Resume or transcript (optional)

THE COVER LETTER

A cover letter introduces you and creates a meaningful context for your portfolio. It shares your frame of reference regarding assessment and informs the reviewer about the type of portfolio you are submitting.

A PORTFOLIO SAMPLER

A portfolio's table of contents can help you envision what it looks like and how it was constructed. There are several tables of contents in Appendix A, "A Portfolio and Transcript Sampler," to help you get a better idea of what a portfolio might contain.

A cover letter is especially important when you submit the portfolio to an unfamiliar reviewer, when you need to submit the portfolio ahead of time, or when there is no interview scheduled and the portfolio needs to stand on its own.

If the reviewer has had only limited exposure to portfolios, he or she may feel apprehensive about the portfolio review concept. A cover letter can clarify expectations and make the reviewer more comfortable. He or she may also be wary of meeting homeschoolers! Your cover letter allows the reviewer to meet you and your style of homeschooling in your own words, rather than relying on images of homeschoolers presented in the media. If you engage in unschooling or base your homeschool program on technology or apprenticeships, the contents of your portfolio may look different from what reviewers expect. Your cover letter prepares them for the type of materials you have assembled. You want the reviewers to focus on the positive value of the portfolio's contents, not shuffle through it looking for a conventional transcript.

A cover letter can also highlight items that you feel warrant special attention. This alerts the reviewer to what you think is most important in the portfolio so that he or she can budget time to discuss these items with you.

Ideally, your cover letter should be kept to one page and be written on letterhead stationery. In it you should:

- State why you are submitting the portfolio.

- Mention that you are a homeschooler.

- Note the basic type of portfolio you are submitting.

- Prepare the reviewers for the type of artifacts they will be seeing.

- Draw attention to one or two items you feel are particularly important and which you hope to discuss.

- State your expectations regarding ownership of the portfolio items.

(You may need to include a self-addressed envelope with sufficient postage if you want the portfolio returned to you through the mail.)

INTRODUCTION AND DIRECTION

Your cover letter should do more than introduce yourself. Use it to direct the reviewer's attention to what you want noticed.

THE TITLE PAGE

This is the easiest part of your portfolio: a single sheet of paper with the name of your portfolio along with the date, your name, and any other information you feel the reviewer needs. When you create your title page use a pleasing layout and a consistent font, which you can italicize, underline, or vary in size as necessary. Plain paper, either white or light colored, is fine but you may want to add a border, either using your word-processing program or desktop publishing software. Paper with a commercially designed border appropriate to the subject of your portfolio could add a unifying touch. Just keep the presentation crisp and uncluttered. You have spent an enormous amount of time collecting, selecting, and reflecting. Don't treat your title page haphazardly! It creates your portfolio's first impression, and first impressions can be lasting. Make sure the reviewer's introduction to your portfolio is a positive one.

 THE TABLE OF CONTENTS

Keep your table of contents to a single page. It shows you've been reflective and selective . . . and that you respect the reviewers' time. They'll appreciate not having to wade through a year's worth of paperwork searching for a few items of importance.

THE TABLE OF CONTENTS

Your table of contents is a list of how you sequenced your supplementary materials and artifacts. It should include the names of your subheadings with the appropriate artifacts listed underneath. However, your table of contents can be more than just a listing of the portfolio's artifacts. Making the table of contents descriptive is one more way you can help prepare the reviewer. If your annotations are short, you can write them next to the name of each item on the table of contents page rather than attaching them to the artifacts.

A table of contents is useful to the reviewer, but it also serves several important functions for you. The final draft of your table of contents is your last-minute management system. It serves as a checklist for all the items that should be ready to go. Is there still an essay to be copied? Do you need to put page tabs on a book in order to locate a passage quickly? Do you have the handheld cassette player? Is the tape cued?

If you need to drop off the portfolio ahead of time, a table of contents makes the reviewer accountable for the artifacts. As the review begins, compare your copy of the table of contents to the artifacts. If you notice something is missing, ask! You want to keep track not only of the items themselves but who has access to them. The reviewer should offer an explanation for the absence of any materials, and indicate when they will be returned.

A table of contents can keep the discussion on track. The table of contents becomes, in effect, your agenda for your meeting. Each item was placed in the portfolio for a purpose, so refer to the table of contents to make sure nothing of importance is overlooked. You and the reviewer will be literally "on the same page" as you move through the process. If there is an item you wanted to showcase but time is running low, a quick look at the table of contents will remind you that it needs to be brought to the table.

After returning home from a review, the portfolio is usually disassembled, and its contents are returned to their places around the house. A table of contents can help you reconstruct the portfolio should you need to make a similar presentation to another audience. It also can remind you what piqued the reviewer's interest should you meet in the future. When creating a college application portfolio or an exhibition of several years' work, review several tables of contents. You will be poised to make your strongest possible presentation, choosing "the best of the best" from your past portfolios.

THE NARRATIVE SUMMARY

The narrative summary tells the story of your portfolio in a compact one- or two-page format. It should not only allude to the contents of the portfolio, but also address what you intended to learn, the experiences you had during the learning process, and how you are able to demonstrate your knowledge or skill. This is another way to prepare the reviewer by creating a frame of reference for what he or she is about to see.

THE ARTIFACTS

I'll talk more in this chapter about collecting, selecting, and sequencing your artifacts for your portfolio. Once you've done that, you'll use your table of contents to check and double-check that all items are present, annotated, and that any technological components needed to display them are in order. Since you want to have duplicates of all your portfolio's artifacts for your records, use the table of contents to check your copies and make sure you are not giving away any originals.

YOUR REFLECTIONS

While you may wish to write reflections for individual artifacts, you also can create a one-page reflective piece that addresses the overall experience represented by the portfolio. Place it either before or after the artifacts so that the reviewer will be able to segue directly from your learning products to your learning process or vice versa.

YOUR RESUME OR TRANSCRIPT

In certain circumstances, it would be appropriate to place a copy of your resume or transcript into your portfolio. Both these documents can be useful when they complement the other materials in the portfolio. However, unless they are requested by the reviewer be sure they have a context before deciding to include them.

 EITHER/OR OR BOTH?

Wondering whether to include a resume **or** a transcript? Consider the **resume transcript** described in Chapter 7, "Transcript Basics." It's an ideal supplement to a portfolio.

Realize, however, that both these items will be reflective of your homeschool experience and, therefore, may not be similar in appearance to those of conventionally educated students. Make sure you identify your resume or transcript in the table of contents so that the reviewer will know what it is.

NOT CAST IN STONE

There is no one prescription as to:

- What goes into a portfolio

- How to organize it

- What is should look like

You get to decide!

But what does a portfolio *look* like? The answer is that *you* get to decide!

Since portfolios are a fairly new phenomenon in educational circles there is no single definition of what a portfolio should look like or what it should contain. Classroom teachers and school administrators struggle with this question, too, because there is no master portfolio prototype sold by a commercial publishing house for school use nationwide. This means that since portfolios are undefined in appearance and content both homeschoolers and traditional educators get to design them in their own way. It is experimental: You match the format to your needs, find out what works and what doesn't, and then try something new next time. Remember, portfolios are an open-ended *process* not a cookie-cutter *product*.

AESTHETICS

A visually attractive portfolio engages the reviewer from the start. It portrays you as an interesting, competent individual and encourages the reviewer to look at your artifacts and written materials with a positive frame of mind. Make your portfolio attractive and vibrant by utilizing the principles of good design. Color, texture, layout, effective use of white space, graphics, appealing fonts, and consistent letterheads are all simple but effective ways to make your artifacts and your portfolio engaging and visually stimulating.

The content of your portfolio is most important, but aesthetics matter, too. Your portfolio should make you look interesting and creative, mature and poised. A polished presentation enhances your portfolio's contents and reflects positively on you, your judgment, and your attention to detail.

 VIVA LA DIFFERENCE!

Most of your portfolio's contents will not resemble the work products of a school. This is true even for those who homeschool in a traditional manner since their artifacts reflect individualized learning rather than group instruction.

As you prepare your written supplements you can use basic design software to create a variety of effects. For example, you can type your annotations on self-stick labels that can be attached directly to your artifacts. Or use clip art to identify the various aspects of an interdisciplinary thematic studies portfolio. You can use desktop publishing tools to turn an otherwise ordinary-looking persuasive essay into what looks like a two-column editorial page opinion piece. Simple tricks like this can make your portfolio look sophisticated and adult.

 MEMORY ARCHIVES AND HOUSEHOLD ARCHIVES: WORKING TOGETHER.

Your **Memory Archives** generate artifacts and information for your portfolio.

Artifacts and information in your **Household Archives** help you remember experiences that should go on your transcript.

Heavy-weight professional quality stationery products available at office supply stores can make your portfolio look mature and reflective. Colored and printed papers can add a touch of whimsy. Just don't get carried away! Your portfolio, which is already bursting with variety, is still supposed to be a unified whole. Lay out your artifacts alongside some sample templates for annotations and reflections. How do they look next to each other? When you start to write, choose a simple font and stick with it. Trust your eye . . .then ask for someone else's opinion! You want to create a dynamic presentation, not an overwhelming one. Remember, white space is good.

Neatness counts. Your artifacts should fit comfortably into whatever container you choose. They should be trim and organized, not sticking out every which way. You should be able to move from one artifact to the next without fumbling.

GATHERING YOUR ARTIFACTS

The goal of this preliminary organization phase is to recall and retrieve at least double the number of artifacts that you eventually want in your finished portfolio. This is because you want to have a large enough pool of items from which to make a selection. Don't forget that a portfolio is comprised not always of the best individual artifacts, but the best combination of items. Each artifact needs to contribute to the strength of the portfolio as a whole, without duplication or extraneous material. In most cases, a finished portfolio will have eight to twelve artifacts. This means that at this point in the process you should be able to develop a "long list" of at least fifteen to twenty-five items. This is the list you will use during the final selection process.

In order to get to your "long list" you'll use three types of tools: brainstorming, the worksheets from Appendix B, "The Discovery Process," and personalized techniques that jog your memory and help organize what you recall.

BRAINSTORMING

When you filled out your portfolio planning sheet in Chapter 3, "Portfolio Basics," you wrote down the names of ten items. These first impressions are valuable, since the items you listed were probably some of the more memorable and meaningful artifacts related to your theme. It has been my experience that, with great consistency, most of these are quality items that move to the next phase of the selection process. If you are the kind of person who knows you can trust your intuition, this list may be the foundation for your portfolio.

The worksheets in the Appendix B, "The Discovery Process," are of two sorts. The "Household Archives" remind you of the items you have in storage and where they are located. The "Memory Archives" help you recall experiences you have had over the past several years. If you have completed these worksheets on an ongoing basis throughout adolescence, you should have a binder full of information at your disposal. Review both sets of worksheets. You will discover not only things that are obvious additions to your long list, but also the memories you will use to write your annotations, narrative summary, and reflections.

If you are starting the portfolio process somewhat later, spend time using the "Memory Archives" lists in Appendix B to reconstruct as much as you can of your past few years. Then, take a look through the places suggested in "Your Household Archives" also in Appendix B to discover what useful information and artifacts are stored throughout your home.

Each of the following techniques is designed to help you not only to remember your experiences and the artifacts that describe them, but also to put them into the patterns and relationships that will make your portfolio a unified whole rather than a collection of isolated items. Moreover, each of these techniques is designed to tap into a different way of processing memories and information. They include strategies that work for visual, auditory, and kinesthetic learners; for list makers and for those who need to use graphic organizers; for those who need to work on paper and those whose personal memories are already housed in their computer's memory. Try several to see which methods work for you. Again, the goal is to remember, find, and retrieve double the number of items your finished portfolio will contain.

Visualize

One of the exciting things about homeschooling is that it is full of integrated learning experiences: trips, productions, early work experiences, project-based learning, hands-on activities, and intergenerational relationships. In these dynamic, complex activities many things may be happening at the same time, but all of them are part of one harmonious whole. Experiences like these create richly detailed memories that are easy to recall when we, literally, put our minds to it.

Guided visualization is a technique that is used to recall events and make connections. It does this by helping re-create a particular experience through a series of questions and answers. The questions are designed to help the listener recall significant aspects of the experience which then can be used to discover artifacts, add context, or write reflections. Although one can read the list of questions to him- or herself, guided visualization is often more effective if done with a partner. One person asks the questions while the other either answers silently, writes a short response, or makes a quick sketch. The questions are designed to move from the external aspects of the scene to the other participants and finally to one's inner perceptions of the event. Guided visualization is best done in a quiet, relaxed environment with few distractions. You will need a blank sheet of paper and either pen, pencil, or markers.

The following questions are just a sample. Create whatever additional questions fit the specific event being mined for memories. Just be sure that all the sensory memories: sight, sound, scent, taste, temperature, and texture are included. Pause between questions so that there is adequate time to think, write, or draw in response.

Visualizing Your Learning

Preparation: Relax your body. Uncross your legs, shake out your fingers. Tense and relax your face, your neck, your shoulders. Take a few deep breaths, in through your nose, then out through your mouth.

The Environment: Think back to the scene. How did you arrive there? Do you remember the weather and what you were wearing? What time of day was it? What sort of light was there? Were you indoors or out? What did you see as you arrived? What did you see in the distance? What sort of furniture? Did you sit down? On what? What about the wall and window treatments? What sort of objects were in your space, on the walls, freestanding on the floor? From your vantage point look around from right to left. What do you see? Does the environment seem cluttered or ordered? Was is quiet? Loud? What kind of sounds were there? Was there any music? Any sounds of voices, machinery, animals? Was there food being served? Did you notice any particular scent in the air? What was the mood of this place when you arrived?

The People: Who went there with you? Who was there when you arrived? Who came later to join you? Was there a crowd? What were they wearing? What were they doing? What did you do with them? What were their voices like? Was anyone the leader? How did people interact with each other? What were they doing, working on, using? What was their mood?

Yourself: How did you feel about going to this beforehand? What was your mood when you arrived? Did it change while you were there? What did you spend most of your time doing? Did you interact with others? Do the activity by yourself? What was it like to move around in this space? How did you use your hands? Did you say anything while you were there? How did people respond to you? What was pleasant about the experience? What was frustrating? Was it tiring? What did you learn that was new? How would you feel about going back? How did you feel as you left? How did you feel when your arrived home? How do you feel about the experience now?

Closure: Now that you've reviewed the event, what patterns and connections do you see to other parts of your life? To other aspects of your learning? What artifact could represent the experience?

Do a Mind Map

Mind maps are a type of graphic organizer. They present information in a visual format so that connections and interrelationships between ideas become more evident. Mind maps are especially useful when trying to create a portfolio where interdisciplinary thinking and activities are the norm, or where the activities are more associative and less sequential in nature. They are excellent for organizing areas that are studied not only in depth, but in breadth, and for material that fits into multiple categories.

The technique is extraordinarily simple. Take the largest piece of unlined white paper you can find (chart paper is ideal, as is the back of wide wrapping paper). In the middle, write the key word describing your portfolio. Circle it. When an associated idea, artifact or experience comes to mind, draw a line from the main circle, write the new word, and circle it. If another concept builds on this new word, add another line branching out from it, then the word, then the circle around the word. Eventually the paper will be filled with associated memories that you can use to build depth and variety into your portfolio.

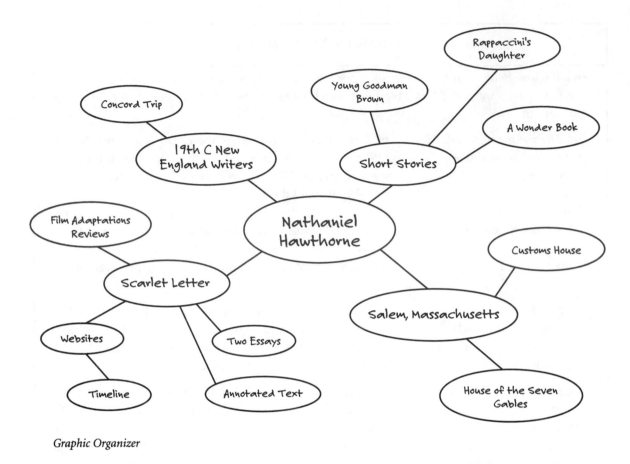

Graphic Organizer

When my son was creating his college application portfolio, this technique allowed him to recall and put into relationship just about all the books he had read during his adolescence. It also showed in graphic format the types of reading he enjoyed as well as areas into which he had not delved as thoroughly. The organizer truly showed a map of his mind as a reader: his likes and dislikes, difficulty level of the books he was reading, the connections between short stories and novels by certain authors, etc. All this information was helpful when he began to write the narrative summary for his literature portfolio. It brought back enough memories so that he could write a comprehensive and authentic summary to complement the selection of artifacts in his portfolio.

Conduct a Look-Around

Each of the spaces in our home tells part of our story, and even a casual visitor would discover much about us just by reading our environment. The books on our shelves, the food on our counter, the newspaper on our coffee table, all give clues to who we are. These everyday artifacts in plain sight reveal much about our interests and our past experiences. Unfortunately, it is often difficult for *us* to take notice of these items or to consider them valuable because they have become so familiar to us. This is precisely where a look-around or walkabout can help you discover artifacts for your portfolio.

The process is simple. You only need a pen or pencil and a sheet of paper. Select a room to inventory. Once you are there methodically gaze around the room from right to left, looking at what actually is there. Looking, however, is not enough. When you take note of an object, name it (actually say the name of the object aloud) and claim it, by writing it on your list. By saying its name and writing it down, you slow down your looking down so you don't scan over items the way you routinely do. A single bookshelf of best-loved books, long forgotten, can yield several portfolio items, as can a dresser drawer or a kitchen shelf. And did you notice the television guide next to the remote? It can become a source for potential artifacts once you realize that you can rip out its pages to document all the documentaries you watch. Don't overlook the obvious!

Sort Your Folders

If you store materials in file folders, this it the time to sort through them. The things that interested you several years ago have made you the person you are today. Your folders contain memories and artifacts, both of which you need for your portfolio. Do not look only in the folders that are labeled with the name of your portfolio's focus. Homeschool learning is largely interdisciplinary. Chances are that you haven't made copies in duplicate and triplicate of a review for the play *Henry IV* so that it could be filed under literature, history, and performing arts. You placed it in whichever folder you thought most appropriate on the day you did your filing. Unless you take at least a quick look through all potential folders, the chances are you will miss out on items and ideas that could add an interdisciplinary note to your portfolio.

 FASTER FOLDER SEARCHES

Make your life easier. Color-code folders so you can tell at a glance the general type of material it contains.

Construct a Timeline

Certain activities are strongly sequential or occur on a cyclical basis. Once you lock these events in place you often will remember other related activities that occurred at the about the same time, adding new connections and complexity to your homeschool memories. Dating artifacts on a continuing and ongoing basis can help you reconstruct a timeline, too. Family calendars, daybooks, diaries, travel receipts, labeled envelopes of photographs, even the dates on computer files can help you discover when you participated in a learning activity and what artifacts might be available to document your experience. Accurate dating can be especially important if you are creating a portfolio for a job search or for college application. A timeline approach is also necessary if you are trying to remember which artifacts would be appropriate for a progress portfolio that demonstrates progress, change, and growth over time.

 MAKE AN ACTUAL TIMELINE

If it helps, use one of these techniques to envision your learning:

- Spread out artifacts across the floor year by year.

- Rip off calendar pages and lay them out side by side.

- Use a roll of shelf paper as a horizontal calendar on which to note activities.

Review Your Bookmarks and Marked Books

The word "bookmarks" in this context refers to Internet bookmarks that return the user to a specific webpage at some future time. Going through your bookmark list for a particular content area will remind you of websites that you used in your studies. Because of the associative nature of the Internet, the hyperlinks on most websites reflect interdisciplinary connections. These relationships can offer you fresh perspectives for organizing your ideas and your artifacts for your portfolio. Your bookmark list may also be a useful tool should you need to reconstruct your learning by downloading and printing out materials you have used.

Books and articles that have been marked with pencil or highlighter are excellent resources for creating context, annotations, and reflections. Because the text is already marked, you can easily skim the material to refresh your memory. Are there insights and connections that you perceive now but which you didn't notice when you first read the book? If so, write them down to use for your portfolio's reflective comments.

CREATING ITEMS YOU NEED BUT DON'T HAVE

If you feel that something is lacking in your portfolio, and most likely something will be, there are several ways you can rectify the situation. If you know what the item is and where it is located, of course, all you need to do is retrieve it. If, however, you have a vague feeling that something is missing but are not quite sure what it might be, do more memory work, perhaps with the assistance of another family member.

 NEED SOMETHING ELSE?

If you find that you're missing something, don't fret. You can:

- Create it

- Reconstruct it

- Reproduce it

- Acquire it

Create work especially for your portfolio. If you feel you need an essay, write one. No problem sets for mathematics? Do a page. Remember, the goal of the portfolio is to show by means of one quality sample that you can do the work. If you only *have* one quality sample, that which has been done specifically for portfolio use, you have achieved your goal. You are looking for quality, not quantity.

Homeschooling often focuses on the process of learning rather than on the creation of an end product. Because of this, powerful learning activities may be underrepresented in a portfolio simply because there were few tangible products to include. If an activity has not produced an artifact, you need to quickly and efficiently reconstruct the event in some concrete way. Make a tape of yourself speaking French. Create a photo collage of a drama production. Print out a blank calendar and enter the hours you spent reading to the sight-impaired. Make your learning visible, audible, or tangible.

Think again about items you didn't seriously consider including in your portfolio because they were too large, bulky, fragile, or valuable. How might you make them smaller, more portable, or more durable? One way is to photograph them; another is to photocopy them. If, for example, you wanted to note a textbook you were using, its name in a bibliography would serve the purpose. But think how vividly you could convey the same information by making a color copy of the book's cover. Consider also whether or not the item needs to be present in its entirety. Could a part indicate the whole?

Homeschoolers can usually boost the credibility of their entire portfolio by including some sort of verification by a source outside the home. You may not have an item available in the house, but can you acquire it? If you need more documentation for a group activity in which you participated, ask other group members to loan you artifacts (especially photographs, programs, news clippings) that they might have. If you forgot to pick up a booklet or a brochure that describes a museum you visited, call the information desk and ask them to send you a copy. If you can't wait for it to be mailed to you, download both text and graphics from the Internet and print them out. If you need a letter of recommendation or evaluation, call and ask for it. (Follow up with a thank-you note or call once it arrives.) If you need grades, licenses, verification of employment dates, or other third-party documentation, photocopy the original you have at home, then place it in your portfolio with an annotation that an official copy has been requested and will be submitted as soon as it arrives.

The more portfolios you create, the better you will become at anticipating which artifacts you will need. If you know ahead of time, you can create or acquire the necessary artifacts during the learning process. Then, by the time you are ready to assemble your portfolio, you will have precisely the items you want right there in your inventory.

At this point you should have reached your goal of double the number of potential artifacts. You're ready to turn your "long list" into your "short list."

MAKING YOUR SELECTIONS

You have determined your audience and goal and settled upon the type of portfolio you want to create, and you know the theme of your contents. Now all you need to do is decide on your artifacts! This is the point at which your collection becomes a portfolio. Throughout this book I have repeatedly stressed that a portfolio is a *reflective selection* of work with a *goal,* a *theme,* and an intended *audience.* You have gone from a household of "stuff" to twenty or so potential portfolio items. Now you are entering the last phase of the portfolio process: You are ready to make the thoughtful, wise, and reflective decisions that define a portfolio.

STAY FOCUSED

No matter how good an item is, if it doesn't meet the criteria of purpose and doesn't fit into the larger scheme of things, it should be set aside. This is one of the most difficult parts of the portfolio process: letting go of quality work that you desperately want to include but which has no place to go. For instance, if you intend to create a progress portfolio that shows growth over time, you cannot put in all your best work. If the reviewer wants only one writing sample, you cannot put in two. If you need to show that you are a team player, you cannot build a portfolio around your individual efforts, no matter how extraordinary they may be. It helps to keep the planning sheet in view, so that you can glance over to it during the selection process to remind you to stay on track.

KEEP THE FOCUS AND THE FLOW

You are your portfolio's:

- **Author:** Select the story you want to tell.
- **Narrator:** Make your story convincing and entertaining.

A portfolio tells a story. Not your whole story, just one part of it. It may help to think of a portfolio's structure as similar to that of a poem, where each word and its placement has a significance that contributes to the whole. One way to determine if you are straying from your focus is to try to tell the story aloud. Because your portfolio is read and reviewed in a sequence, your story is told in that sequence, too. How does it "read"? Does it make narrative sense? Is there a smooth transition in your story as you move from object to object? Or does it sound choppy? Did something in the story seem jarring and out of context? That could indicate something that is not aligned with your overall goal and ought to be removed. You should be able to flow from one artifact to the next, confident that each item has a context and its proper placement.

You may have an artifact you intuitively know has a place in the portfolio, but you cannot find the words to describe why it fits. If you cannot explain to yourself why it belongs in your portfolio, then the reviewer surely will not understand. The item needs clarification. Keep it off to the side, being alert for a flash of understanding as to how it fits into the picture. As you select and eliminate other items, you may discover that your ambiguous item indeed has a place. Perhaps it can support another more essential artifact even though it is not a key element itself. This is when you need to trust your instincts and remember that creating a portfolio is an art that requires an intuitive eye as well as a structured format.

MAKE ASSESSMENTS

In selecting the final items for your portfolio, you will need to judge, critique, and assess each item from your list of twenty using the following criteria:

- Context and purpose
- Quality
- Credibility
- Clarity

You can use the "Artifact Assessment Worksheet," found in Appendix B, to organize your evaluations. Notice that on the worksheet there is no hard and fast rating scale for each of these four criteria. Remember, this is not an objective assessment (see Appendix C, "Helpful Words and Terms") where the scoring system is predetermined and predictable! Instead, *you* will determine how purposeful, successful, believable, and clear each artifact is based on what you know about your audience.

Context and Purpose

Three key question can be used to assess context and purpose:

- *Is it exactly what they want?* If you are creating a product-oriented portfolio you will need to include certain mandated items. If the directions for assembling the portfolio expressly say not to send certain types of items, follow these dictates.

- *Does it show what the reviewer hopes to see?* This more open-ended question requires that you know the content and standards that the reviewer is looking for regardless of the type of artifact being submitted.

- *Does this piece contribute to the whole?* Every piece should have a rationale for being in the portfolio. Taken together, all the artifacts should contribute to the unity and cohesiveness of the portfolio making it an interlocking whole.

Be sure you know what is required, what is optional, what is left to your discretion, and what probably should not be sent. A piece without purpose, which does not have a context, calls the whole portfolio (and the judgment of the portfolio's creator) into question.

Quality

How good is it? When assessing quality you need to evaluate an artifact from two vantage points: how good *you* think it is, and how good *the audience* will consider it to be. All too often the creator becomes involved with his or her work and loses perspective—either seeing flaws too vividly or inflating an item's importance. Remember that one of the goals of the portfolio process is improved self-assessment. How objective can you be as you evaluate each item?

 INDICATORS OF QUALITY

Here are some questions to ask as you critique each item:

- Does it show what I know or can do?

- Does it show evidence of complex learning and higher-level thinking?

- What are my reviewers' criteria?

- Does this artifact meet that criteria?

- How well does it meet their criteria? Is it excellent, adequate, poor?

- Does it meet **my** standards of excellence?

- Does it meet **their** standards of excellence?

However, even if you know that a piece has value, you still need to consider the audience's view and ask, *What constitutes quality to this particular audience?* The more you are able to discover about your audience's criteria and its definition of quality (see the preliminary planning sheet that you filled out in the previous chapter) the more closely you can assess whether or not a particular artifact will meet their standards.

This is the time to "think rubrically," critiquing each artifact's position on a quality scale from exemplary to unacceptable using the variables that you feel your audience will utilize to judge your work.

Credibility

How believable is it? As excellent as your work may be, your audience needs to be convinced. In order to believe in you, your reviewers need to believe in your artifacts. Of the four criteria used to assess portfolio artifacts, credibility is probably the most difficult for homeschoolers to establish. You are wise to think about credibility from the very start, so when you select artifacts from your collection later, they will have a certain level of credibility attached to them. Unfortunately, conventional indicators of credibility may not apply to the type of artifacts homeschoolers tend to acquire or create. In these circumstances, the question becomes how to add credibility to homeschool projects and products.

 CREDIBLE EVIDENCE = DOCUMENTATION + CONTEXT

Without context, even grades, test scores, awards, and letters of reference can be confusing or misleading. They will have greater credibility when you give them context either in the narrative summary or with individual annotations.

This leads to a another question, *What constitutes credibility to this particular audience?*

Some audiences want plenty of numbers, figures, and calculations because this is what they feel constitutes credible evidence. When presenting a portfolio to this type of audience, homeschoolers need to determine how to add a quantifiable aspect to their work. One way would be to create a rubric and give numerical values to the quality indicators: 6 being exemplary, 5 being very good, 4 being adequate, etc. A rubric would allow the reviewer to compare a sample and its rubric to determine if your numerical evaluation matched his or hers. Including one rubric in a portfolio should give evidence that you could assess other items this way if you choose.

Dates can be important to reviewers. Sample entries from logs and diaries, dated and handwritten, might be considered credible evidence, as might receipts, photos with the date printed on the back, or a series of geometry papers whose dates indicate they represent one sample per month for the course of a year.

Other reviewers feel comfortable about evidence if it is presented in a familiar format, perhaps as an official document complete with date and school or governmental seal. Once again, homeschoolers need to ask how they can add a touch of tradition to a portfolio whose work products do not look like those from a conventional school. This can be as simple as creating a homeschool letterhead and logo for all your "official" paperwork, dating it and signing it as you would an official document.

Many reviewers do not trust their own ability to judge a portfolio of homeschool work, and for them, third-party verification adds credibility. Again, this can be as simple as a letter from a mentor, an instructor, or another person knowledgeable about the student's work. Another way to add verification is through publication. If there has been a newspaper article about you that is relevant to the theme of your portfolio, make sure you save the clipping for your files. If you had a letter, opinion piece, or article published, keep a copy of the original. A slightly grainy photocopy of a newspaper clipping is far more credible evidence than a perfect hard copy of the same article printed from a diskette at home.

Your annotations contribute to an artifact's (and your) credibility. You may have documentation that you consider credible evidence, such as an award, a list of references the reviewers could contact, even a transcript with a grade from a course you took at a community college. However, documentation lacking a context can be confusing or misleading. It certainly isn't as strong as the same artifact annotated for the convenience of the reviewers. Do indicate in your annotations if an item is a reconstruction of an experience—for example, a practice schedule written after the fact, or photographs that were staged and taken after the event being described. Being forthright about the origin of an artifact can add points to your personal credibility.

Quantity

Do you have enough evidence to prove your case? Your portfolio should be lean and streamlined, but it also needs to be comprehensive and complete. While you want to avoid obvious duplications, there may be occasions when several similar items should be included. If, for example, you developed a business communication skills portfolio you would want several artifacts representing each of your skill areas: letter writing, oral presentations, telephone skills, and electronic communication skills. A portfolio of only four items, one per area, would make a weak presentation. You want to make sure that all of your portfolio's internal divisions or subheadings are adequately represented.

Although a portfolio is supposed to be a representative sample of your work, some audiences want quantity. This can be especially true at the local school district level if an administrator assumes that the portfolio will be an unabridged work folder. In this situation, you need to know what is actually required of you by law so that you can clarify this legal information (and your definition of a portfolio) to your school official. For more suggestions on this topic see Chapter 5, "Presenting the Portfolio."

 THREE KINDS OF QUANTITY

There are several kinds of quantity when it comes to the contents of your portfolio:

- **Number:** How many artifacts do you have?

- **Variety:** How many types of artifacts did you include?

- **Range:** How much learning have you covered?

Transparency

How clear is it? Clarity is more fully explored in the section below on annotations; however, realize that what is crystal clear to you may appear ambiguous or downright confusing to your audience. If an artifact is less than "transparent," you need to include an explanation. This is one place where having your portfolio read by what is termed a "critical friend" can help. He or she can offer feedback on where you need to make your evidence more self-evident.

> ### TRANSPARENCY
>
> An artifact is clear to the point of transparency if:
>
> - Its title is self-explanatory.
>
> - Its format is familiar to the reviewer.
>
> - Its context is instantly recognizable.
>
> If an artifact doesn't speak for itself (and most don't), annotate it!

Clarify how an artifact meets your reviewers' needs. Highlight this in your annotation, stating how a particular item is aligned with exactly what the reviewers said they were looking for.

Clarify, too, what you want the reviewers to notice. If they don't know what to look for, chances are they won't see it! It is to your advantage to make the reason for *any* artifact's being in your portfolio as clear as possible, but if one merits particular attention, make sure you draw the reviewers' attention to it.

ADDING YOUR VOICE TO YOUR PORTFOLIO

Although your artifacts should be able to speak for themselves (and for you!), they usually need a little prompting. You will be giving them a bit of support so that they can better support you. This help comes in three forms:

- Annotations

- Reflections

- A narrative summary

Even if you do not intend to present your portfolio for review, I urge you to complete this part of the process. Memories can fade, and a year or two later you will be wondering why you considered an item important. If you hear yourself saying, "What was this about?," you know you should have written an annotation! It is especially important that you annotate artifacts if you intend to develop a progress portfolio, a learner reflection portfolio, or comprehensive portfolio for college application. Do not rely on your memory! Homeschooling is so rich and full that at times it becomes kaleidoscopic. Take time to reflect on learning and put experiences in context.

ANNOTATIONS

Annotations tell the story that the artifact represents. If you have made wise selections for your portfolio, you will have a rationale for every item. You know what each artifact is, what it means, and why you chose to include it. Your reviewers need to know this, too. Annotations become especially important if you will not be combining an interview with your portfolio review. If a portfolio needs to stand on its own, everything must be perfectly clear.

Annotations are necessary for full communication of your portfolio's purpose. Many reviewers, especially those whose familiarity with adolescents' work is limited to school-based products, will

TO ANNOTATE IS TO . . .

Annotations need to accomplish the following three objectives:

- **Note:** Describe what the artifact is.
- **Connote:** Tell how it implies learning.
- **Denote:** Tell why it is a significant part of your story.

not see evidence of deep, important learning when looking through a portfolio. Where you see a rich interdisciplinary study of the Battle of Gettysburg, they see a collection of travel souvenirs. Do not expect that they will discern the significance of the portfolio's contents on their own. Instead, find ways to help them perceive and appreciate the learning that the artifacts signify.

Some artifacts can stand on their own without annotation—but they are few and far between. Make it a policy to annotate every item in your portfolio. In fact, it is wise to jot down informal annotations at the time you create an artifact or before you store it away. This can be done by writing data on the back of the artifact, using a highlighter to draw attention to pertinent information, paper-clipping relevant articles together, or using sticky notes to record your comments. Even though record-keeping should be ongoing, it ought not to be burdensome. Informal annotations should contain just enough information to jog your memory in the future: the date and a few words that explain the artifact's context. It is much easier to write formal portfolio annotations later if you have informal ones available to help you.

When writing formal annotations, you can either create a form like the one below and attach a completed copy to each portfolio item, or you can build your annotations into your table of contents, describing each item for the reviewer at the start. The table of contents method adds a touch of unity, but if you need more than a few words to annotate an item, use attachments.

Artifact Annotation
Date: _____
Descriptive Name: _____
Context: _____
_____
Rationale for Inclusion: _____
_____
_____

Help yourself by helping the reviewer. Write your annotations in terms familiar to your reader, avoiding homeschool-specific phrases he or she may not fully understand. If you want the reviewers to notice something in particular, make sure you mention it in the annotation. If they know it's there they will be more likely to look for it and find it. In this way, you are using annotations to direct the reader's attention to precisely those things you want to highlight. This extra direction is important. Chances are your reviewer will overlook subtleties simply because your portfolio is so stimulating and engaging!

It is also wise to connect your annotation to the needs or expectations of the reviewers. If you know they are looking for someone who is methodical and organized, make sure you use those words when writing your annotation. By stating that the artifact demonstrates those particular qualities, you make it easy for them to consider you an attractive candidate.

Two last notes on writing your annotations. If you are using an artifact that comes from a group project, clarify your role and the extent of your participation in the activity. And if you submit written work make sure you indicate whether it is included primarily as a writing sample, as an essay in another subject, or as an interdisciplinary artifact showcasing both disciplines.

Ideally, you should have someone outside the family who will read through your portfolio and offer feedback for improvement. If he or she feels any specific artifact, or the portfolio as a whole, is still lacking in clarity, work to improve your annotations. Remember your goal: clear to the point of transparency.

REFLECTIONS

Annotations tell about your artifacts. Reflections tell about yourself. Because they require you to think about yourself as a learner they will be far more useful to you than they will be to an outside reviewer. When you write your reflections, you will be prompted by introspective questions that ask you to think about the way you think, learn, process information, and use your skills. This "thinking about thinking" is termed *metacognition*. Colleges expect that you will be able to engage in this type of thinking, and they look for its evidence in your application essay.

Being a reflective learner permits you to address the questions outlined in Chapter 1, "Evaluating, Documenting, and Communicating Your Homeschool Experience":

- Who am I ?

- What do I need?

- What do I know?

- What am I able to do?

- What do I want to do?

- How have I changed?

While the entire portfolio process requires higher-level thinking skills, your written reflections make this mature, sophisticated type of thinking visible. They clarify in writing what your artifacts imply. Writing reflections throughout adolescence allows you to track your growth as you move toward adulthood. Because the questions listed above often feel undefined and amorphous,

 YOUR SIGNATURE PIECE

Your reflection animates your portfolio. When you write it, your personality and voice should come through loud and clear.

portfolios help by grounding the questions in something tangible: the artifacts. Artifacts allow you to write about yourself by focusing on something external. Because of this, your reflections will be far more specific—and presumably more useful—than answers to questions asked in isolation.

For personal use you will probably write a paragraph-length reflection for only one or two of your portfolio's artifacts. When submitting a portfolio for review, you can either create short reflections for each artifact or write a longer reflective piece for the portfolio as a whole. Usually, even this more comprehensive reflection would be limited to one page. If you are presenting your portfolio to a reviewer outside your family, you need to decide how much of yourself you want to share in your reflections. Some of the questions in the list below may seem better suited to personal exploration, others for external review.

Reflection requires the same perspective you used to create your portfolio. When it comes to the questions, make a judicious selection. Do not attempt to answer them all; pick just two or three to act as prompts. The idea is to answer a few questions in depth rather than giving quick, shallow responses to the whole list.

Reflections on Myself as a Learner

- Why did I pick this piece for my portfolio?
- What did I learn about the subject?
- What did I learn about the process?
- What did I learn about myself?
- Why was this important to me?
- How did it change me?
- What new questions arose?
- What did I find most challenging about this piece?
- What does this tell about my past experiences?
- What does this mean for the future?
- What new direction is it pointing me toward?
- How could I improve my performance?
- What do I need to do next?
- What does this piece tell about:
  - Me
  - My life
  - My achievements
  - My personality
  - My likes and dislikes
  - My strengths and weaknesses
  - My knowledge and skills

NARRATIVE SUMMARY

There is nothing mysterious about writing a narrative summary. Your portfolio tells a chapter of your life story. During the selection process, I suggested that you tell that story aloud, moving your way through the portfolio, artifact by artifact, to determine if the story "made narrative sense." At this point in the portfolio process, you need to write that story down. While the annotations and the reflections are written by the student, the narrative summary may be developed by either the parent or the student, or by both working together.

The narrative summary is a short piece, a page or two in length, that addresses three major themes:

- What I wanted to learn

- How I learned it

- How I demonstrated or applied what I learned

In educational circles those three divisions would be called curriculum content, instructional practices, and assessment. You simply call them your learning story and you tell it as engagingly as possible.

Your narrative summary should do more than move from artifact to artifact. Remember the items that didn't make it through the final selection process and into the portfolio? They had a part to play in the story, too, and the experiences they represent should take their place in the summary.

The narrative summary will be placed near the top of the pile when you assemble your portfolio. It will inform the reviewer about the story your portfolio tells before he or she delves into the artifacts. The summary gives the artifacts a context so that the reviewer will better understand the structure of your portfolio. The narrative summary will also give the reviewer enough information to ask meaningful questions and to engage in discussion and dialogue about the portfolio's contents.

If you are creating portfolios for personal use, I urge you to write narrative summaries. Not only will they come in handy when you develop your college application portfolio and your comprehensive transcript, but they will record your adolescent learning in a powerful way. Because homeschooling is such an all-encompassing endeavor, narrative summaries do more than chronicle a student's academic history. Taken together they are the story of his or her life.

BRINGING THE PIECES INTO FOCUS

Presumably, you have all your artifacts ready. Nothing is missing or unfinished. You have assessed your artifacts for purpose, quality, credibility, and clarity, knowing which of them need annotations. Perhaps during the assessment process you have eliminated a few items that were not as useful, good, credible, or clear as you first thought. Presumably, all the remaining artifacts are worthy candidates for inclusion. Now you need to move beyond the individual items and think of the overall portfolio. How does each of the remaining artifacts fit into the portfolio's overall plan and design?

 DECISIONS, DECISIONS

If you find yourself asking:

- Should I leave it in?

- Do I take it out?

Then ask yourself:

- Does it fit into the overall plan?

This would be a good time to go back to the portfolio evaluation rubric in the previous chapter. Remember, that particular rubric was not designed to evaluate the portfolio's *individual* components. Rather, it was devised to rate the quality of the portfolio as a whole. So, review the scoring criteria and keep them in mind as you make your final selection.

For a final portfolio of twelve items, try arranging the artifacts into three subdivisions. Experiment with a number of combinations until you see a pattern that has all your strongest artifacts evenly distributed among the three categories. Which of the items can play supporting roles? Which have no slot to fill? If you find the resulting organization dull and predictable, rearrange the objects until you devise a more creative and sophisticated package.

Does each artifact make your learning visible? More importantly, do the artifacts in combination show that your learning was deep and complex? What does your portfolio tell about involvement in tasks requiring higher-order thinking skills? Does you portfolio have evidence of research, communication, reasoning, problem solving, and technology skills? Check the section, "Your Learning Self: Bloom's Taxonomy," in Appendix C to review the types of skills you want to demonstrate through your portfolio.

Does the portfolio as a whole make visible the traits you brought to your learning experience or acquired as a result of it? Characteristics such as accuracy, resourcefulness, enthusiasm, cooperation? Use the list in the section, "Your Personal Traits," in Appendix C to see which personal attributes you would like your portfolio to display.

Create Diversity

Your portfolio should be unified, but it should also be vivid and dynamic. As you finalize your selection, take a look at your remaining materials with an eye toward achieving balance by means of variety.

You can create variety in your portfolio by choosing artifacts of diverse:

- Formats
- Disciplines
- Sources
- Points of view
- Colors, textures, and dimensions

Learning products come in such a variety that it would be a shame if you limited your portfolio to only one or two formats. Even a portfolio on the works of Nathaniel Hawthorne needs not be composed solely of five-paragraph essays analyzing his short stories and *The Scarlet Letter.* How much more engaging and true to your homeschool program it would be if the portfolio contained two well-crafted essays; an essay in progress; a slim paperback copy of *The Scarlet Letter,* highlighted and underlined; reviews of the three film versions of the novel; a timeline showing Hawthorne in relation to his fellow New England authors; a brochure from the Customs House in Salem, Massachusetts, where Hawthorne had been employed; a photograph of yourself taken at the House of the Seven Gables; and a list of Hawthorne-related websites embedded in the narrative summary.

 BEYOND 8½" × 11"

Your story can be told in many ways. Don't limit yourself! You can use:

- Sketches
- Menus
- Ticket stubs
- Graphs
- Maps

Check the "Artifacts and Evidence" list in Appendix B for more ideas!

Even though you want to keep your artifacts close to your portfolio's focus, you need to acknowledge that most homeschooling is interdisciplinary in nature. In fact, while the theme of your portfolio should be narrow, it probably will not be tightly circumscribed by the school's major academic disciplines. And even if you were creating a trigonometry portfolio, think about crossing disciplinary boundaries to include, for example, pencil sketches of early surveying tools.

Homeschool learning comes from a variety of sources, and these should be represented in your portfolio, too. Coursework, independent study, employment, travel . . . all are part of your composite learning. Try to include evidence from at least two or three of your learning sources.

A portfolio can benefit from the connections and interrelationships that show your knowledge at work in the world beyond home and homeschooling. Including artifacts from several perspectives—both inside and outside your family—not only demonstrates the breadth of your learning, but also can add verification and credibility to your portfolio.

MAKE THINGS MANAGEABLE

You can become overwhelmed if you ask, "Where do I put everything?"

Instead, ask yourself, "Where should I put *this*?"

YOUR PORTFOLIO'S SEQUENCE

Think of the type of portfolio you set out to create. If you are putting together a progress portfolio, each section's artifacts will go from early attempts to more polished work. A process portfolio that moves the reviewer though a series of events should be arranged chronologically. Both single discipline portfolios and those describing thematic unit studies can be arranged topically. If you are developing a showcase portfolio, consider sequencing your artifacts for dramatic effect, with earlier items paving the way for your more impressive ones later in the stack. Try several sequences until you come up with one that is not only logical but also effective in telling your story.

Hit the Floor with Your Archives

Once you have created your "long list" and have an idea of the type of portfolio you're aiming for, go get the items from their storage spaces. Spread them out on the floor so you can see items in relation to each other. Move them around. Put them in positions that suggest new patterns and relationships. Ideally, you should do this with a partner. In addition to getting another perspective, it will give you the opportunity to process the layout aloud. I cannot emphasize strongly enough the importance of this arranging and rearranging and this talking back and forth.

This part of the process will make it clear which items tell your story better together and which can stand alone. It will give you a feel for the overall look of the finished portfolio. If it lacks variety with twice as many artifacts as necessary, it will look incredibly dull when only half the items are left. This process will help you discern which are the collection's essential items and which play supporting roles. It will also suggest if something is missing.

MAKING IT PORTABLE

A portfolio is supposed to be portable. If you can lift it, it qualifies! The basic rule is that the container should match the contents. You may have a sleek paper product portfolio that fits into a file folder. Or you may need a milk crate to cart your portfolio to a review. Between these two extremes you have a great deal of options.

 HOW TO HOUSE IT

Portfolios don't need to fit into folders. Try housing them in:

- Boxes
- Baskets
- Tote bags
- Websites

All Shapes and Sizes

If you have both paper documents and small artifacts, you might consider using a large three-ring binder with work samples and artifacts slipped into plastic sleeves. Albums or scrapbooks make excellent holders for your portfolio if you want to create a more permanent collection and not return the artifacts to storage. A collage portfolio is another choice. Make it on poster board that has been scored and folded in thirds so the portfolio can be made more compact for transport then stood on a table for presentation. In cases in which the portfolio's artifacts have been separated from its written material, the reflections and narrative summary can be presented in an accompanying folder or binder.

For larger items try boxes, wicker baskets, plastic shopping baskets, or a canvas tote. If you have items that are too large, fragile, or awkward to carry with you or mail, take snapshots of them. Either place the pictures in plastic photographic sleeves or mount them on heavyweight paper. If you have many oversized pieces of flat work, take a cue from visual artists who use large portfolio cases to transport and display their paintings and drawings. Check out an art supply store to see the variety of sizes and formats available. Some portfolio cases even have plastic sleeves bound into them for display purposes so that you can simply flip through the portfolio, artifact by artifact, page by page.

If you need to mail your portfolio, you may receive instructions from the reviewers regarding how they want it packaged. Follow their instructions meticulously, especially in a high-stakes situation. Post offices, parcel services, and office supply stores will have packing suggestions for sending your artifacts though the mail safely.

 MULTIPLE MULTIMEDIA PORTFOLIOS

In schools, students are lucky if they can create a digital portfolio in one of their subject areas. Homeschoolers can create multimedia portfolios in the traditional academic disciplines, and then some!

Technology Options

Chapter 6, "Using Technology in Portfolios," discusses this topic in greater depth. However, you want to differentiate between using technology *in* your portfolio (for example, adding an audio cassette, videotape, or diskette to your wicker basket) and using technology *as* your portfolio by digitizing your artifacts and storing them on a portfolio website.

Realize that the reviewer needs to have technologies compatible to yours in order to access your information. If he or she doesn't, you will need to recreate your portfolio using simpler, more universal technologies.

READY TO GO

Let your portfolio "rest" for a few days once everything has been assembled. Then, come back to it with the rubric from the preceding chapter in hand. How do you think it rates? Is there anything you want to upgrade? If not, then your portfolio is (almost) ready to go.

If you think your portfolio is ready, it's time for a front to back read by someone you trust. You have created, revised, and edited your portfolio. By now, there are no major omissions, your

QUICK CHECK

Ask yourself:

- Have I included everything?

  Cover letter

  Title page

  Table of contents

  Narrative summary

  Reflections

  All the artifacts

  Resume or transcript

- Is everything in the proper sequence?
- Did I evaluate the portfolio against the rubric?
- Did I have the portfolio proofread?
- Have I made two copies of everything?

Now you are ready to go!

annotations have made things perfectly clear, and the portfolio's appearance is polished and professional. All you need is proofreading help. Get someone to do this for you! Do not try to proofread it yourself. You will have looked through your portfolio so many times that you are no longer likely to catch any minor mistakes. You need someone with a bit of distance to notice what you just don't see any more.

Once it's proofread and fine-tuned, it really is ready to go—almost! The key word for finishing off a portfolio is *triplicate*. Whenever you prepare a portfolio for review, make two copies of every original. If possible, give the reviewer a copy and keep the original and the duplicate in your files.

Congratulations! You have just gone through one of the most demanding of all learning tasks: self-evaluation. Not only have you documented your activities, you have put them into perspective, discovering how they fit into your life as a learner today and what they suggest for your future. Be assured that your next portfolio will be different from your first. As you move through adolescence toward adulthood, your needs will change and so will your portfolios. You undoubtedly will modify the suggestions in this book and personalize them. Knowing what the portfolio process entails will allow you to experiment with new approaches, keeping what worked and discarding what didn't. You have the freedom to format your portfolio any way you wish. By now, you know the rules by heart. It's simply a matter of collect, select, and reflect. Good luck!

ADDED DIVIDEND

Build homeschool portfolios as an adolescent, and you'll know how to develop employability and professional portfolios as an adult.

C H A P T E R   5

Presenting
the Portfolio

For homeschooled students, the most illuminating portfolio reviews are usually the ones they do for themselves or with their parents. Reviewing one's own achievements can offer new insights about the future and help the student appreciate growth that up to this point went unnoticed. When homeschooling parents review their son or daughter's portfolio, they can see where their parental influence has facilitated learning and what they might do differently in the future. Portfolio reviews done to direct future learning or enhance parental involvement are called formative reviews.

For the purposes of this chapter, however, we will assume that the portfolio review is being done by someone outside the family, and that the focus is not about the future but about what has already been accomplished. This type of review—one that sums up what has been achieved—is termed a *summative review*. In general, homeschool portfolios are evaluated by three types of outside reviewers: local school administrators, college admissions officials, and prospective employers.

 INTERVIEW, REVIEW, REVIEWER

When both you and your portfolio are in the reviewer's office, it's an interview. If your portfolio is there without you, it's a review. In either case, the person who looks through your portfolio and evaluates it is the reviewer. Remember, your portfolio may be evaluated by a committee of reviewers, too.

When you submit a portfolio for review, you may choose (or be required) to attend an interview. In these circumstances, you will be able to discuss the portfolio's contents and put them in context. At an interview, the student and the portfolio form a composite of *who I am* and *what I've done.*

At other times, the review of the portfolio takes place without your being present. When this is the case, the selection of what goes into your portfolio becomes even more critical. You'll need to achieve clarity, credibility, and context through your artifacts alone. These three key concepts are addressed in depth in Chapter 3, "Portfolio Basics," and Chapter 4, "Creating Your Portfolio."

Whether you are submitting a portfolio to a school, a college, or an employer, you need to learn how to prepare for the review, how to present yourself if you are submitting your portfolio in person, and why it is important to debrief soon after the interview is over.

DOCUMENTATION FRUSTRATION

For homeschoolers, documentation portfolios can be frustrating. In most cases the reviewer wants to see only end results, best work, or outside documentation. A portfolio that meets these expectations may have fewer samples of student work and more third-party paperwork, such as scores from standardized tests, transcripts from outside courses, letters of recommendation, and verification of course completion. The student's work is there in *proxy* form, with the documents substituting for authentic products of learning.

 SHOWCASE PORTFOLIOS

Showcase portfolios present your most polished work—artifacts designed to impress your audience. You might also include documentation from persons outside the family who can attest to the quality of your work.

These expectations can pose a problem since most homeschoolers have few of these official-looking documents in their archives. What can you do? Sure, you can give the school what you've got and hope for the best. But as I describe later in this chapter, this has proved a discouraging route in my experience. I discovered that the presentation of a documentation portfolio would go more smoothly when I handled it in one of two ways: Either my sons had to purposefully create the kind of materials that school officials expected to see, or I needed to create annotations written in educational language for each piece of work submitted. Both these strategies are discussed in Chapters 3 and 4.

THE SCHOOL ADMINISTRATOR REVIEW

Generally, when you submit a portfolio for review by school officials, your primary goals are to meet minimum legal requirements and to continue homeschooling in the least restrictive manner possible. You hope the portfolio will make your school officials less suspicious and less concerned—less inclined to press for greater control, accountability, or oversight of your child's education. Theoretically, the portfolio review should make your homeschooling easier and less complicated. By coming across as competent, prepared, and knowledgeable, you set a positive precedent for your child's future dealings with the school system, and for those of the next homeschooler who comes into the building.

Even if your local officials do not advocate homeschooling or are suspicious of alternative assessment, they are still bound by the laws of your state to respect your right to homeschool so long as you meet the minimum legal requirements to which you are subject. Remember—because they sometimes forget—that administrators do not create laws, they implement them.

DETERMINING THE PARTICIPANTS

Before making arrangements for the meeting, check your state's homeschooling law to see if it clarifies who needs to be present for a portfolio review. This is still another area where you should know the minimum requirements for compliance with state law. You may discover that there are no set guidelines for who should be in attendance. Generally, however, schools assume that for a portfolio review the child will appear along with one parent. If you envision a different scenario, if your child will not be present, or if both parents plan to attend, let the school know. You should expect that the school will let you know beforehand which staff members will attend the meeting, and you can extend the same professional courtesy to them by informing them of who from your family will arrive for the review.

 THE "REGULAR" SCHOOL-HOMESCHOOL CONFERENCE

The following three people are typically present:

- One student

- One parent

- One administrator

Any variation (two parents, no student, other administrators) should be clarified beforehand.

One last word of caution: I have no problem with either of my sons sharing their portfolios with college admissions officials or employers without my being there. Nor am I uncomfortable having my sons converse informally and off the record with our local school officials. They are poised and articulate young men. However, I never permitted them to sit for a formal portfolio review at the school alone, without either my husband or myself being present. This is because every portfolio review done by a school administrator and logged in your child's records needs to be considered a high-stakes review that can impact your freedom to homeschool. Because of this, your attendance as the primary educator and the person legally responsible for homeschooling is imperative.

THE AGENDA

Before you attend a review of your child's portfolio, you should fully understand the school's motivation for the meeting. Is it to . . .

- Rubber-stamp the portfolio and check off a year's progress?

- Evaluate the portfolio by giving the student a pop quiz on its contents?

- Engage the student and parent in meaningful dialogue about how this year's work aligns with the student's future plans?

- Criticize the parent for doing things "all wrong" regardless of how much evidence of learning the portfolio contains?

I have personally experienced all these scenarios, and it was only when I became more experienced and confident that I realized that *I* was the one who needed to set the tone and the agenda. I needed to inform the school of my expectations rather than settling for those of the person chairing the meeting. Setting your agenda and communicating effectively will be discussed later in the section, "Preparing the Reviewer."

KNOW YOUR REVIEWER

Before you begin to assemble your portfolio, try to find out which staff members will be involved in the review, especially who will chair the meeting. However, merely knowing which person or persons will be in attendance is not enough. You need to learn more about who these individuals are. You should try all of the following approaches:

- Reflect on any prior experience you had meeting with them.

- Listen to the firsthand accounts of others (both schooled and homeschooled) who have dealt with these individuals.

- Keep abreast of current events at the school by reading the local newspaper and checking out the school's website. (If your town is constantly trumpeting its standardized test scores, you may have a clue as to how it views portfolios and alternative assessments.)

Your own experience with an individual is invaluable, but learning about others' (both home-schooled and schooled) experiences with the reviewers is helpful, too. If, for instance, you learn that an administrator invites homeschoolers to a coffee hour twice a year to listen to their concerns, you will have different expectations than if you hear that parents typically leave the office in tears. At the same time, as with anything learned secondhand, all such information should be taken with a grain of salt. One principal we encountered was considered a weak administrator by many parents. However, we found him to be one of the finest public school educators we had ever encountered.

 WHO IS YOUR REVIEWER?

Homeschoolers should be aware of school administrator responsibilities:

- **Superintendent:** The executive officer of the school system; he or she will typically meet with homeschoolers only in small districts.

- **Director of Curriculum and Instruction:** Responsible for what is taught (the content of school programs) and how it is taught (the instructional methods used).

- **Building Principal:** Responsible for the tone and culture of the school, scheduling, supervision of teachers, interface with parents, and public relations.

- **Vice-Principal:** At the secondary level, often concerned with student discipline.

- **Director of Special Education:** Responsible for reviewing learning problems that may be eligible for special education services under Federal or state law.

- **School Psychologist:** Usually a team member in situations dealing with discipline and special education.

- **Educational Statistician:** A specialist in testing and measurement, responsible for standardized testing of students, interpretation of test results, and presentation of those statistics to the public.

- **Guidance Counselor:** Responsible for shaping a program of courses matched to a student's abilities, interests, and career goals, and for maintaining student records for the college application process.

Determine the chair's formal occupational title before you meet with him or her. If, for example, you meet with the vice-principal in charge of scheduling, you can expect a very different meeting from one chaired by the head of curriculum and instruction. In some school systems, the guidance department deals with homeschoolers; in others it might be the Special Education office. The everyday job requirements of the reviewer will shape the way he or she views your portfolio. This is why it is important to determine which lens will be used to look at you and your work.

A reviewer's job description is only one aspect of him or her. You also need to determine what role the reviewer is playing and understand his or her personality. Will he or she be there as an educator or as an administrator? As a mentor who offers suggestions because he or she is concerned about your child's growth and development, or as a gatekeeper who judges how the homeschool experience meshes with the school's expectations? On the one hand, you may encounter administrators who consider themselves primarily as educators. These are the people who will want to chat with you about individual portfolio items and discuss educational philosophy. At the other extreme, there are those administrators who want you simply to drop off the portfolio so that, in the privacy of their office at a time convenient to them, they can place a checkmark next to each item on their list of requirements. These are the situations where the administrator is passing little if any judgment on the quality of the work. He or she wants only to have created a paper trail should someone in the district raise the issue of how homeschoolers are monitored.

Then, too, there are administrators who feel they don't have the ability to evaluate your portfolio personally and instead pass it along to other staff members with more expertise in a particular subject area. This is when it is critical to determine ownership of the portfolio (see the section, "Portfolio Ownership," below). Even if you have built up a positive and trusting relationship with the administrative team at your school, you probably do not know individual teachers. While homeschooling may be discussed occasionally in the professional journals that are read by administrators, information on homeschooling is woefully lacking in periodicals aimed at teachers. Unfortunately, both the National Education Association and the National Parent Teacher Association have come down as disapproving of homeschooling, so it's unlikely that most classroom teachers have read articles depicting homeschooling in a favorable light.

 ## MORE THAN PHYSICAL OWNERSHIP

Even if you ultimately take the portfolio home, you still want to clarify who gets to see it while it's at the school.

Because they are most familiar with the strategies needed to evaluate a roomful of children with efficiency, classroom teachers may be taken aback at the sometimes informal appearance of items in a homeschool portfolio. For a teacher who distributes typewritten tests, corrects them in red ink, and enters letter grades into a roll book, drawings and logbooks may appear suspect.

Suppose, for example, that you live in the Midwest and have just returned from a family vacation to Florida. In your science portfolio you have placed excepts from your travel log and a selection of brochures from your trip. You are excited about how much you learned about aerospace science, the Everglades, and the coral reef ecology of Florida's east coast. You feel the artifacts you selected would be suitable prompts with which to engage a science teacher in meaningful discussion. If the administrator whisks your portfolio away and hands it to a teacher who believes that perfect attendance is a requirement for an A, that vacations take away from school time, and that education happens only inside a classroom, you will be at a definite disadvantage. You will have no way of explaining why those artifacts are there and what they represent.

Even if such a teacher is willing to sit down with you to discuss the portfolio and your trip, you will have a very slim chance of convincing her that a family vacation was an educationally valid alternative to classroom study. At best she might be able to view it as a field trip: nice, interesting, but only supplementary to the "real" learning that happens in a classroom. At worst? Unable to comprehend the artifacts of real-life learning, she dismisses your portfolio, and you, as fluff. Your experiences are dismissed and devalued, and the science requirement you expected to fulfill is still left open on the checklist. No matter how self-confident and supported you are, these kinds of experiences are wearisome.

I learned that it is wisest in the long run to offer school officials only the minimum amount of documentation that fulfills their administrative requirements. It is important to revisit your state's minimum legal requirements for homeschool assessment and to structure your portfolio around them. Because homeschooling is an exciting venture and test scores and paperwork can appear very dry, we may be tempted to share more dynamic samples of our children's learning. Nevertheless, keep the goal of the portfolio review clear. You are not trying to convert administrators to your personal educational philosophy. Rather, you are trying to fulfill legal requirements while protecting the homeschooling freedoms of yourself and others.

As a person excited about new models of learning, I had to face the fact that sometimes a school may be more concerned with fulfilling administrative requirements than it is about contemporary models of education. I remember a portfolio review that I thought was far too brief and cursory, one in which the reviewer engaged in very little meaningful dialogue with my son about his work. Instead, she kept looking over to a checklist of courses required for graduation to determine how my son was fulfilling the requirements. When my son and I debriefed after the session, I mentioned how discouraging it felt. To which my son reassuringly replied, "It was OK, Mom. She's an administrator, not an educator!"

Of course, he was right.

PREPARATION

PREPARING YOURSELF

As a former first grade teacher, when I walk into school for a portfolio review, I instinctively think "Show and Tell." This is the essence of a review with an interview. Generally, you *show* your portfolio and you *tell* about its contents. Sometimes, however, it is wise to show and keep quiet, answering only the specific questions raised by the interviewer. On still other occasions, you may want to engage the reviewer in dialogue or direct the conversation. In large part, your approach will depend on your knowledge of the reviewer and your comfort level dealing with him or her.

In order to prepare yourself for the interview, it is useful to rehearse the meeting ahead of time by role-playing. While family members can do this with each other, I have found it much more effective to have trusted friends act as interviewers. A veteran homeschooler can be an excellent choice, but my best mock interview was conducted by a group of friends who were teachers. And my most rigorous practice occurred one-on-one with a friend who is a Harvard-educated building principal. In each case, I asked my interviewers to make it tough on me, and they obliged. They knew the vocabulary, the issues, the hot buttons to push; and I learned to stay cool and composed. I cannot overestimate the usefulness of this technique. When you walk into a school building after having been thoroughly grilled by caring friends, you will be poised, polished, professional, and ready to meet the challenge ahead of you.

 A MILLION HOMESCHOOL QUESTIONS

There's no end to the number of questions people ask! However, they tend to begin in a few predictable ways. Use the following prompts to generate role-playing questions:

- I read somewhere that homeschoolers . . .

- Why did you . . . ?

- Aren't you concerned that . . . ?

- How can you possibly think that . . . ?

- But what about . . . ?

- How many . . . ?

As homeschooling parents, you are both parent and instructor/facilitator. Recognize that even though you are both parent *and* teacher you may need to compartmentalize yourself during an interview. At any moment you may have to decide whether the parent *or* the teacher in you is speaking. In addition, throughout the interview you need to be constantly alert to your role as your child's advocate. If the administrator starts to veer off-topic into areas you wish not to discuss, you quickly need to bring the conversation back to the portfolio and its artifacts—to keep the talk "on task," as educators like to say.

PREPARING YOUR CHILD

Similarly, once you have a feel for what may be expected of you, prepare your child. Let your son or daughter know what the agenda will be, who will be in attendance, the type of questions you anticipate, and the role you see yourself playing. I have found it useful to take each artifact in the portfolio and have both of us review it aloud a day or two before the review. Ideally, your son or daughter should be well versed in the portfolio's contents, the rule being: If you can't discuss it, it doesn't go in. Chatting about each piece ahead of time will allow you to both refresh and share your individual insights about the piece's significance. This way you can work together as a student/teacher team during the interview if that strategy becomes necessary.

The Importance of Parental Support

While your son or daughter is the person best able to describe the artifacts in the portfolio, your presence is an invaluable asset during an interview. If you see that an item in the portfolio is being overlooked, bring it up for discussion. If you detect that the reviewer lacks context for a particular artifact, remind your child to add it. If there is educational jargon that needs to be used to better explain a concept, use it.

HOMESCHOOLERS SPEAK

I continue to be impressed by the oral communication skills that homeschool students display when speaking to school officials. Remember that most high school students rarely talk to their building administrators, and if they do it is usually because of behavioral problems. Students discussing their work in a thoughtful, reflective manner is a somewhat remarkable occurrence for central office personnel.

Even though I had a great deal of confidence in my children's ability to think on their feet and show what they knew, I was always wary of the portfolio review interviews. Yes, my sons were articulate, but they were still young and, as such, vulnerable to aggressive or inappropriately probing questions. Again, this is where your role as your child's advocate becomes important. If there are areas you consider off-limits, make sure your child knows what they are. If they arise during the interview, let your child know he or she can turn to you and say, "Mom, maybe you'd like to handle this." If your child fears that the interview will become awkward or stressful, devise a signal that will alert you that he or she needs intervention. It is critical that you create failsafe mechanisms so that the portfolio review does not stray from the artifacts you have brought to discuss.

 SHOW YOUR ENTHUSIASM

Remember that even if the only reason you are presenting your portfolio to the school is to fulfill minimum legal requirements, the tone you set is important. My toughest, most rigorous practice interview was with the Harvard-educated principal, but she also gave me the warmest, most gentle piece of advice. "You look so serious and you love this!" she exclaimed, "You've got to smile more!" She told me to write the word "Smile" above my agenda on my yellow legal pad. Throughout the Superintendent's meeting, every time I saw that word "Smile" that's exactly what I did.

PREPARING THE REVIEWER

Just as you need to prepare yourself and your child for a portfolio review and interview, you need to prepare the reviewer. There are three areas that you want to clarify before walking in for your appointment:

- **Assessment literacy:** familiarity with alternative assessment

- **The agenda:** your expectations for the meeting

- **The ownership of the portfolio:** to whom does the content of the portfolio belong?

Assessment Literacy

Recognize that you are not alone in wanting to use a portfolio as an evaluation tool. Many contemporary education researchers favor authentic reporting instruments for *all* students—the researchers are in your corner on this issue. Furthermore, authentic assessments and reporting systems are well suited to the practice of home education. In fact, a case can be made that book reports, multiple-choice tests, and indeed all other types of nonauthentic assessment exist because schools have not figured out how to make authentic assessments "scalable," that is, manageable for large numbers of children. We homeschoolers, however, do not need to deal with scalability issues. We are close to our students, we observe them carefully, and we can evaluate and assess using a rubric when necessary.

 AUTHENTIC ASSESSMENT

In authentic assessments, the student applies knowledge or skills in real-life situations. He or she may perform a task or create something tangible, but in either case, whatever is assessed is a natural outcome of the learning process, not an artificial add-on.

Understand, too, that there is an area of educator professional development called "assessment literacy." This term refers to how knowledgeable teachers and administrators are about the wide array of evaluation tools. While we would hope that the person reviewing the portfolio is well versed in authentic assessment and has a sophisticated level of assessment literacy, it pays to be realistic. Administrators are most familiar with testing and other *quantitative* tools that supposedly measure learning. Even if they are familiar with *qualitative* assessment tools, chances are these methods are probably not widely used in their school.

Sharing accurate information about homeschooling law with your administrators usually works to your advantage, primarily because we homeschoolers are more informed than they on the subject. Similarly, realize that you may be better informed about authentic assessment than your school administrators. Thus, in order to clarify your expectations regarding portfolios and alternative assessment, you may find it useful to provide administrators with information in this area, too.

 ASSESSMENT LITERACY

A reviewer with high assessment literacy . . .

- Has a working knowledge of what he or she is assessing

- Knows that diverse products can be used for assessment

- Is open to the idea of using these alternatives to evaluate progress

When communicating with my administrators, I always found my best source for information was not homeschooling magazines. Rather, I looked to the professional journals my administrators read (or should be reading) to keep abreast of educational trends and research. Here are a few that I found helpful:

- *Educational Leadership,* published by the Association for Supervision and Curriculum Development: www.ascd.org/pubs/el/elintro.html

- *Education Week* and *Teacher Magazine:* www.edweek.org/edsearch.cfm

- *Phi Delta Kappan,* the journal of the international education fraternity: www.pdkintl.org/kappan/kappan.htm

- *School Administrator,* the magazine of the American Association of School Administrators: www.aasa.org/SA/contents.htm

By searching these websites using key words such as "portfolio," "rubric," "authentic," "assessment," etc., I discovered articles that my Superintendent and building principals found credible and noteworthy. Then I would print out a copy of the article and clip it to my letter setting the agenda. Alternatively, you could mention the article's title, along with the issue in which it appeared and the URL of the website where it is located.

Again, your goal here is not to convince your administrator to adopt alternative assessment practices for his or her building or school system. Rather, you want him or her to realize that you are making an informed and valid educational choice in selecting a portfolio for reporting, that you have done your homework regarding assessment, and that you will not to succumb to arguments about standardized tests being the only valid measure of student learning. In short, you are holding your administrator accountable to professional standards for assessment literacy. And by sharing professional resources, you are claiming your status as a well-informed educational practitioner, as well.

The Agenda: Setting Your Expectations for the Meeting

Although a telephone call can set the time for the interview, I discovered that it was important to write my administrator a brief letter highlighting what I perceived to be the agenda for the meeting. I found this to be useful no matter how well I knew or trusted the individual chairing the meeting. By formalizing my agenda and expectations first, I put a structure or shape to the meeting. I was not responding to the school's agenda; they were responding to mine. This strategy came about after sitting through several agenda-less meetings at the middle school level. These were meetings where my son and I were put on the hot seat and were forced to defend whatever the administrator found unfamiliar in our curriculum, portfolio, or methodology. We eventually realized that the administrator chairing these meetings had never bothered to look through the portfolio. He was winging it, trying to cover up his unpreparedness by blustering. The irony, of course, was that he was holding us to standards for academic accountability while being professionally sloppy himself. Here is what I do now, in advance and in writing, in order to hold our administrators to appropriately high standards:

- Write a letter covering the agenda
- Arrange for a timely preview of the portfolio
- Clarify ownership issues

When you write your letter outlining your agenda, you are clarifying your expectations about a number of things. First and foremost, you want to set a *positive tone*, stating that you believe this is going to be a cordial, productive, and professional meeting. It is also helpful to restate the *day, date, and time* of the meeting in the letter, perhaps noting that you expect it to last no more than half an hour. This is mutually useful. Your administrator has other job obligations that he or she needs to attend to, and you want to create a graceful exit.

Next, you need to state your *definition of a portfolio:* a reflective and representative selection of work. This is to ensure that the administrator does not expect to see evidence for everything done during the past year. You then need to clarify that this is a portfolio review, and as such *conversation will be grounded in the portfolio's artifacts.* This is an extraordinarily important point to clarify. Your child should be asked to discuss only what is in the portfolio, not what is missing from it. If, in your narrative summary (see Chapters 3 and 4), you refer to activities, travel, or projects, etc. for which you chose to include no artifacts, the administrator might legitimately inquire about these experiences. However, the discussion should be a *review of the portfolio,* not an inquisition regarding things not there. This is a critical point, and one you need to be alert to as your child's advocate. If the administrator loses sight of his or her role as a reviewer, it is crucial that you bring the conversation back to an artifact and shape the discussion around it.

 SOMETHING MISSING?

Does the administrator think something is missing? It may be that:

- The information is present, but not in familiar format.

- The information is there, but the reviewer has not read deeply enough into the materials.

- The subject anticipated was actually not on the semester's agenda.

- Other subjects were substituted for those on the original educational plan.

Questions about perceived program omissions should be directed to the parent as the educational facilitator, not to the student.

Sometimes there will be additional issues you'll want to discuss while meeting with school officials, and if so you should state these in your letter as well. We were once interested in discussing the dual enrollment program that gives high school students (including homeschoolers) access to courses in the state college system. In this situation, we mentioned in our agenda-setting letter that we would like someone from the guidance department to attend the meeting in order to share program information with us.

Your letter is a good place to mention that you would like to have your child's records available at the meeting for your review. Usually, a school requests a day or two's notice for parental review of a child's cumulative folder. Your letter will give them the advance notice they need in order to comply with the open records law in your state. It is always good to take a quick look through the folder. Not only will it give you an idea of how the district's records look (which can be useful when thinking about how you will configure a transcript), but it will also allow you to question anything which you find that strikes you as confusing or inappropriate.

Another important item you need to address in writing is the ownership of the portfolio's contents. Before making a statement regarding this, you should check your state's regulation—but in general, just because you are sharing the portfolio with the school does not mean that you are giving it to them, or that they may keep it for any length of time they wish, or that they may share it with others without your permission. It would be helpful to clarify for the school which, if any, items you would not mind leaving with them, such as your narrative summary. If there are artifacts you intend to leave at the school, make sure they are copies, not originals.

Finally, while it is entirely proper to take notes during the meeting, if you intend to make a tape recording of the meeting for any reason, let your administrator know this in advance. Showing up with a cassette recorder, even if it is just to take notes, can be threatening and may well put the reviewer in a defensive mode. If you feel you need to make a recording, approach the subject

PORTFOLIO OWNERSHIP

Avoid awkwardness. When you submit your table of contents, indicate with an asterisk the items you choose to leave with the administrator after the meeting. Things left unmarked go home.

tactfully, letting the administrator know, for example, that you want to have a record of the interview for your spouse who can't attend, or because you are using the review formatively and want to document his or her feedback, or simply because you want to free yourself from taking handwritten notes so that you can more fully participate in the discussion. You would not want the administrator to surprise you with a spur-of-the-moment taping; offer him or her the same professional courtesy.

NOTE TAKING

Make sure you bring a notepad to the review. As the meeting progresses, you want to put the following points in writing:

- Verbatim comments by the reviewer

- The reviewer's answers to your questions

- Dates or schedules for future meetings

All of these details can be addressed in a one-page letter similar to the sample on page 96.

THE PORTFOLIO PREVIEW

One way to hold your administrator accountable to a professional review is to have him or her *preview* the portfolio. This increases your chances of a thoughtful, reflective review rather than a hasty, impromptu one. How much lead time you allow is important. While you want to avoid handing the portfolio over for the first time when you walk into the interview, you also want to avoid its being out of your hands for too long. You want to give the reviewer enough time to look through the portfolio, but not enough time to pass it around to others for comment, make copies of all the work, call together a committee, etc. The key is to treat it as you would any business meeting. You want the reviewer neither underprepared nor overprepared, but appropriately prepared. A ten- to fifteen-minute review of the portfolio with time afterward to reflect on its contents should be more than enough for a competent professional to determine what he or she would like to discuss with you.

TWO ARTICLES TO SHARE

Check out FairTest's article "The Value of Formative Assessment" at www.fairtest.org/examarts/winter99/k-forma3.html. The *Phi Delta Kappan* article at www.pdkintl.org/kappan/kbla9810.htm would be a good enclosure with your cover letter.

Heueristics . . .

Loretta Heuer, M.Ed.
333 Jackson Street
Holliston, MA 01746
(222)555-1436
e-mail: LorettaMCH@aol.com

January 17, 1999

Dr. Mary Ellen Rizzo
Holliston High School
Hollis Street
Holliston MA 01746

Re: Grade 11 Home Education Program for Jefferson Heuer

Dear Dr. Rizzo:

We would like to confirm our meeting with you 8:45-9:15am, Thursday, January 28th, to review Jed's portfolio of first semester work. We will drop the portfolio off at your office Wednesday the 27th so that you can preview it before we get together. There will be approximately eight to ten artifacts in his portfolio, each of which he is prepared to discuss with you as time allows. It has been a productive few months, and Jed is looking forward to showing samples of his work to you.

We will also need to modify Jed's second semester home education program, which differs from what we anticipated in September. In November Jed applied to Massachusetts College of Art through the state's dual enrollment program and just recently finalized his course selection. Because she dealt with the administrative details of Jed's dual enrollment we would appreciate if JoAnne Cummings, his guidance department liaison, could join us to answer several questions we have about the program.

As usual, we are requesting that Jed's cumulative folder be available for review when we meet and that our narrative summary of this past semester be placed in it along with the portfolio's table of contents.

As we begin this second semester, we look forward to continuing our positive and collaborative relationship with the Holliston Public Schools.

With warm regards,

ENC: Phi Delta Kappan, October 1998, "Inside the Black Box: Raising Standards Through Classroom Assessment"

> ## THE PORTFOLIO PREVIEW: TIMING IS EVERYTHING
>
> For a morning conference, drop off the portfolio the day before at the close of school. If you're meeting in the afternoon, bring it to school early that morning.

Of course, allowing access to the portfolio ahead of time is no guarantee that the reviewer actually will look through it. As I mentioned before, one of our middle school principals had every opportunity to preview my son's portfolios in advance, but didn't. After two very negative meetings, it became clear that he was not prepared. Before our third review, I was able to address the issue, stating that I wanted this next meeting to have a different tone and be focused on the portfolio and its artifacts. It is important that a portfolio review does not turn into a cross-examination of you and your child.

PORTFOLIO OWNERSHIP

It is a sinking feeling. The conversation ends, the reviewer stands up, she thanks me, shakes my hand, leaves the portfolio on her desk, and then comes around to escort me to the door. I assumed that I would leave with the portfolio; she assumed it would stay with her. It is an awkward situation that is best prepared for by clarifying the ownership of the portfolio beforehand. This can be done in several ways.

When you write your letter about the meeting's agenda, include a sentence that lists which artifacts you choose to leave at the school. By stating what stays, you imply that the rest goes home with you. For example, you may want your narrative summary to go into your child's cumulative folder. The table of contents may be included, too. In this case, its being in the folder would serve as a memory aid for the next time you meet. If you want to leave certain pieces from within the portfolio, they can be noted with an asterisk on the table of contents. By extension, things left unmarked go home.

Suppose, however, that the administrator says, "I'd like to keep this," at some point during the meeting. In that case, feel free to graciously decline, saying that you need it for your own records. On the other hand, if it is something you feel comfortable leaving, you can always say you would be glad to make a copy and mail it to the school. This happened to us once at the high school level. In our homeschool group, we had dissected fish, frogs, and a fetal pig. To spur discussion on the ethical treatment of animals, I printed out website articles debating real versus virtual dissections. I included copies of these in my son's science portfolio to illustrate that we were addressing these issues in our home biology program. The principal had obviously previewed the portfolio, for when we met he asked if he could have copies of the articles for his staff. Of course I gave them to him. But offering curricular materials is different from leaving student-produced artifacts. If an administrator asks for something you don't want to leave, say no. If he or she doesn't automatically offer you the portfolio back at the end of the meeting, *ask for it!*

Surely it is wise to make copies (or have duplicates) of everything in the portfolio. In fact, it is probably sensible to present the copies rather than the originals whenever possible. This way, even if an item is left behind you have your own original documentation in your files. This is not unusual. Remember, even art students who do three-dimensional work in ceramics, sculpture, and mixed media present their portfolio of work on photographic slides. Certainly a middle school principal should accept a photograph of a science activity as long as it is given appropriate clarity and context in the narrative summary or with an annotation attached.

One last note: Perhaps after reading this far you have come to the conclusion that the whole review-by-interview process is too fraught with potential problems and you are tempted to distance yourself from the school and just drop the portfolio off at the main office. Understand, however, that if you decide not to have an interview, you are giving up a great deal of control. You will not be able to predict who will review your portfolio, what context they will give it, where the contents eventually are filed, what notes and annotations the reviewers make, and whether or not you will ever get it back. However many missteps we and the administrators made at the beginning, our family was always convinced that the interview offered us far more control. Fortunately, you have the opportunity to learn from our mistakes . . . and our successes! For us, the interview model offered greater control and entailed far less risk. Consider your decision carefully.

DURING THE REVIEW

Remember that when you, your child, and the reviewer engage in a discussion of the portfolio's contents, you are doing one of two things. Either you are fulfilling a legal requirement for homeschooling in your state, or you are volunteering nonessential information to your school district. In either case, you need to be prudent, alert, and knowledgeable. While the portfolio "says" something about you, your child, and your homeschooling, the words that you say during the interview count for a great deal. This is why you should carefully consider whether you want to present the portfolio in person or simply submit it for review, as well as whether you want to present the portfolio on your child's behalf or have your child there to discuss his or her work. Remember that your goal is to homeschool with minimal restriction.

As mentioned earlier in this chapter, preparing for the review through role playing can be valuable. Your practice questions at home will help identify which pieces your child feels comfortable discussing and which ones seem to make him or her tongue-tied (Omit the latter!). One of the major rules we had for portfolio presentation was if my son couldn't discuss it glibly, it didn't belong in the portfolio.

WEARING DIFFERENT HATS

During the interview, you need to assume the multiple roles of parent, educator, and advocate in order to guide the conversation to the artifacts when necessary. This may take the form of cuing your child by mentioning an item that has not yet come up for discussion. There is supposed to be a dialogue going on between the student and the administrator with you acting as the monitor and facilitator. Dialogue, of course, is not a pop quiz. So, if this starts to happen, you, in your role as advocate, need to step in and redirect the conversation back to what you know is in the portfolio.

In the end, quizzing will most likely come back to embarrass the administrator rather than your child. It was painful to watch a middle school administrator try to remember his own high school algebra and quiz my son on factoring. All three of us knew he was grasping at straws, trying to appear knowledgeable about something he had forgotten but thought that he should know because the students in his building were studying it. If he had been less threatened and more professional, he could have asked my son about problem-solving procedures or what the diagram next to the equation meant. Instead, it was a sorry picture of an adult trying to cover his own feelings of inadequacy in mathematics by aggressively quizzing a youngster. By redirecting his attention back to the portfolio, I was actually helping both him and my son out of an awkward situation.

GUIDING THE DISCUSSION

Your narrative summary is the brief commentary in which you can refer to learning experiences that are not reflected in the contents of the portfolio. You need to share what you've written with your child in advance and be certain he or she is comfortable discussing its contents. If, for example, you mentioned certain books, your child should be able to allude to them in conversation. If you visited Civil War battlefields and included them in the social studies section of your narrative, they, too, are fair game for a reviewer's questions. In fact, discussion on the narrative may need to be prompted by the parent, especially if you start to feel that the reviewer hasn't adequately previewed the portfolio and has no idea of what you did during the past semester!

 NO SURPRISES

Show your son or daughter the narrative summary well before the meeting. If he or she does not feel confident discussing its contents, you need to do one of two things:

- Use the narrative to prepare your child for the interview.

- Revise the narrative to better reflect your child's perception of his or her learning.

In addition to listening to what the reviewer is saying, you also want to watch his or her body language, eye contact, engagement with your child, etc. Observe the observer as carefully as you would your child because you will be reviewing the reviewer when you debrief after the meeting. Naturally, you probably will be taking some sort of notes during the meeting. This is to be expected, but don't forget to also keep in mind the questions in the section below, "Debriefing," to attune yourself to some things you will want to observe as the interview is underway.

If the reviewer is perceptive and reflective, he or she probably will attempt to explore how the student sees his or her growth over the past semester or year. This is entirely appropriate from the reviewer's perspective, but you want to ensure that you stay alert in order to protect your child's and your family's privacy. If there are areas that you wish to remain off-limits during the meeting, let your child know what these are in advance so he or she doesn't venture there. If the conversation appears to be gravitating toward one of these issues, be prepared to redirect it back toward the permissible areas you have established for discussion: the portfolio and the narrative.

VIEWING YOUR CHILD'S SCHOOL RECORDS

When it comes time to review your child's school record, you'll need to remember that schools fulfill a variety of functions nowadays and that they maintain a host of records and data about students and their families. Material about students' physical and mental health, learning disabilities, and family history are held in both paper and electronic files. While it is almost impossible to access all the information that is held electronically, you should at least ask about the electronic records the school keeps on homeschoolers.

PRIVACY ISSUES

During interviews with school officials, homeschoolers should be alert to inquiries that are non-educational. Check your state's law, and you will probably find that homeschoolers are not required to answer questions about the student's:

- Family responsibilities

- Social contacts

- Health and medical history

- Religious or political views

Your district will probably have some sort of folder for paperwork relating to your son or daughter. Since you have a right to see the contents of your child's cumulative folder, and because you requested it in advance, expect that it will be made available to you at the portfolio review meeting. Make sure to leave time during the meeting to take a look through it. If something looks questionable or inappropriate, make a note of it, and then check your state's law on student records to see if it is something that schools are permitted to keep on file.

If you discover extraneous information that you do not wish to be included, request that the school remove it from your child's folder. Inappropriate material released to a college or an employer could have major impact on your child's future. This is why a regular, periodic review of your child's cumulative folder is important. Also, if the person reviewing your child's portfolio signs off on the work by adding a note to your child's folder, ask that a copy be mailed to you to be kept with your records at home.

CLOSING THE INTERVIEW

When the time comes to close the meeting, refer back to the table of contents you created to help you make a graceful exit. Ask for the portfolio back, and run through the table of contents to ascertain that all the items you originally submitted are still present. If certain items are to be left with the school, this is the time that *you* remove them from the portfolio and hand them over to school officials. Obviously, if items are missing, ask where they are. Now, with portfolio in hand, stand up—you are ready to leave.

DEBRIEFING

Debriefing is a tool used to critique the interview based on what went right, what went wrong, and what you'd like to change next time. This is your opportunity to get down *in writing* what transpired during the past half hour, while the words and impressions are fresh in your memory. This written record is important in charting your course for future interactions with the school.

 DEBRIEF IMMEDIATELY

The sooner you debrief, the better. If you can do it in the school parking lot, fine!

Understand that the reviewer is probably sitting in his or her office at the same time, recapping the meeting in personal notes. While these notes will not go into your child's cumulative folder, they may well be referred to before meeting with you next time. You want to do the same kind of record-keeping for yourself, noting the following:

- Your first impressions
- The "minutes" of the meeting
- How you and your child felt
- Your instinctive conclusions

Once you are out of the building, quickly jot down everything you can remember about the review. What was your overall impression of the meeting? Whatever it was, name it and write it down. Then move on to specifics—anything that happened during the meeting ranging from questions that were asked about the artifacts, to which particular items piqued the reviewer's curiosity. Next, move from facts to feelings. How did you and your child feel about the experience? Finally, write down whatever generalizations or patterns you perceive.

The checklist below, "Criteria for Reviewing the Reviewer," can give substance to the gut feelings you had during and immediately after the meeting. It includes criteria you may want to consider when assessing the reviewer's competency in four areas:

- Professionalism
- Interviewing skills
- Assessment literacy
- Interpersonal communication skills

If you and your child differ on your perceptions, make note of that. Later, when the tension and information have cooled off a bit, review your notes to see if you want to add anything you might have forgotten or if you have new insights in a particular area.

Criteria for Reviewing the Reviewer

Professionalism

- Did the reviewer give evidence of being prepared for the meeting?
- Did you feel the reviewer was open-minded toward homeschooling as an educational option?
- Did you feel you were respected as a colleague and fellow educator?
- Did it appear that the reviewer had an agenda different from yours?
- Were all your agenda items covered at the meeting?
- Was your time respected? Were you kept waiting? Did the meeting go on longer than expected? How did the reviewer handle interruptions?
- How would you rate the reviewer's overall professionalism?

continues

Criteria for Reviewing the Reviewer (cont.)

Interviewing and Questioning Skills

- To whom were questions mainly directed?

- Did the reviewer try to quiz the student?

- Did he or she ask open-ended questions?

- Did the reviewer's questions attempt to elicit higher-order thinking?

- Did he or she attempt to seek the student's opinions on issues?

- Did the reviewer ask probing personal questions?

- Did his or her questions show knowledge of the content areas?

- How did the reviewer deal with areas in which he or she did not have expertise?

- Did he or she attempt to engage the student in dialogue?

- Did you ever feel that you or your child were being grilled or cross-examined?

- How would you rate the reviewer's overall skill as an interviewer?

Assessment Literacy

- Did the reviewer ground his or her questions and comments in the portfolio and narrative summary?

- Could you direct his or her attention back to the artifacts if the conversation wandered?

- Was he or she concentrating primarily on administrative details or on the portfolio's contents?

- Did he or she treat the review as a formative evaluation and offer feedback?

- Did the reviewer consider it a summative evaluation and rate or grade the portfolio?

- If it was graded, was the reviewer using a clear rubric that you were aware of when developing the portfolio?

- Did the reviewer appear conversant with the concepts and vocabulary of authentic assessment?

- How would you rate the reviewer's overall assessment literacy?

Interpersonal Communication Skills

- How were you welcomed into the reviewer's office?

- Did the reviewer make eye contact with you and your child?

- What body language or physical mannerisms did you notice during the interview?

- Did the reviewer seem to enjoy the review? Did he or she seem engaged?

- Did he or she seem bored with any aspect of the interview?

- Was there anything that you tried to discuss that the reviewer avoided?

- Was there anything in the portfolio that captured his or her attention?

- From friendly to hostile, how would you rate the reviewer's treatment of you and your child?

- Did the reviewer mention any personal information during the interview?

- How would you rate the reviewer's overall interpersonal communication skills?

The notes you take in the debriefing process should assist you in planning future meetings. Perhaps you found the administrator overly friendly and her questions inappropriately probing. The next time you will probably redirect her attention back to the portfolio sooner. If the reviewer went over every artifact with a fine-tooth comb and kept you at the meeting far longer than expected, you will know next time to schedule the conference first thing in the morning and to be absolutely firm about a specific exit time.

If you need to follow up the meeting by requesting additional information or sending the school copies of artifacts, remember that including a brief thank-you note never hurts. Even if it doesn't find its way into the administrator's personal notes, it will be remembered as evidence of your professional demeanor in dealing with the school.

PORTFOLIOS FOR LEGAL PURPOSES

Unfortunately, some homeschooling families find that they are faced with *extraordinary* legal requirements, such as divorce proceedings, a child custody case, or intervention by the state's department of social services. In these situations, a court-ordered portfolio review might be required.

Even if traditional educators don't use authentic assessments on a schoolwide basis or feel comfortable with them in their classrooms, they are at least aware of alternative assessment practices. Social workers, guardians *ad litem*, attorneys, and judges, on the other hand, know little if anything about contemporary methods of educational assessment. Information on the subject just does not cross their desks in the course of their everyday work. Thus, it is naïve to assume that they will understand homeschooling in general, and authentic assessment in particular, without your setting a clear research-based foundation for them. This is where the mainstream professional education publications mentioned above and in Appendix D, "Print and Internet Resources," can serve homeschoolers well. If under a court order to provide documentation of learning, homeschoolers will want to use every available resource to bolster their case. The information in these periodicals can help build a strong, clear, and credible foundation to support the appropriate use of student work portfolios in such extraordinary circumstances.

PORTFOLIO PRESENTATIONS YOU *WANT* TO DO

So far, this chapter has dealt with portfolio reviews that you *need* to submit to in order to continue homeschooling. The information has been addressed mainly to parents because they are the persons legally responsible for homeschooling. The following two sections touch briefly on the portfolio presentations you *want* to do, the ones that extend the homeschool experience into the future.

 ON-CAMPUS INTERVIEWS

Only a small number of students actually request on-campus interviews. Schooled students probably will be okay omitting the interview. Homeschoolers, on the other hand, should schedule one.

There is one key difference between presentations aimed at college admissions and employability and the required presentations that you've read about previously in this chapter: *The rules of the game have changed.* I cannot emphasize this strongly enough. Up to this point, you have been playing your cards somewhat close to your vest, trying to give your school district the minimum amount of information legally required in order to continue to homeschool unencumbered. In most cases, it didn't matter if the school agreed with your family's educational philosophy or choice of instructional methods. They didn't even have to *like* you! Your goal was educational freedom of choice when faced with compulsory attendance at governmental schools.

Now, however, all your strategies need to be reconsidered. You want the interviewers not only to think your educational background was good, if not excellent, you want them to like you. In fact, you want them to like you so much that they will ask you to live on their campus for the next four years or will offer to place you on their payroll. This is not the time to be reticent, coy, or protective about your homeschooled lifestyle. Instead, you want to celebrate it and show how it adds value to your candidacy.

Here are a few other suggestions before you head off to a college or job interview:

- Don't bad-mouth public schools! Whatever your personal opinion about the state of American education and the role of government in it, recognize that you have been granted an extraordinary educational opportunity. Millions of other kids have not been so lucky. There is no need to be arrogant about the choices your parents made or allowed you to make. Remember to be gracious about the way your life turned out and grateful to those who helped make it happen.

- Realize, too, that the persons interviewing you probably went to conventional schools, their children probably go to them, and you are asking to join their college or workplace community which is probably filled with people who have been traditionally educated. The interviewers will expect you to get along with people who have been educated differently from you. Being argumentative and smug about your homeschooling is downright foolish and counterproductive . . . for you, and for the next homeschooler the admissions counselor or employer meets.

- Do get your contact's business card. You will want it for future reference, but right now you also need it for a different reason. One of the most important things an interviewee can do is to send a handwritten thank-you note to the interviewer. It is a small act that takes only a few minutes, but it is one more way to cast yourself in a favorable light. And the business card? Check and double-check when you write the note and address the envelope. You'll make the best impression if you spell the interviewer's name correctly!

THE COLLEGE ADMISSIONS INTERVIEW AND PORTFOLIO REVIEW

It will be helpful to read Chapters 9, "Preparing for College Admissions," and 10, "A Homeschooler's Comprehensive College Application," along with this section. They deal with how to get to know your audience (the college and its admissions committee), as well as how to construct a comprehensive application packet.

Some colleges require interviews, some suggest them, others don't use them at all. In most cases, the interviewer is a college official, but at other times he or she is an alumnus. Alumni reviewers are often used when the school is far enough away from the student's home that visiting the campus for an interview would be difficult.

Homeschoolers should try to make a campus visit whenever possible for several reasons: A campus visit gives you a better feel for the school and helps you decide if it is a good match for you, your current interests, and your future goals. Additionally, since on-staff admissions officials have met with (and accepted) homeschooled applicants before, they will be more familiar with homeschooled adolescents than most alumni. An on-campus interview also allows you to begin developing a relationship with a member of the admissions committee that decides who is admitted and who is not. If at all possible, try to make your portfolio presentation to an admissions officer who will be part of that committee. Realize that the admissions committee may have questions about your homeschooling that a face-to-face meeting can answer. In fact, the person who conducts your interview may well turn out to be an important advocate in moving your application, complete with its homeschool transcript and portfolio, through the admissions process. If an admissions official is wary of homeschooling for any reason, then an interview is an excellent way to dispel any misconceptions and mistaken assumptions he or she might have. In person, you can defuse most of the homeschool myths and stereotypes portrayed in the media. Finally you, your portfolio, and your transcript, when seen together, should create a portrait that tells the admissions official whether you and the school have found a match in each other.

 ANOTHER QUESTION A COLLEGE MIGHT BE ASKING ITSELF

"Who is this kid . . . really? I mean, his *mom* wrote the transcript!"

Most college guidebooks have sections on handling college interviews, and it pays to read several in order to get an overall picture of how the interview fits into the whole application process. You'll find there are several admissions issues that are unique to homeschoolers, and I've addressed those in the next few sections.

WHY SCHEDULE AN INTERVIEW?

Why bother traveling three hundred miles to spend a half hour talking with a college admissions official? And what role will your transcript and portfolio play during the meeting? By and large, your answer to those two questions will depend on where you are on the application process timeline.

At the beginning of your college search, you may have found fifty schools that seemed to have potential. I hope you were then able to narrow the list to twenty, then ten. Once you've narrowed the field down this far, you may want to go on an *informational interview*. Your goal in this type of interview is to gather specific information about a college's admissions policies toward homeschoolers. At an informational interview, you can discuss both your aspirations and your concerns as to how as a homeschooler can best format his or her application. Of course, you will also be setting a foundation for the future if you eventually decide to apply to the school. It will be valuable for you to already have a contact on the admissions staff to look to for guidance. In addition, you will have demystified homeschooling a bit, and you will have made yourself a known quantity, not simply another "prospective."

Once you know where you want to apply, you should schedule a portfolio review and interview to better gauge your chances for admission. By arranging to have your transcript and portfolio reviewed by an admissions counselor, you can ask for feedback on how you might strengthen your application. (If you have read the earlier chapters, you will recognize this as a *formative review*.) This is also a good time to discover how the college would like you to format your materials.

Once you have filled out the application form, assembled your portfolio, and formulated your transcript, you are looking at your last-chance, one-on-one review and interview. This is when you will leave your packet at the admissions office and hope that your interviewer will champion your cause when the full admissions committee meets. In this case, you are going in for a *summative review and interview*, where you are summing up whatever you wanted to say and display.

Regardless of when you schedule your interview and portfolio review, you will have many of the same goals. These are discussed more fully in Chapter 9, "Preparing for College Admissions," but basically you want to accomplish the following objectives:

- Put a face on a heretofore anonymous homeschooled candidate

- Be remembered for being an interesting and poised individual

- Allay concerns about academic competency

- Answer questions about your homeschool program

- Show a good match between yourself and the college

Bringing your portfolio to the interview allows you to deal with these issues in concrete, nonverbal ways. Your portfolio complements your interpersonal communication skills and, along with your transcript, creates a credible and consistent portrait of you, the applicant.

What Questions Might a College Ask?

When you were younger, you probably became annoyed at the predictable questions people asked about homeschooling over and over again at the supermarket, park, and playground. Later, you were probably advised by your parents on how to field these same questions if asked by school officials. But now you really have to come up with sound, reflective answers because, more likely than not, some of those same predictable and seemingly intrusive questions will be directed at you during your college admissions (or employability) interviews. This time you need to avoid any and all defensiveness and respond instead as a mature young adult with full, rich, complex answers.

Again, you need to remember that the rules of the game have changed. You will be asked these questions because college officials and employers genuinely want to know why you believe homeschooling has prepared you for the adult world. And because you want to be accepted for their freshman class or be hired by their organization, you need to feel more comfortable about telling them what they want to know.

Incidentally, homeschoolers learn a great deal by careful observation, and homeschooling parents do much of their teaching by modeling. Over the years you have probably heard your parents answer many of these questions again and again. This time, however, you want to be sure that you are giving your own well-thought-through responses, which may differ from those of your parents. Realize, too, that you most probably will need to give these answers while your parents are sitting with you at the interview. For this reason, I would strongly advise you to share your responses to the questions below, and other similar questions, with your parents beforehand. Part of the rationale for rehearsal is to avoid surprises in unfamiliar and somewhat stressful situations.

PREPAREDNESS

Quite frankly, you are probably incredibly well prepared for a college admissions interview. Because homeschoolers interact with people of many ages, you have greater experience talking conversationally to adults than do most of your traditionally schooled peers. Furthermore, by engaging in self-reflection through the portfolio process during adolescence, you already have

---

Homeschool-Specific Questions You Should Be Prepared to Answer

- How has homeschooling provided you with opportunities for leadership?

- How has homeschooling provided you with opportunities for service?

- Tell me about an important project that you were able to complete because you were homeschooled.

- Tell me about a typical homeschooling day.

- How do you think homeschooling has prepared you for college?

- How has homeschooling affected your relationships with kids your own age?

- Is there anything you disliked about homeschooling?

- Do you think you would homeschool your own children?

- How did you decide what to study?

- What sort of outside interests do you have? (This is a tricky one because homeschoolers tend to blur the line between curricular and extracurricular activities.)

- Why does a college classroom atmosphere attract you after having been homeschooled for high school?

- If you had to do it over, what about homeschooling would you do differently?

thought about many of the issues likely to be raised at an interview. By the time you have scheduled your interview, you will have done your homework, investigating colleges to find that good match of student and program which, of course, is a hallmark of homeschooling. Don't forget that your portfolio will be an asset to you at the interview—as a prop to support you, to offer credibility to your comments, and to spur the conversation. Just having created a portfolio makes you immensely more prepared than many students that show up for an admissions interview.

If you feel the need for extra preparation, role playing is always a good idea. You probably have already used this strategy to rehearse other scenarios over the years. However, rehearsing for an interview is not the same as memorizing lines for a play. In this case, your goal is to become comfortable phrasing your answers during practice sessions in order to feel more relaxed when it is time for the interview.

THE PARENTS' ROLE

Regardless of whether the student is homeschooled or not, parents often sit in on an interview. I would like to think that we have been unobtrusive, allowing our children to answer questions on their own. However, parents do have a role to play. First and foremost, they can take notes. Much information is going to move back and forth between the applicant and the interviewer. Get down important points so you can refer to them later. Because colleges are interested not only in the student but the educational background from which he or she comes, homeschooling parents are in a unique position to explain whatever facets of their son or daughter's high school program need clarification. Because homeschooling parents will have trained themselves to be acute observers at conferences with local school administrators, they can utilize these same skills at college admissions interviews. In fact, many of the same questions suggested above for reviewing the reviewer will also apply to a college admissions portfolio review.

 PARENTS . . .

- Let your son or daughter take the lead.

- Take written notes of any names, dates, comments to follow up on later.

- Answer any questions asked about your homeschool program.

- Debrief immediately after the interview.

Finally, parents can help debrief after the meeting is over. Try to leave some time open following the interview rather than immediately going on a tour or to some other organized activity. We found that we needed only ten to fifteen minutes together as a family to collect our thoughts in private. That short time proved incredibly valuable both for helping us evaluate the school throughout the remainder of the visit, as well as for future reference when we had to compare all the schools we visited and evaluate the relative merits of each.

THE EMPLOYABILITY INTERVIEW

The difference between the college admissions interview and the employability interview is that if you succeed in the former, you pay money to *them*, but if you pass the latter with flying colors, they pay *you!*

CAREER CONSULTANT

Create an employability portfolio for your own use. You can use it as your personal consultant to discover a career that:

- You love

- Makes good use of your skills

- Allows you to earn a living

Because of the flexible scheduling homeschooling permits, you may have had time to explore many career options, and perhaps you have even investigated one or two areas in depth. Once you discover some attractive career options, you may want to go on informational interviews to get a better feel for the different jobs. If your only information has come from reading and research, this type of interview will help fill in the details by letting you hear directly form people working in the field. It can help you become more realistic about the entry-level experience and education expected, job responsibilities that are invisible to outsiders, personal attributes necessary for success in the field, etc.

Individuals, even busy ones, are usually glad to take time to answer your questions if they know you are serious in your intent and have done enough basic research to ask intelligent questions. Put the relevant information that you have collected into a folder and bring it to the interview. Your materials will demonstrate your sincerity of purpose while serving as a springboard for questions and discussion. Here again, your folder will serve as a prop to get the conversation going and to keep it on target. After the interview, you will probably take the portfolio home with you since it is one of your self discovery tools.

 WHEN YOU'RE READY TO APPLY

You've gotten past the informational interview stage and you're ready to apply. In addition to your work samples and artifacts, you should have the following things in your employability portfolio:

- A completed application form

- A transcript in resume format

It also helps to have *your* questions about the job handy. Remember, interviewing is a two-way conversation with each side trying to discover more about the other.

When you are actually applying for a job, the scenario is different. In this case, your portfolio can serve to document not only your interest but also your existing level of competency to do the job. You may want to create a portfolio in the classic sense of the term: a *selection* of artifacts, beyond just the contents of your research folder. The portfolio may need to be left with the interviewer, so make sure you retain copies of everything in it and that it follows the guidelines for clarity and credibility discussed earlier in Chapter 4, "Creating Your Portfolio." It may be passed along to others, and it will have to showcase you and your accomplishments through the artifacts alone.

What Employers Want to See

When preparing your portfolio and getting ready for the interview, it will help if you can document more than your interest in the field and your quality education. There are other qualities employers are looking for in a candidate, and they may question how homeschooling helps you meet the following criteria:

- Competence

- Dependability

- Common sense

- Manageability

Let us assume that your prior work—whether paid, unpaid, or project based—meets the competency requirements of the job. Your portfolio probably has evidence of this, but you will still need to address the remaining three criteria in your portfolio and conversation.

Did you know that employers consider themselves lucky when their workers consistently show up for work? Amazingly, many workers don't come in to work regularly and on time! Thus, anything you can do to verify a dependable work ethic will go a long way toward your being hired. A letter of reference from a prior employer or volunteer coordinator would help here. A note of caution: If asked about a typical homeschool day, you would be wise not to emphasize the flexibility factor to the degree that it would make an employer worry that you are undisciplined. Homeschooling, as we know, has its own internal structure, scheduling, and discipline, but these factors are all but invisible to the rest of society. Most likely your interviewer will be most familiar with adolescents whose schedule is that of the school day, where arriving on time for first period class implies reliability. You will need to determine how you can show a prospective employer dependability that goes beyond punctuality.

Common sense is fairly uncommon, it seems, which is why employers value it so. Employers are looking for problem solvers who can exercise good judgment. They may not see how homeschooling provides opportunities for devising commonsense solutions to problems every day. What can you put into your portfolio that shows evidence of problem solving and mature decision-making?

While you want to be able to display that you can think and act independently, you also don't want to overplay those attributes. What you need to keep in mind is that, while employers value independence in their workers, they also want employees to be what is termed "manageable." Therefore, you want your portfolio to show that as a homeschooler you are not too independent for the job. A letter from a past supervisor describing how you followed through on suggestions or worked as part of a team will prove valuable. Incidentally, highlighting teamwork abilities can be important because homeschoolers are so often depicted as working in isolation. Think ahead to how you can confront and dispel this stereotype when talking with your prospective employer.

PREPARING FOR YOUR INTERVIEW

When going for a job interview, the rules mentioned before still apply:

- Know your audience.

- Prepare yourself.

- Prepare the interviewer.

It is helpful to get information on both the organization itself and the person who will be interviewing you. Most organizations, even small ones, have a mission statement. This is a document that is often on display in the workplace, telling why the organization exists, how it intends to do business, etc. Of course, in addition to the mission statement you can utilize print materials, ads, websites, newspaper articles, and word-of-mouth references from others who know the organization. Find out, if possible, the exact title of the person interviewing you and what that title means. It is frustrating to discover that you incorrectly assumed the person who met with you could make the hiring decision when in reality he or she was just screening applicants. This is why it is important to have your portfolio ready to be seen and evaluated by those who haven't met you in person.

Your portfolio is one way to show that you are competent, dependable, sensible, and manageable. Your answers to the interviewer's questions is another. Practice role playing in question-and-answer format. In addition to the questions listed above for the college admissions interview, think of how you might answer ones specific to your job experience as well as some of these:

Employability Questions You Should Be Prepared to Answer

Dependability

- How will your homeschool schedule affect how you will do this job?

- Tell me about a typical work day in your past job.

- How do you handle repetitive tasks?

Common Sense

- What kinds of decisions did you have to make on your past job?

- What kind of problems did you have to solve?

- Tell me about responsibilities you had. (Here you can mention homeschool responsibilities as well.)

Manageability

- How has homeschooling provided you with opportunities for teamwork?

- What were your former co-workers like?

- Why makes this job appeal to you?

- Is there anything you disliked about your past job?

WHAT COULD YOU PUT INTO YOUR EMPLOYABILITY PORTFOLIO?

Use your portfolio to answer employer questions about:

- **A typical work day:** printed reconstruction of your daily schedule

- **Repetitive tasks:** time sheet annotated with the type of work done

- **Decisions made:** sample of work done independently or under your leadership

- **Problems solved:** diagram or written report showing the final result

- **Responsibility:** letter from a former employer

- **Teamwork:** photo of you and your colleagues engaged in a project

When filling out a formal application, you will most assuredly find a box for listing your school and educational background. Don't leave it blank. Note that you have been homeschooled and then use your portfolio and interview to show your employable qualities. Many of the unique jobs that homeschoolers take, however, are not ones that require a formal application. They come about through networking and informal contacts. In this case, the prospective employer probably already knows that you have been homeschooled and is prepared to ask you pertinent questions about it. You can help your employer get a better understanding of you and your qualifications by including in your portfolio a copy of a resume, your homeschool transcript, and/or the narrative summary that was discussed in Chapters 3 and 4. These are quick reference tools that he or she can scan to help ask more about you and your experience. Don't be shy about having them in your portfolio, ready to pull out and use if the situation calls for them.

OTHER TYPES OF INTERVIEWS

SCHOLARSHIP INTERVIEWS

Your portfolio will also serve you well in several other types of interviews. Scholarships often require that the candidate be interviewed by a committee, and having sat for several college admissions interviews will help you answer the academic, extracurricular, and service questions that the committee is most likely to ask. If you have not yet been on an admissions interview, you should still prepare by reading the "Interviewing" sections of several college admissions guidebooks (see Appendix D for suggestions). Be prepared for committee members to express an interest in homeschooling, of course, and have comfortable answers ready for them. Often, scholarship

DON'T LEAVE IT BLANK!

Colleges are getting used to how homeschoolers fill out application blanks. Employers, however, may wonder if you have dropped out of school (or have been expelled!) when you leave the lines for school name and date of graduation blank. Make sure you clarify that you have been homeschooled and that you have graduated from your homeschool program. This is one more reason to have your homeschool transcript ready in your portfolio or stapled to your application form.

committees are looking for a uniquely qualified individual. Having a portfolio that documents your achievements can only add to their impression of you as a candidate with competency, organization, and potential.

VOLUNTEER INTERVIEWS

If you are trying to land a position in a volunteer organization, read through the employability interview section earlier in this chapter. Many of the same employer concerns exist; the only difference is that you will not be paid for your work. Volunteer supervisors and coordinators are still looking for dependable, sensible, cooperative people to do the job. Interviewing with a portfolio will give them clear, credible evidence of your capabilities.

MEDIA INTERVIEWS

Finally, a word about interviews with the media. For most of us, it is flattering to be asked to speak about homeschooling. It is even more exciting to see our picture in a magazine or to watch ourselves on TV. However, I have had mixed experiences with members of the press that lead me to urge you to consider the following issues before saying yes to a reporter who calls requesting your participation in an interview.

First, know that there are different types of reporters: education reporters, feature reporters, and local reporters. The *education reporters* I have worked with have been knowledgeable, and their articles have been balanced, accurate, and informative. I trust them and have been comfortable working with them.

Feature reporters, on the other hand, are looking for an interesting angle, perhaps a story on homeschooling for a special back-to-school issue. Most feature writers are general reporters with no background in educational journalism. The extent of their knowledge about homeschooling may consist of a couple of homeschooling articles that were themselves full of misconceptions and stereotypes. Feature writers also tend to want to add human interest and drama to their articles. One way they do this is by asking negatively phrased questions, by editing what you said to imply

 INTERVIEWING THE INTERVIEWER

Every reporter brings something of his or her background to the interview. Before you consent to be interviewed for a feature on homeschooling, get answers to the following questions:

- How long will the interview be?

- What is the purpose of this story?

- What sort of tone do you expect it to have?

- Have you ever interviewed homeschoolers before?

- Who else are you interviewing?

- What is your educational background?

- Where do your own children go to school?

conflict, or by finding someone who is willing to counter whatever statements you made. Unfortunately, when written according to this formula, the finished articles come across as superficial and stereotypical and are basically inaccurate and misleading.

Local reporters usually want to keep on good terms with all segments of the community, so manufacturing conflict is not to their advantage. Still, they may ask questions about your homeschool curriculum, schedule, or lifestyle that you would prefer to keep private. It is important to know that one of the ways that school officials keep abreast of community issues is to read the local paper. I guarantee that someone will bring the story about your homeschooling to their attention.

Because of these issues, it is imperative that you clarify your ground rules for the type of questions you will answer and that you state your expectations for the tone of the resulting article. You may also want to stipulate that only handwritten, not tape-recorded, notes be taken. Parents should always be present when their children are interviewed by the media and they should feel comfortable reframing and rephrasing the reporter's questions if necessary.

Finally, I have learned to treat every media interview the way I would a school administrator's interview: Ground it in the portfolio. By doing this, you keep the reporter's attention focused less on your child and more on the products of homeschool learning. This is one way to help the reporter show the world that homeschooling is a true alternative model of learning, not just mom and child at the kitchen table.

CHAPTER 6

Using Technology
in Portfolios

This chapter gives a brief overview of how technological tools can be used to document learning. Homeschoolers tend to focus on the process of learning rather than on the creation of tangible products. However, in order to create a portfolio we are looking for credible artifacts. Since we usually do not monitor learning through traditional paperwork, we may have few book reports, quizzes, or essays available to document learning. The question for homeschoolers is how to turn the process of learning into credible products. This is where technology can help.

WHY TECHNOLOGY?

Sometimes, however, technological solutions are more than appropriate; they are essential. This is true in cases where any of the following applies:

- The reviewer requires that technology be used for submission.
- A performance needs to be viewed or heard at a later date.
- The process of learning needs to be documented because it did not result in a tangible product.
- The artifacts are too large to evaluate in the reviewer's office.
- The artifacts are about technology itself and exist only in virtual form.
- The portfolio can be viewed best in a nonlinear format.
- The portfolio has been designed to be interactive and invites the reviewer's response.
- The components of the portfolio exist in several media, and technology can unify the project.
- The family's system for archiving is based mainly on technology, and the original artifacts are no longer available.
- Technology can bring energy and variety to an otherwise dull portfolio.

MANY LITERACIES

Homeschoolers have always known that there is more than one type of literacy, that there is more to "read" than words.

When colleges and employers accept portfolios as evidence of learning and mastery, they often request (or require) that information and artifacts be sent to them through technology. This is not really new. Students applying to art school, for example, have always been expected to submit their portfolios in slide format if they are not able to have their portfolio reviewed in person. Nowadays, however, many colleges offer the option of online applications, and employers routinely accept digital resumes. When a college or employer asks for a digital submission, you need to be ready to respond.

Audio- and videotapes allow you, the student, to demonstrate a skill for future review, and these dynamic recordings can encompass more than just the performing arts. Leading a meeting, working with toddlers, or identifying plants on a nature walk are all instances in which a tape would show credible evidence of learning that is being applied in context. In instances where the learning process needs to be documented, even simple photographs can be solid evidence. Most physics experiments, for example, result in data, not a tangible product. An experiment caught on film at key points would show learning in action. When it comes to literature, homeschoolers tend to talk about books rather than write about them. A tape of your family's book discussion would show not only that you had read the book, but also that you were able to analyze and interpret it.

Some artifacts are just too large and bulky to bring to a review. Remember: A portfolio is supposed to be portable! If you can't carry something to the reviewer's office, share it on film, video, or a website instead. Or perhaps, as in the biological sciences, you are unable to bring in your artifacts because they have wilted, spoiled, or been used up. Drawings are low-tech solutions, but think, too, of digital materials such as photographs on a biology website that show the specimens you have been working with. Most likely, these will be better springboards for discussion than the actual organisms.

When your work exists *only* in a virtual format, you need technology to reflect what you know. For example, paper-and-pencil graphing is no longer used in higher-level mathematics courses. If you want a reviewer to see your overlaying graphs in trigonometry, you will need to program them into your graphing calculator. Similarly, if your artwork is focused on digital animation, it can only be displayed through technology.

 DIGITIZED PERFORMANCES

Even if an activity doesn't result in a product, you can use technology to create a record of your performance when you:

- Give a speech
- Participate in a group
- Lead an activity
- Demonstrate a skill

Electronic portfolios move your artifacts out of the hierarchical, linear format to a more associative learning format. For example, when my son Jed was applying to institutions for the creative arts, an art school wanted to see visuals, a school for the performing arts needed to hear a dramatic interpretation, and a scholarship committee wanted a writing sample. We were able to satisfy each requirement with an electronic portfolio on 19th-century poet William Blake. Each reviewer could proceed through the portfolio in a different sequence, clicking on whichever of the following links most closely matched the school's interests:

- The text of Blake's poem "The Tyger"
- Jed's essay interpreting the poem
- A page featuring links to literary analyses of Blake's poetry
- Jed's watercolor painting of the tyger
- Blake's own painting of the tyger, from a museum in Australia
- An audio clip of Jed reading "The Tyger"
- An audio clip of a professional actor reading the poem
- A page with links to additional sites for Blake and other 19th-century poets

There was no correct or incorrect way to proceed through the portfolio, so individuals could choose the route that made the most sense to them.

When information and artifacts exist in the same medium, there is a sense of coherence and unity. This is true even in books where the text and its accompanying illustrations exist in the same format: ink on paper. Similarly, you can toggle between graphs and equations on a graphing calculator, showing how both represent the same mathematical concept. This unifying effect is even more dramatic on a website. Once artifacts are digitized and organized into a web-based portfolio they can be viewed in relation to each other instantly. This can make context and connections much more evident. See "Creating a Web-Based Portfolio" later in this chapter for more about digital portfolios.

As families become comfortable with technologies, they tend to use them more frequently. Letters on paper may be supplanted by e-mail. Drawings are scanned, then saved on diskettes. Digital cameras take pictures that are stored on diskettes or your hard drive rather than in photo albums. In short, families have begun to archive their memories and artifacts in electronic formats, and certain physical artifacts that formerly offered tangible evidence of learning no longer exist.

Technology with its colors, bells, and whistles can add much-needed energy to artifacts that routinely show up in a portfolio. Even something as mundane as a review of a Shakespearean play can take on a sense of wit and irony, as when my son used desktop publishing software to create a tabloid satire based on *Macbeth*. The mock newspaper showed that he had read the play, knew the plot, and could discuss the characters' motivations. And the technology he used allowed him to write about the play's events and characters in a variety of styles—from weather reports to horoscopes to obituaries—and to present the information in an engaging and enjoyable manner.

Finally, use technology if you love it, are comfortable with it, and think about life in terms of it. If technology is second nature to you and part of your identity, you could be faulted for *not* using it! Of course, you need to remember that when you create a portfolio or a transcript for anyone other than yourself, you need to keep your audience in mind. Consider their general comfort level regarding technology and the specific hardware and software they need to order to receive and review your materials.

IS TECHNOLOGY RIGHT FOR YOU?

As wonderful as technology can be, avoid getting caught in the technology trap. Focus instead on whether or not technology is *useful* for what you are trying to achieve. The key is to select the right technology for the job, and in many instances sophisticated technology is unnecessary. A sheet of paper with pencil calculations might be an appropriate low-tech solution, as would a hard copy of an essay printed from a word processing program. A file folder purchased at Gettysburg that is filled with brochures, entries from a travel journal, and a plastic sleeve of photographs (another use of technology) can show off a unit of study on the Civil War quite well. Low-tech solutions are also good when the physical act of paging through a group of artifacts and laying them out for comparison is warranted.

You should also avoid using technology if you know the person reviewing the portfolio is uncomfortable with technology or if *you* are uncomfortable with it yourself. A note to parents: Realize that your teenager may be quite adept at using technology and may be well equipped to create and maintain the technological components of his or her portfolio. Don't let your insecurities stand in the way of a project at which he or she might excel.

CHOOSING THE RIGHT TECHNOLOGY

Once you've decided what you want to show or demonstrate, you need to determine which technology is going to serve you best. Begin to think in the plural form of the word "technologies" since there are many products that can help you create, store, and display portfolio artifacts. While it is tempting to seek out commercial software designed to create educational portfolios, remember that most of the software on the market has been developed for school use and contains features that are specifically school-related. Furthermore, most school software packages are designed to be used at the school's level of technology, which may be less sophisticated than what you already have at home. Because of this, you will probably want to develop your own portfolio storage and record-keeping systems using the same powerful software you use for handling everyday chores.

WHAT DOES EACH TECHNOLOGY DO WELL?

What can a certain form of technology do better than its alternatives? Digital photographs embedded in a report can *show* progress that words can only describe. E-mail can show ongoing

 ANOTHER TOOL

Portfolios can alert you to your growth, knowledge, skills, and interests. Use technology to develop portfolios that foster self-discovery.

dialogue between correspondents in a way that handwritten letters cannot, simply because of the time it takes for letters to be mailed and delivered. Similarly, if you wanted to share an interesting magazine article you could clip it and then mail it; on the other hand, you might read the same article in its online format, save it as an Internet bookmark, and then forward it via e-mail or place a link on your website. If fast, efficient transmittal of information is what you want, each of these technologies does it very well.

HOW MUCH TECHNOLOGY DO I NEED?

Strongly consider how much sound and motion you need to add to your portfolio. Suppose you have given a speech and want to include it in your portfolio. Is it enough to present the text along with a still photo of yourself at the podium? Would an audiotape be enough? Or would it be better to show the presentation on videotape? How about a 60-second video clip on your website? Remember, however, that you don't want to overload your portfolio with sound and movement. Keeping a good balance between text and technology is important.

HOW CAN YOU DEMONSTRATE ACHIEVEMENT?

Your web-based portfolio might have a page detailing an award you received along with the following links:

- A scanned copy of the award

- A digital photograph of you receiving it

- An audio clip of the spokesperson's comments about you

- The text of your acceptance remarks

- A link to the website of the organization granting the award

WHAT CAN MY AUDIENCE HANDLE?

You've heard it before, but it bears repeating: Know your audience! People vary so much in their approach to technology. Unless you are developing a portfolio solely for self-discovery and personal reflection, it is critical to consider what will happen to your portfolio when it arrives at the other end. Will the reviewers take the time to find a VCR to view your tape? How much of your speech will they want to spend time watching or listening to? If you present something on diskette, is the file format readable on their system? Do they need to download certain software in order to view your video clip? How long will it take your webpage to load, and will they wait that long? While technology can add a positive dimension to your portfolio, keep in mind that it should enhance your presentation, not detract from it. Technology limitations certainly shouldn't cause your reviewer to skip over your work.

TRYING IT OUT

Regardless of which technology you use, the traditional methods for creating portfolios and transcripts still apply. You need to determine what you have, what you need to create, what your focus is, what artifacts contribute to that focus, and how best to format your content for your intended audience. The emphasis should be on using technology to do these things more efficiently and to increase communication with your audience. Technology should not be thought of as a gimmick; nor should it be equated only with computers or thought of as simply an electronic file cabinet.

Work through the following exercises to begin thinking about how you can use technology effectively.

Exercise 1: Using Your Existing Technologies

1. Select an area of homeschooling for which you are developing a portfolio:

   _____

2. How you can use each of the following technologies to make your portfolio more dynamic?

   Camera

   _____

   Digital camera

   _____

   Scanner

   _____

   Video recorder

   _____

   Commercial videos

   _____

   VCR

   _____

   Telephone

   _____

   Audiocassette tapes

   _____

   Recorded music

   _____

Recorded speech

_____

Word processor

_____

Spreadsheets

_____

Databases

_____

Graphing software

_____

Clip Art

_____

Desktop publishing software

_____

Drawing programs

_____

Animation programs

_____

Color printer

_____

FAX machine

_____

Family website

_____

E-mail

_____

continues

Exercise 1: Using Your Existing Technologies (cont.)

E-mail attachments

_____

Chat logs

_____

Sound clips

_____

Video clips

_____

Internet links

_____

Graphing calculator

_____

Educational software

_____

Reference software

_____

Writable CD-ROMs

_____

VIRTUAL OR TANGIBLE: THE BASICS ARE THE SAME

As you begin thinking about all of the opportunities technology can afford, don't forget the basic principle that a portfolio is a _thoughtful_ selection of items. While technology can collect and inventory a tremendous amount of information about learning, you still need to exercise discernment when selecting (or rejecting) items for your portfolio.

You need to remember that while your archives may be bulging, your portfolio needs to be streamlined and manageable. Just because you have a great many artifacts doesn't mean you need to use them all! When developing any portfolio, it pays to focus on a few areas and then develop them in depth.

In addition to its specific subject matter, each portfolio needs an overall organizational theme. Is your portfolio going to highlight where you are today in a variety of subject areas or show growth over time in one discipline? Will it focus on varied expertise in one skill area (for example, writing in several styles) or present research that you've done in depth? The basic ways to organize portfolios are also discussed in Chapter 3, "Portfolio Basics."

Even if you intend to use your portfolio only for home use, sequencing artifacts is still important. Digital artifacts need to be as thoughtfully arranged in a virtual portfolio as paperwork would be in a file folder. This means creating folders and file names that remind you, or encourage the viewer, to look though the portfolio's contents in the order you feel is most compelling. Perhaps you would like to show progress over time toward mastering a specific skill. Or perhaps you want to show *final* mastery of a broad range of skills. Whatever organizational style you choose, make sure it's understandable and that you stick to it!

A SAMPLING OF VIRTUAL PORTFOLIOS

The range of options for creating electronic portfolios is beyond the scope of this chapter, but to start you thinking about a few of the options, here are three approaches, ranging from simple to quite complex:

- A diskette combining text and other media

- A diskette with text and embedded hyperlinks

- A web-based portfolio

MULTIMEDIA DISKETTES

The first idea that may come to mind when thinking about digital portfolios is a simple diskette containing a variety of media: text, photographs, drawings, charts, and audio clips that can be distributed for review. While this model can work, especially in a personal portfolio for home use, there are several issues to consider.

USING TECHNOLOGY: TWO WAYS TO GO

- You can put text, sound, and images on diskettes or tapes and include them **in** your hand-delivered portfolio.

- You can put them on a website and use the Internet **as** your portfolio.

Certain types of files fill up a diskette very quickly. Animation, for example, because of its dynamic nature, takes up a great deal of space and does not leave room on a diskette for much else. To handle this situation, animation would need to be saved on one diskette and complementary text on another. While this sounds like a practical solution for displaying two types of information, it defeats the purpose of displaying them seamlessly or simultaneously—of using technology to create unity across several media. One way to address this would be to use writable CD-ROMs that can hold much more information and many more images than a conventional $3^1/_2$-inch diskette. Creating a web-based portfolio, as discussed below, provides another solution.

Diskette portfolios intended for use outside the home might run into compatibility problems: Can the hardware, software, and human being at the receiving end read your portfolio? Check beforehand. Another issue is that of security. Institutions are often reluctant to use diskettes from outside their own system for fear of contracting viruses. In fact, many organizations have policies that prohibit using diskettes that have not been cleared through their security system. It is important to ask about this in advance. Remember: *Knowing your audience* is one of the primary rules for creating portfolios and transcripts. If the reviewer cannot, or will not, read your diskette, you need to provide other alternatives that will demonstrate what you know.

EMBEDDED HYPERLINKS

One of the simplest ways to add technological sophistication to your portfolio is to embed hyperlinks in text. A plain list of Internet web addresses lacks a frame of reference, but embedding them in text puts them in perspective. If the hyperlinks you have used can be thought of as evidence of learning, then they need to be put into context. When used properly, hyperlinks can also round out an otherwise mundane report, adding color, sound, dimension, and an element of drama and surprise.

If you are using an up-to-date word processing program, you can add Internet connectivity to your writing by typing or pasting an Internet address directly into your text. Once you press "Enter," the address will turn into a hyperlink. When the word processing file is stored on a diskette or e-mailed as an attachment, the link can be activated when the receiver opens the file while he or she is connected to the Internet. A click on the hyperlink will bring the reviewer to a site that adds context and richness to your subject matter.

You can insert hyperlinks into the educational plans or narrative summaries that you submit to your school system. This is a good way to document curriculum resources that are not text-based. For example, suppose I wanted to document a virtual frog dissection that was part of my son's biology program. When I write my narrative summary, I would paste the website's address into the text. Then I would copy the file to a diskette, which I would give to my administrator. As he reads my narrative, a click on the link would bring up the resources. If his system were incompatible with mine or if he were forbidden to use outside diskettes due to school security policies, I still could send this as text in an e-mail. The example on p. 125 shows a biology curriculum with embedded links.

All sites are not created equal. Think twice before using one that is primarily text. Remember, you want to ask, *What does this technology do particularly well?* If the answer is that it adds color, photos, and interactivity, then link the reviewer to sites with those features. Something that is mostly text, such as an online essay about the ethics of dissection or a webpage of step-by-step dissection instructions, could be printed out and included as hard copy. The web address will be printed at the bottom of the page should your reviewer want to visit the site.

Because we were creating this biology portfolio for our local school system, I was the person responsible for writing the narrative summary. Students, however, should also find this technique easy to use, especially when building a diskette portfolio to document web-based learning. Since the links are descriptive, the student can concentrate on writing text that is reflective. In such instances, when you are constructing your own learning packages, your immediate audience probably will be limited to yourself and your family. However, keep in mind that you may find

Biology

Spring dissections included the roundworm, segmented worm, http://spider.albion.edu/fac/biol/pearson/annel.htm, frogs (both male and female), and fetal pig.

Before dissecting the frogs, Jed and his partners reviewed the University of Virginia's virtual frog dissection web-site: http://curry.edschool.virginia.edu/go/frog/.

This helped them understand the sequence of procedures and the care with which incisions must be made. In addition to directional terms such as dorsal, ventral, superior, and inferior, group members needed to understand vocabulary for systems and organs. Previewing this on the virtual frog dissection site was incredibly useful. When the boys finally got their frogs, they were able to label the external characteristics and make clean, deft incisions. The goal was to have each student identify and name each organ made visible though dissection and to understand its function. I am confident that all participants remember their frog's 3-chambered heart, the yellow fat deposits, the egg mass in the female, and the curly small intestine that resembled a phone cord!
http://curry.edschool.Virginia.EDU/go/frog/organs/Layer2/home.html.

The fetal pig dissection took many sessions, each devoted to a particular system of the organism. The pig was accompanied by several larger specimens (sheep's brain, sheep's heart, and sheep's eye) that could be studied in greater detail. Again, the goal was to notice mammalian similarities. Because the fetal pig's skeletal system could not be easily studied, comparison of mammalian skulls was done by studying models pictured at http://skullduggery.com/skulls.htm.

Throughout the dissection lessons, a human anatomy book was always nearby to make connections between the pig's anatomy and our own. To complement this we also used an interactive CD-ROM, *Bodyworks 5.0,* that showed human organs from various perspectives and described their functions more fully.

diskette portfolios useful in the future, when you are describing to colleges the depth and breadth of your independent study.

WEB-BASED PORTFOLIOS

Web-based portfolios provide powerful answers to two important questions, *How can I show what I know?* and *How can technology better manage student work?*

Web-based portfolios are websites that hold whatever work and artifacts you choose to display. Like traditional portfolios they hold selections from your master collection and are focused, streamlined, clear, and targeted to those you invite to review it.

Several problems are eliminated with web-based portfolios. Since Internet websites can be accessed from any computer, PC or Mac, the compatibility issue becomes moot. It doesn't matter if you and the reviewer have different platforms. Nor does it matter if you wrote your essay or designed your graphics with software different from that of the viewer. All that is necessary is that the computer used to view the page has the appropriate downloadable software needed to play your audio and video clips. Access to a web-based portfolio is easy, since only one piece of equipment, the desktop or laptop, is needed to view a variety of media. The reviewer doesn't need to set up a VCR or find a cassette player; he or she just needs to connect to the Internet. Web-based portfolios also eliminate some of the security concerns regarding using infected diskettes and downloading attached files.

In addition, a web-based portfolio permits sharing your student work with a wider audience than would be possible with a portfolio filled with tangible objects. It allows you to display not only your showcase pieces, but also works in progress, perhaps with a mentor or research partner who lives at a distance.

Web-based portfolios also deal with the issue of storage. Since the products of even four home-schooling years can fill file cabinets to the bursting point, digital storage may become an attractive option. Web-based portfolios also encourage student ownership of learning and assessment. Because website maintenance is usually ongoing, you will be reviewing and reflecting on your work regularly.

A web-based portfolio can unify materials that have been created in several media, displaying the connections you perceived among various portfolio components. For example, my son was engaged in a historical research project that entailed documenting children's gravestones. One of his tasks was to take photographs of the markers using a digital camera. The result was a web-based written report combined with thumbnail photos of the stones, each of which could be clicked in order to see a close-up of the carved inscription. Not only did this create a moving and powerful presentation, but it also digitally preserved artifacts that were in danger of deterioration.

Finally, web-based portfolios can be useful when you have an interdisciplinary artifact to display. If you consider one of your science reports to be evidence of your best writing, it can be cross-referenced so a viewer would find it by looking in either science or English. A scanned-in photograph of a quilt that you made might be accessed from your mathematics, art, women's studies, and American history page. A web-based portfolio is an extraordinarily useful tool for showing relationships, adding clarity and context, and helping the viewer better understand your learning process, your growth, and your accomplishments.

A successful web-based portfolio shares these attributes with other high-quality web-based products. Any type of website ought to be:

- Attractive
- Multisensory
- Cohesive
- Rich in content
- Maneuverable
- Interactive
- Audience- or stakeholder-oriented

Before applying this list to portfolios, consider how these qualities would operate in the corporate world. How would a company attract customers using the Internet? And how would it close the sale? First, the company would use text, color, movement, and perhaps sound in the ad, displaying all these media on one page in order to create a synergy that results in a powerful image. Effectiveness on the web goes beyond attractive design and meaningful content, however. A well-crafted online site is maneuverable. It allows the potential customer to move through the entire website, traveling along a route that meets his or her needs. A good advertising website is also interactive. It encourages the customer to make choices en route by offering options at critical points. Just as using two- and three-dimensional design principles is important when creating a traditional portfolio, utilizing good website (not just webpage) design techniques is necessary when organizing a digital one.

CREATING A WEB-BASED PORTFOLIO

Approach creating a web-based portfolio as you would if you were designing a generic website. Use the same web design principles, but remember that a portfolio is different from a personal homepage. A traditional portfolio shouldn't include everything you like and everything you've done well—and neither should a digital one. A homeschool portfolio, indeed *any* student or professional portfolio, needs to be more than just a random collection of files and links. A portfolio needs thoughtfully selected contents, and it also needs a theme, a format, and an audience.

ORGANIZING YOUR CONTENT

A portfolio's contents must be organized according to some sort of plan. If you know that the people most likely to view your portfolio would want (or expect) to see material in the traditional high school disciplines when they visit your website, make sure those areas are highly visible on the site's homepage. Suppose you want to create a web-based portfolio based on the major school subject areas of English, Mathematics, Natural Sciences, Social Sciences, Languages, and The Arts. Most websites are too large to look through thoroughly, so you need to direct your audience's attention with major headings. If you use an outline approach, these categories will determine your subcategories. For example, a link on the Literature page might bring the viewer to the list of poetry you read during the past year. From there a link might lead to a page showcasing Irish poets, and then finally to a page about Irish Nobel Prize winner William Butler Yeats where you

USEFUL TO HAVE ON YOUR WEBSITE

Use your web-based portfolio to:

- Showcase work you are most proud of

- Display items too difficult to physically send or transport to a reviewer

- Answer frequently asked questions about your work or homeschool program

have placed a copy of his poem, "The Lake Isle of Innisfree," an audio clip of you reading it, and a reflective essay you wrote about it.

This hierarchical approach, however, is not the only way to organize your material. One of the most useful aspects of a website is that it allows and encourages associative connections. Because of the interdisciplinary manner in which many homeschoolers construct their learning, a web-based approach is an ideal way to demonstrate the interconnectedness of subject matter and family life. Thus, a viewer could arrive at the Yeats page using a route very different from the one described above. For example, beginning at a page about family travel, the viewer could click to a page devoted to a trip to Ireland; then to a page featuring lakes, cliffs, coastlines, and other natural features the family visited; then to a page on the actual Lake at Innisfree (complete with a photograph, of course); and finally to the Yeats page with the poem, audio clip, and essay.

In addition to showcasing the artifacts of which you are most proud, your web-based portfolio is an ideal place to answer the most frequently asked questions you have to deal with as a homeschooler or to situate frequently requested items, such as a transcript. Once an item has been added to your website, it is easy and efficient to send its web address via email to whoever wants or needs to see it.

DISTRIBUTION ISSUES

When a traditional portfolio is assembled in manila folders and briefcases, it usually has limited viewership. But a digital portfolio can have virtually unlimited distribution. It can be a delight to share your web-based portfolio with family, friends, and mentors, and you may find it useful and efficient to show it to schools and employers. You can even flick it to a reporter who wants to know more about homeschooling. List it with a search engine and researchers who type in the words "homeschool" and "portfolio" will find you.

This limitless potential may sound exciting, but be cautious. Going public with pages that are under construction can backfire if your viewer finds all the mistakes your proofreading missed. Furthermore, since your portfolio is your alter ego, sharing it means you are sharing yourself. You need to be alert to the personal information your work communicates. How much of that do you want a local school administrator to see?

Privacy and security concerns extend to the internal links you add to your site, too. For example, if you put a letter of recommendation into your digital portfolio, you should respect the writer's privacy by deleting the address and phone number. Although teens should assume increasing responsibility for their web-based portfolio, parents should exercise oversight just as they would if a high-stakes portfolio were being presented in person.

WEBPAGE DESIGN ISSUES

You probably will use a general website construction package rather than a school-oriented portfolio program to design your web-based portfolio. Because of this you will need to build in portfolio features when designing your site. This section will give you a few things to keep in mind.

GETTING STARTED

You can construct your first website using free downloadable programs on America Online, Yahoo!, Geocities, Talk City, or other Internet hosts. These are good places for a beginner to practice. As you become familiar with website design, you will probably investigate comprehensive packages such as Microsoft's FrontPage or Vizact, or Macromedia's Dreamweaver. No design sense? Try *The Non-Designer's Web Book: An Easy Guide to Creating, Designing, and Posting Your Own Web Site* by Robin Williams and John Tollett.

Read through the list of artifacts in Appendix B, "The Discovery Process," to get an idea of what you can put into your portfolio. Remember, however, that before you can put an artifact into a web-based portfolio it needs to exist in digital format. This means that you will need to digitize any item that exists in paper or three-dimensional form. Run physical documents through a scanner to convert them to word-processing documents or pieces of electronic art. Take pictures of artifacts with a digital camera or scan existing photos that you have. Connect your stereo to your computer and rerecord audio artifacts into your computer. Web design books can offer instructions for your specific conversion needs.

Even if items already exist digitally on your hard drive or on diskettes, you may want to rename them as you build your portfolio. Filenames should include a date so that you can easily organize digital artifacts chronologically when you want to create a year-by-year model for viewing. Furthermore, it should go without saying that you should have a hard copy or a back-up copy of *everything*.

Creating Your Homepage

Your cover letter and table of contents would be the first two items visible when opening a traditional portfolio. In a web-based version, both these features should go on your homepage—the place your viewer enters your website. When a traditional portfolio is housed in a manila folder,

THE ADOLESCENT'S ROLE

Teenagers should become increasingly responsible for the . . .

- Ownership,

- Management

- Maintenance

. . . of the virtual artifacts on their portfolio websites.

a reviewer can leaf through it quickly, getting an overall idea of its contents. Because this is not possible for a digital portfolio, the subjects you list as titles in your table of contents should be clear to the point of transparency. This is not the place to be cute or coy. The same holds true for naming your links. They should be descriptive and unambiguous. If you want the reviewer to look at items in a particular order, make that clear in the name of the link, too.

> **WELCOME TO MY DIGITAL PORTFOLIO**
>
> Your homepage introduces the viewer to your entire website. It acts as a digital cover letter, making that important first impression. Plan it carefully.

Every portfolio item should have a context. In a traditional portfolio, this is usually done by an annotation on the table of contents. However, since a web-based portfolio can contain many more items than a traditional one, an annotated digital table of contents would become cluttered and confusing. Thus, it would be better to add a contextual note to an individual item's webpage.

> **BE EFFICIENT**
>
> Once you decide on a layout model that includes all the information you want to share, save the format as a template. Having a template means you won't have to start from scratch in order to use the same webpage design for the next artifact you want to display. Using a template is another way to add a sense of unity to a portfolio filled with a wide variety of artifacts.

Creating a Webpage for Each Artifact

What might an artifact's page look like? Decide how your reviewer might want to see artifacts in reality, and then create a webpage layout that includes all that information in a virtual way. If you are communicating to an educator, here is a skeletal outline of what you might include on an artifact's page. These assessment terms are ones an educator would find familiar:

1. **Goals:** What did you want to learn or do?

2. **Assignment:** What was the specific learning task you performed?

3. **Criteria:** What constitutes quality work?

4. **The Artifact:** text, graphic, audio, or video

5. **Rationale:** Why is this item here, and what is its context?

6. **Assessment:** How good is this piece of work?

7. **Reflection:** What did you learn? How have you changed?

If you are including a digitized performance, remember that a short clip is all you will be putting on the website. You will need to determine if this small amount of information is enough to help the viewer or listener understand your work. Certainly, if you are applying to a conservatory, a few seconds of digitized sound is not going to be enough. But suppose you want the listener to know that you enjoy playing several different styles of music on your violin. In this case, audio clips of classical, bluegrass, and Scottish fiddle music would be delightful.

Curricular and Extracurricular Links

You also need to determine how to link your homeschool experiences to the established canon of learning used by schools. Much of what you have done as a homeschooler may not fit neatly into traditional subject area categories. That is fine. By using your creativity you will be able to frame your experiences to show, for example, a history curriculum with far greater depth and breadth than that of most public schools. In addition, the quality of your artifacts will attest to the standards of your homeschool program.

Remember, too, that travel, volunteerism, and work opportunities—the experiences that schools usually term "cocurricular" and "extracurricular"—may be the fundamental way that learning is configured in your family. When developing your portfolio website, be sure to treat these as legitimate curricular experiences. In short, if you can find an educational link, create the hyperlink. For more on the subject of constructing courses from experiences see Chapters 7, "Transcript Basics," and 8 "Creating Your Transcript."

Letting the Website Speak for Itself

When you personally bring in your two- and three-dimensional portfolio for review, you can verbally fill in details and add the force of your personality to the presentation. Virtual portfolios, on the other hand, need to be treated just like a portfolio that has been mailed away or dropped off at a reviewer's office. If you are not there to complement it, your portfolio needs to stand alone and to stand in for you. Because of this, it is critical that you fine-tune and proofread your website. You want it to be polished and professional. Make sure your internal links work. Check and double-check external links to determine if they are still current. Proofread it again. Send yourself an e-mail through your site to make sure viewers can reach you. Test it out on friends before going public. And when you're certain that it's ready, proofread it again!

 FEATURES TO ADD TO YOUR WEB-BASED PORTFOLIO

Simplify navigation and communication with two built-in features:

- A back-to-home button
- An e-mail reply form

WEB PORTFOLIOS AND THE FAMILY

Both parents and adolescents need to be aware of several concerns related to homeschoolers' web-based portfolios: time, shared decision-making, and educational security.

Once you've decided to develop a web-based portfolio, it will take time to:

- Learn how to create a website
- Learn how to digitize artifacts
- Design a web-based portfolio
- Install and test the site's dynamic features
- Maintain, update, and upgrade the portfolio

Is a Web-Portfolio Right for Your Family?

Again, it is necessary to go back to the two fundamental questions: *How can I show what I know?* and *How can technology better manage student work?* If a web-based portfolio is an effective and efficient way to display what you know and what you can do, and if it helps you better manage the products and processes of homeschooling, *and* if you get a kick out of working with technology, then go for it! Perhaps you already have a website up and running and you feel it is relatively simple to create a portfolio section off the master site. In this case, a web-based portfolio makes sense. It is a continuation of your homeschool experience with technology.

 THE PARENTS' ROLE

While parents may allow their teens considerable freedom in developing personal websites, they need to exercise more oversight for web-based portfolios. As the primary educational facilitators, they should routinely monitor the site to ensure:

- Its material is aligned with the homeschool program.

- Identifying information is not inadvertently posted.

- It remains a portfolio rather than a personal webpage.

Perhaps you don't have a personal website but would like develop one. A web-based portfolio may provide the motivation you need to get started. On the other hand, you may feel that the time invested in learning about web design would be better spent doing other things, or maybe you already have an archival, storage, and presentation system that meets your needs, or your administrator wants to meet with you in person and discuss original work samples. If so, then leave the web-based portfolio for another time and just concentrate on creating the best handcrafted portfolio possible.

Privacy, Security, and Family Concerns

In many families, adolescents are more technologically savvy than their parents. But if collaboration is important when developing traditional portfolios, it becomes even more so for electronic ones. Because a web-based portfolio can be accessed by anyone with an Internet connection, parents need to be alert to what is on the site. While there are general issues of personal safety and family privacy that need to be addressed, there are educational concerns as well.

Each family needs to be aware of its state's minimum legal requirements for homeschooling. School administrators, like anyone else, can access a web-based portfolio if they know its web address. Homeschoolers need to be aware of the public nature of web-based portfolios and think carefully about placing anything in their portfolio that might compromise their ability to homeschool. It is important to read about the issues regarding portfolio reviews in Chapter 5, "Presenting the Portfolio."

A web-based portfolio not only stands alone, it stands open for anyone to see, critique, use, and distribute as he or she sees fit. Your vacation plans, reading list, personal interests, and reflective essays may all be there. So might your resume and transcript. This is one more reason to emphasize that any portfolio, but especially a virtual one, is comprised of *thoughtful selections*. And while

BE CAREFUL!

To access a school-based web portfolio, a viewer needs to pass through several built-in security filters that protect a student's portfolio from universal access. However, homeschool portfolios usually lack this type of privacy. Therefore, parents need to decide if they want their son or daughter's portfolio listed with a search engine.

portfolios can be used for formative purposes—to improve learning and instruction by assessing works in progress—you probably don't want your first drafts up on the Internet for your Superintendent to see. Instead, a web-based portfolio may be a good place to showcase your best, most polished work. If you choose to place lesser-quality work online, make sure it carries an annotation that clarifies its context and its rationale for being there. Just as parents and their children would sit down together for a strategy session prior to a portfolio review held on school premises, it is important that the family preview the web-based portfolio before it is launched.

A FEW LAST WORDS

How else will technology affect assessment? For starters, your resume, transcript, or curriculum vitae can be digitized and then forwarded to colleges and potential employers with a click of the mouse. You can use instant messages to get feedback from your mentor while struggling with a particularly difficult math problem. You can gather in a chat room with your writing partners for a group critique of a short story that you have written. And soon, the face-to-face conference with your local school administrator may become a videoconference.

Homeschoolers are ahead of the curve—whether by including technology *in* portfolios, perhaps as a programmed graphing calculator demonstration, or by using technology *as* a portfolio, making it entirely web-based. You should realize that most school systems are just beginning to experiment with portfolio assessments at the high school level. For them, incorporating technology into portfolios requires a dramatic shift in their assessment policy. It is a major change and an expensive undertaking. Currently, only a few schools have what are called "media stations" that allow students to add audio and video elements to their records. Realize, too, that even if a

PERSONAL, ACADEMIC, AND EMPLOYABLE TRAITS

Did you design and develop your own website? Good! Design and develop your own web-based academic portfolio? Incredible! This fact alone reveals your:

- Initiative
- Perseverance
- Creativity
- Organization
- Independent learning

schooled student develops an electronic portfolio, it will probably cover only one academic discipline, perhaps writing. Homeschoolers, on the other hand, have the freedom to use technology to cut across subject area boundaries and to integrate whole-life learning into their record-keeping and assessments.

Just the fact that you have used a variety of technologies in your portfolio or have set up your portfolio online is a statement about your competency. Schools, colleges, and employers do not come across young persons with this degree of organization, problem-solving skill, and follow-through everyday. It marks you as an aware and self-aware young adult.

C H A P T E R   7

Transcript
Basics

Transcripts and portfolios are two sides of the same coin. Portfolios take your learning and present it as a collection of tangible objects; transcripts, on the other hand turn your learning into letters of the alphabet with plus and minus signs that are significant to the traditionally educated community. If you have already assembled a portfolio, you may have felt as if you were putting together a three-dimensional figure out of Lego bricks. In contrast, writing your transcript will be decidedly two-dimensional—more like a jigsaw puzzle. In fact, the analogy is so apt that one of the planning strategies described later in this chapter uses a puzzle motif to help you literally lay your learning out in front of you.

Transcripts are similar to spotlight portfolios in that they report on all facets of your learning at one point in time, usually at either the end of the semester (or year) or at the conclusion of your entire secondary experience. Because they usually accumulate your learning over several years, they are termed a *cumulative* reporting tool. Homeschool transcripts also can be considered similar to resumes or showcase portfolios, where your best personal and academic self is on display.

 NO WASTED WORDS

Transcripts are usually written in an educational shorthand consisting of the following:

- Numbers
- Letters
- + or – signs
- Clean, efficient prose

Unlike portfolios, which are richly detailed, interdisciplinary, and have no set shape or form, transcripts are tightly organized and traditionally formatted. In general, they use a highly symbolic code consisting of five letters of the alphabet (A, B, C, D, F) to summarize a teacher's opinion. Transcripts do not describe anything. They merely report. This is why it is appropriate to consider them to be high school report cards.

A high school transcript is a concise document that presents an academic snapshot of a student's adolescence. Although scanning a transcript is a time-efficient way to get an overview of a student's activities, it doesn't tell the reviewer what was *learned*. Because the reviewer does not know the content of what was taught, he or she really has no idea of what the student actually knows. A traditional transcript consists of the name of the course and the number or letter grade awarded by the instructor. Notice that I did not say "the grade that was earned by the student." Grades are awarded by teachers according to a particular formula that they devise. A different weighting of tests, participation, and homework would result in another formula and, perhaps, a different grade. Grades appear objective because they are crisp and symbolic, but they are essentially subjective, based on a teacher's opinion.

 THE FOUR-C TRANSCRIPT

Your homeschool transcript should be:

- **Compact:** a one- or two-page document

- **Cohesive:** having a sense of unity

- **Comprehensive:** covering many areas of learning

- **Cumulative:** showing several years' work

If transcript grades are a shorthand for teacher assessment, what does this mean for you, a homeschooler whose primary educational facilitator is your parent and who is being guided toward ever-increasing self-assessment? It means that *you* get to write the rubric, evaluate your learning, and create your transcript! And because the educational activities of homeschoolers are significantly different from those of schooled students, homeschool transcripts reflect what was actually learned during adolescence.

There will be directions in the next chapter on how to format your transcript to look like a traditional one. But there are other more descriptive options for you to consider. Whichever format you choose, during the transcript process you will be looking at the past four to six years—perhaps even your entire K-12 experience. You will give definition and shape to your learning, distilling all your homeschool experiences into a compact document that communicates not only what you did, but also who you are, what you know, and what you can do.

RESISTANCE TO CREATING YOUR TRANSCRIPT

Because homeschoolers integrate learning so deeply into their lives, personal and emotional issues may arise when faced with creating a high school transcript. While creating portfolios can be an ongoing activity throughout the high school years, a homeschool transcript may be a once-in-a-lifetime event. There may be approach and avoidance, bursts of energy and periods of writer's block. What often comes across loud and clear, even if the words are not voiced, is the message, "I can't *do* it! I feel overwhelmed."

There are many reasons for this crisis of confidence, the first of which is that creating a transcript *is* an enormous undertaking. But there are many more issues that could be lurking underneath the resistance and undermining the process. Creating a transcript can call up very powerful emotions about one's learning: what was done and left undone, what it means to be in transition from one learning venue to another, and most important, what it means to grow up. A homeschooler's transcript is more than an academic document. It is an autobiographical statement.

If you are the parent, observe your son or daughter as carefully and as kindly as you would in any new problem-solving situation to discern what the underlying concerns might be. If you are the student, attempt to locate what is making you feel blocked or stuck. Look through the following statements to see if one or more sounds familiar. Once you have insight into your fears, you can face them, confront them, and develop strategies to defuse them. Then you can get on with the project at hand: creating your transcript.

Obstacles to Developing Your Transcript

- I had all these experiences, but I didn't really learn anything.
- I didn't do anything while homeschooling.
- I did so much I will never remember it all.
- I don't have the self-discipline to do everything I need to do.
- I can't put all this down in writing.
- I can't put numbers and grades on my learning.
- I don't like talking about what I've learned. Learning is too personal.
- I'm too shy to talk about how well I've done. It sounds like boasting.
- They'll think that what I did wasn't real learning.
- They'll never think the things I did *for fun* was real learning.
- They'll think my mom will say good things about me just because she's my mother.
- After I do all this work they won't accept me/hire me anyway.
- I'm just not ready to do this.
- I'm only a kid! This is too important to be left to me.
- I need help!
- This is too big a project.
- I don't know how to start.
- I don't know what I'm doing.
- I never wrote a transcript before!
- This is the end of homeschooling. Once I finish my transcript, it will be all over.

OVERCOMING CHALLENGES AND CONCERNS

Admit it. You probably wouldn't be creating a transcript unless you needed to. But try to view it from another perspective. You *get* to create a transcript, and in doing so you will be looking back on your life as a homeschooler from a new, adult perspective. Most teenagers, with their transcript hidden deep in their school's computer database, don't have a compelling reason to take a long and reflective look over the past few years. As a homeschooler you have that opportunity.

Nevertheless, homeschoolers face several challenges as they go about compacting all their learning into a single efficient document.

RECORD-KEEPING

When organizing a transcript it is an enormous help if you have kept detailed records. Homeschoolers, unfortunately, tend not to engage in meticulous record-keeping. They are too busy doing things, being active, and learning on-the-run. If it is still early in the teenage years, you can do some long-range planning. Make it easier to create a transcript later by starting to use the worksheets in Appendix B, "The Discovery Process," right now. Reconstructing a lifetime of learning is possible, but if you need to rely on memory alone, it will take more time, energy, and coordination.

Whether you are starting early or late, it may help your confidence to know that in some ways, designing a transcript is easier than developing a portfolio. In a portfolio, you need to show tangible products as evidence of learning. With a transcript, you are not faced with that task. As long as you can document for your own files that something did indeed happen and that learning did occur, you can use that information on your transcript. You do not need to reconstruct the activity and represent it through an artifact. This means that when you delve into your household archives it will not be for the artifacts themselves, but for the memories they bring back.

TIME

Homeschoolers organize and calculate time differently from the way schools do. Exactly when learning occurred or how long it took is considered irrelevant.

Homeschooled adolescents may finish algebra in the eighth grade, take two years to complete the same material in grades nine and ten, or take no formal algebra but work though a dozen SATs in a prep book. Time as a variable does not matter so long as they have mastered the content they wanted to learn. While most high schools do not give credit for courses taken before ninth grade, homeschoolers who use mastery—rather than time—to frame learning need not divulge when their learning occurred or how much effort it took. Because of this, you may want to think back to the late middle school years when developing your transcript.

 THE "WHEN DID WE . . . ?" SYNDROME

Use your family calendar or, better yet, a homeschool logbook to track down when you engaged in activities that should appear on your transcript.

Homeschoolers' daily schedules vary so much from that of schools that trying to calculate "time on task" for transcript purposes becomes an absurdity. Schools usually award one Carnegie unit for 120 hours of classroom seat time, calculated as one 45-minute period per 180-day school year. Block programming uses a 90-minute period for 90 days. But, time in a classroom is not the same as time on task. Research has shown that less than half of classroom time can be considered on

TRANSCRIPT TIMING

Decide when the best time is to create your transcript:

- At semester's end (January, June, and August)

- Annually

- For homeschool graduation

- For college admissions or employment

task. And, of course, time on task is not necessarily student learning time. Furthermore, a semester-length course at the college level is calculated as 3 class hours per week for 13 weeks. During this 39-hour semester, students are considered to have covered material equivalent to that taught in a 120-hour year of high school! (A college semester of foreign language, for example, covers a year-long high school course.) In short, the numbers are arbitrary. So what's a homeschooler to do? Try to calculate the number of hours spent reading or playing chess or visiting Mexico? Of course not! *Focus on mastery rather than time!* Then, if necessary, convert mastery to "a year's worth" or "a semester's worth" of learning as you, the parent and primary educator whose signature will appear on the transcript, see fit.

You might choose to create an *annual* transcript for each year of high school. This would be appropriate if you are taking courses through a correspondence school, distance learning center, or a local college. Several annual transcripts can then be put together to create a *cumulative* transcript.

Many homeschoolers however, do not use closed-end coursework. Instead, they spread their learning of many subjects over several years. In such cases, each traditional "school year" would end with everything labeled "incomplete"! This type of learning is incremental and is best described in a single *comprehensive* transcript that covers a continuum of learning over time. Normally a comprehensive transcript is developed toward the end of adolescence.

It would be wise for those who structure time more flexibly to experiment with one or two transcript models early in adolescence to discover how well each matches the way their family homeschools. If you will eventually need to incorporate both coursework and incidental learning into one transcript, you may want to tally completed courses on an annual basis and create a comprehensive transcript for ongoing learning as you move toward college or employment.

If at all possible, work on your transcript the spring before applying to college, and then finish it during the summer. The college application process is demanding, stressful, and time-consuming. Recalling and reflecting on your learning, writing your transcript, completing your application packet, and going on campus visits all at the same time may be just too much to handle. This timing would mean that the work done in your final year at home would not appear on your transcript, or that it would need to be described as "in progress." This is no different from that which occurs for traditionally schooled students, who apply to college with their Junior grades and note their Senior courses with grades pending.

DEFINING YOUR STANDARDS

Homeschoolers, by not participating in the public school system, are usually not bound by state or local curriculum and performance standards. This doesn't mean that they lack high standards for quality work, of course, but when preparing a transcript for employers or colleges, the family's standards need to be made clear. Colleges always want to know how rigorous a school's program is; homeschools are no exception. This is another situation where it helps to think in terms of rubrics and ask *What constitutes quality work?* Understand that when colleges are looking for this information it is to create a context for the student's learning. The school is trying to evaluate the *program* so as to more accurately evaluate the student. For homeschoolers who have scrupulously avoided program evaluation with their local authorities, the idea of articulating their standards may be disconcerting. Just remember that by this point in a student's life program evaluation is no longer a legal issue but an educational one. When colleges and employers look at your child in relation to a whole pool of applicants, they will want you to put the homeschool experience into context for them by sharing program information. Just as the student engages in self-assessment during the transcript process, parents need to assess both their program and their child in order to write the school and student profiles described in Chapter 10, "A Homeschooler's Comprehensive College Application."

Homeschoolers can look at their overall program from the following four perspectives:

- Content

- Intensity of learning

- Level of rigor

- Graduation standards

CONTENT

When you apply to a college or seek employment, you need to show a match between yourself and the school or the job. Schools will want to know what you did during adolescence and how it relates to their institution or organization. If you intend to study or work in the sciences, for example, you will be expected to show evidence of science content in your homeschool program. Did you have an academic experience (coursework or incidental learning) similar to that of a conventional high school, covering basic content in basic biology, chemistry, and physics? Or, did you study an interdisciplinary science, such as oceanography? Or engage in applied science by working at an organic farm? Your transcript will need to list areas of knowledge and skill.

 ACADEMIC CONTENT: "WHAT" YOU LEARNED

When writing your transcript you need to recognize the academic content of your learning regardless of how you homeschooled. Then you need to take these three steps:

- Document it

- Describe it in words

- Translate it into a language your reviewer understands

HOW WIDE? HOW DEEP?

The title of each "course" on your transcript should indicate if it was:

- A survey course

- An in-depth study

- An interdisciplinary, thematic learning experience.

INTENSITY

Any subject can be studied with varying degrees of intensity. When you write your transcript it should communicate as accurately as possible the intensity you brought to each area of learning.

A survey approach allows for a wide view of a subject. You acquire a large amount of factual knowledge without going into any one aspect of the subject to any great depth. Most high school courses are survey courses, as are most introductory 101-type college courses. Survey courses are ideal for getting a broad perspective on a subject or for becoming more culturally literate. They are also useful for getting a taste of the subject to determine if you find it interesting enough to pursue further. If you find that you are covering a great deal of material, whether through a course, informal learning, or independent reading, you can probably describe your learning as a survey course.

On the other hand, you may have pursued a subject in depth, studying and learning all you could about one particular facet that was important or interesting to you. Perhaps you have a significant passion for Ernest Hemingway's writing, and have spent months reading all the Hemingway you could. If you find that you return again and again to one section of the library, consider yourself studying the subject in depth. If you have built up a personal collection of specialized books, tools, or other artifacts around one narrow focus, you can legitimately state that you are engaged in serious study.

A third approach to learning is to study a subject thematically, treating it as complex, multifaceted, and organic. Thematic learning allows the student to move between traditional subject areas in an associative way—seeing connections, for example, between the art, history, religion, and politics of the Reformation. This interdisciplinary learning, often described as thematic unit studies, is less likely to occur in a comprehensive high school where teachers are members of a single academic department and survey courses covering the large amount of material needed for mandated tests are the norm. Homeschoolers whose programs are based on thematic unit studies should not fear including interdisciplinary coursework on their transcripts. Content from the traditional disciplines is surely there, just rearranged in fresh and interesting combinations.

RIGOR

Rigor is where content and quality meet. Schools want to know how intellectually strenuous your learning was. This is not so much a personal question, asking if your mastery of a subject came through a great deal of effort. Rather, it means as compared to other schooled students, how sophisticated was your content and how high was your achievement? Was it an honors course? Honors level work is often easily accessible to homeschoolers because they have flexible time to pursue a subject, freedom to use a wide variety of resources, and opportunities for sophisticated discourse with their parents or mentors. But because homeschooling is a personalized endeavor, comparing one's accomplishments to those of other students is not a frequent event. Learning for one's own sake, or learning for learning's sake, is usually more important. However, when dealing with an applicant pool in which each student college will want to know how much higher-level thinking is reflected by the course grade.

To evaluate the rigor of your learning, look through "Bloom's Taxonomy of Learning" in Appendix C to see where on the continuum from knowledge to evaluation you feel your mastery of a subject lies. You may have done fairly simple knowledge-oriented work in American Literature, or you may have probed four novels in depth, discussed them at length, and explored their characters' interactions in written work included in your portfolio. If the latter, discuss with your parents or mentor if it should be considered honors level work.

GRADUATION STANDARDS

What does granting a diploma mean? For school systems it implies that a student has met the basic requirements for graduation and is therefore ready to move beyond high school's structured learning to a more adult phase of study or work. Keep this idealized definition in mind, because homeschool parents also note when their young adult children are ready to move from the homeschool high school experience to another phase of learning.

A school's graduation standards are usually listed in a one-page document called a school profile that is included with the transcript in a student's college application packet. Each high school has its own criteria for graduation, so it would be expected that each homeschooling family will, too. Is yours quantitative: requiring that your child has covered a certain amount of material or taken a certain number of courses? Is it qualitative: requiring that you could see evidence of independent research? Perhaps you had a specific goal you foresaw back in early adolescence. Or, maybe you just knew the time had come. The family's graduation standard is simply "how we knew." However you knew, now is the time to articulate that knowledge.

GRADES

In addition to explaining your standards, you will also need to describe your grading system. Even if you kept careful records and have clear standards of quality, you will encounter a problem since much homeschool learning is not organized into school-like courses and classes and most homeschooling parents do not give formal end-of-term grades to their children. When you start to envision how your family's method of homeschooling will mesh with a comprehensive transcript, you might ask: *How can we transform what doesn't look like school into a transcript that looks as if it were issued by a school?* If you believe that transcripts need to contain letter and number grades

 GRADES FOR A NON-GRADED PROGRAM

Even if grades were not a part of your family's homeschool program, you may choose to include them on the transcript. Because certain scholarships are based on grade point average, you should check with each school's financial aid office before you begin formatting your transcript.

you may wonder how you will deal with the issue of grading. If your homeschool program was non-graded, does this mean that you need to compromise your educational philosophy? The answer is that you don't necessarily need to create a school-like document. There are clear, efficient, alternative transcripts discussed later in this chapter that communicate effectively to colleges and employers.

GRADES AND ALTERNATIVE ASSESSMENT

Teachers who use alternative assessments need to develop classroom grading systems that factor in activities, assignments, and participation. Parent-educators need not feel shy about exercising this same authority when they need to give grades.

As far as adding grades to a transcript, there are several ways to address the issue. First, because we live in a ratings-driven culture, there will be numerous opportunities for even the most unschooled homeschoolers to receive grades and scores in their various activities. Although we never graded my sons' homeschool work, each of them did receive scores for orchestra seating auditions, college courses, CPR certification, SAT exams, etc. These will be the grades and scores you will include on your homeschool transcript. They will come mainly from outside sources, rather than from within your family, and will complement your non-graded portion. Second, you can follow the lead of certain high schools and colleges where grading is optional and the student can request an "S" for satisfactory completion of the course. He or she then includes a written evaluation by the instructor as part of the transcript. Since homeschoolers using mastery rather than seat time would only put on their transcript those activities that they have successfully completed—i.e., the things that they have learned—a grade of "S" seems redundant. However, an "S" with written feedback can be considered a legitimate transcript entry.

WHAT THE AUDIENCE WANTS TO SEE

Homeschoolers need to discover what their audience wants to know and then communicate that information in a clear, efficient format. What *you* think is important, meaningful, and powerful about your homeschool learning may not be what a prospective college or employer wants to read about in your transcript. This is not because they are unconcerned about these things, only that the transcript may not be the best place to present them.

Colleges and employers have a two-fold view of the transcript. They see it as a *reporting tool* that describes your academic experience and a *prediction instrument* that helps gauge whether or not you will succeed in their environment. The predictive use of the transcript goes beyond simple academics, however. Admissions officials and employers read between the lines of your transcript, looking for clues about your interests and your personal traits to help them determine if you and they are a good match for each other. As a homeschooler your transcript will definitely mark you as unique, but the clearer your transcript is, the more effectively it helps distinguish you from the

ALIKE BUT UNIQUE

You want your transcript to show that you are a good match for the school or organization, that you'll fit in. On the other hand, your transcript needs to differentiate you from the rest of the applicant pool.

rest of the applicant pool. However, bear in mind that your transcript should not only reflect positively on you, it should also defuse any homeschool stereotypes the reviewer holds.

EFFICIENCY, CLARITY, CREDIBILITY

Your transcript needs to be concise. It should be time-efficient to read and easy to understand. College admissions officials read and evaluate hundreds of student application packages from September through March each year. Narratives take time to read and interpret, and are best left to the essay portion of your application packet. Limiting your transcript to only a few pages increases the likelihood that it will be read thoroughly rather than scanned.

In addition to being brief, your transcript needs to be clear. When describing alternative educational practices, utilize language that is user-friendly for the reviewer rather than homeschool terminology tar. Colleges and employers are most familiar with transcripts written in an alphabet soup of ABCDFs, Hs, SATs, APs, CLEPs, etc. If you have developed your own homeschool grading or coding system, make sure you provide a key to explain what your symbols mean. Do not make your grading system convoluted and difficult to understand.

Most high schools use weighted grading systems to assign quality points for course difficulty and to determine a student's rank in class. Because each school's formulas are unique, colleges often find it difficult to interpret a transcript grade unless they have dealt with students from the school in prior years. Since this will probably be your first encounter with a particular college's admissions staff, you will have no track record to familiarize them with your grading system. Thus, if you intend to assign grades, be clear from the start as to what they represent. And if you do not give grades for work in your homeschool program, say so. Otherwise, it may appear that you are avoiding the issue in order to downplay lesser quality work.

If you decide to write a brief narrative transcript, realize that your writing skills will be under intense scrutiny. How tightly can you write? How clear and unambiguous is your prose? Unfortunately, the more descriptive and detailed your narrative, the less useful information it may contain for a reader who just wants the facts. This is why it is imperative to inquire in advance what each college on your list expects to see and if a narrative transcript would be appropriate.

It is wise to include more than self-assessments and parental evaluations in your transcript. Third-party sources vouching for you—either by grades they awarded or letters of reference—can produce a halo effect, increasing the credibility of the sections of your transcript written by the family.

YOUR PERSONAL TRAITS

Your transcript should do more than showcase the academic side of your homeschool experience. You need to create a transcript that allows your personality to shine through and display the qualities that colleges and employers are looking for in candidates.

 JUST THE FACTS

A winding and long-winded narrative may leave the reader wondering why you aren't being direct or if you're avoiding something.

One needs to be realistic, however, and acknowledge that many persons still have misconceptions about homeschoolers. If homeschooled adolescents present a program strong in the traditional academic areas having used a commercial curriculum, they may be pegged as passive, knowledge-based learners. Those who have unschooled might be stereotyped as being undisciplined and lacking a general knowledge base. Of course, the best way to dispel these myths is for schools and employers to get to know homeschoolers personally and to see firsthand their college or on-the-job performance. But first, homeschoolers need to be admitted or hired. This is why your transcript needs to report both your academic knowledge and your cross-disciplinary skills. This combined agenda can be achieved by determining the traits that colleges and employers want in their students and employees (and which they may fear homeschoolers lack), and then making certain these traits are clearly mentioned where appropriate in your transcript, student profile, and school profile.

Abilities Colleges Want Their Students to Have
• Independent thinking skills
• Higher-level thinking skills
• Creativity
• Ability to learn through lecture
• Ability to participate in discussion-based learning
• Oral and written communication skills
• Note-taking skills
• Research skills
• Ability to engage in teamwork
• Ability to interact with persons from diverse backgrounds
• Participation as a member of the college community
• Self-discipline
• Perseverance
• Time-management skills

EMPLOYABILITY

While most college admissions officials have met homeschoolers and seen their alternative transcripts, employers are less likely to have had that same experience. Anticipate their concerns and write your transcript to reflect the traits they would like their employees to have.

When an employer looks at your transcript, he or she will be looking for many of the same personal traits that colleges want to see in young adults, but some traits are unique to the workplace. The following list of traits and abilities constitutes what are termed employability skills.

Whether you are job hunting or applying to college check Appendix C for "Blooms' Taxonomy of Learning," the "Department of Labor's Dictionary of Occupational Titles," and the list of personal traits for additional vocabulary you can use to highlight your skills and your unique personal qualities.

Traits and Abilities Businesses Want Their Employees to Have
• Competency necessary to do the job
• Understanding the scope of the job
• Responsibility
• Honesty
• Punctuality
• Organization
• Flexibility
• Attention to detail
• Ability to meet deadlines
• Ability to follow instructions
• Ability to work without supervision
• Ability to participate in group or team work
• Ability to work with people from diverse backgrounds
• Written communication skills
• Ability to read and understand employment related materials
• Ability to use mathematics
• Ability to read charts, graphs, and other displays of data
• Ability to use materials, tools, and equipment carefully

TRANSCRIPT PROTOTYPES

Portfolios are so new that their format and contents are largely undefined. Resumes are changing to become more contemporary. But transcripts stay the same: course names with their letter grades, neatly arranged in four yearly blocks. This is because transcripts are format-driven documents. The transcript template has become so standardized that it is difficult to envision alternatives, develop them, and put them to large scale use. Even something as simple as arranging courses thematically according to subject area—grouping together all a student's science courses to show a progression of learning, for example—is a radical departure from the norm. (See Appendix A, "A Portfolio and Transcript Sampler," for how this could be achieved.) Changing the structure of transcripts means changing the look and the contents of students' permanent records. This is a major systemic change that most schools are reluctant to undertake. Homeschoolers, on the other hand, have a great deal of freedom to envision and create alternative transcripts. The only restriction to keep in mind is that a transcript needs to communicate efficiently and effectively to the reader.

The type of transcript you create depends to some degree on your method of homeschooling but, more importantly, on the college to which you apply. If you know the type of transcript the school of your choice expects, or is willing to accept, then your job has been made easier: Follow their guidelines. You still can use the suggestions in the following chapter to remember and reconstruct your learning as you shape it to fit the school's specifications. Most schools, however, are less specific when asked about homeschoolers' transcripts. In this more typical situation, you will need to make an educated guess as to which transcript model would be most effective.

When left on your own to create a transcript, you need to make decisions about its structure, its content, and its format. The content will showcase your personality and academic achievement, the format will demonstrate your organizational style, but the structure of your transcript describes a particular philosophy of education. The five transcript prototypes described below range from compartmentalized and numerical to holistic and qualitative. Each is based on two fundamental elements: graduation standards and the primary questions it should answer for the reader.

The formality of your transcript does not need to reflect how you approached homeschooling. Regardless of how you homeschool you can use *any* of these five structures to create your transcript. Some models will match the manner in which you homeschooled more comfortably than others, but even if you were unschooled you can develop a transcript with a traditional image should you want or need to. Think of your learning as fluid and the five prototypes as containers that can hold it. The containers don't change your learning; they simply give it a form. By doing so they allow you to shape your learning, *however* it occurred, into a document that is easy for your reader to comprehend.

EXPERIMENT

When my son was getting ready for college, we experimented with all five prototypes, creating transcripts that would appeal to different audiences and different types of schools.

Appendix A contains a collection of transcripts, all based on the same homeschool experience, that of my son, Tad. Notice how the information is dressed up or down, depending on the prototype used. Some of the transcripts are clinical and detached, others more conversational and relaxed. While each transcript gives the reader a different first impression of Tad, all accurately reflect his adolescent learning. Each transcript would appeal to a different audience. When he petitioned our local School Committee for a diploma, for example, he used the course equivalency model based on Carnegie units. When applying to Brown University, where Exit Exhibitions were developed, an Exit Exhibition transcript/portfolio model was the obvious choice. Same student, same learning; different audience, different transcript.

Be aware that most businesses have limited experience with alternative transcripts. Consider the nature of the organization you want to work for in order to determine if it would be wise to take a more conservative approach when designing a transcript for your job search. The following section will familiarize you with the five transcript prototypes to help you decide which will serve you best.

THE TRADITIONAL TRANSCRIPT

The traditional transcript issued by most high schools and colleges looks very much like a course schedule. It differs only in that the room number where the class meets has been replaced by a letter grade. It is designed to answer the following questions:

- *What were the names of your courses?*

- *Did a course last for a semester or a year?*

- *What grades did your teachers give?*

The variables necessary for graduation are credits and time. Depending on the length of time the course met, the student will be awarded a specific number of units or credits. By acquiring enough of these, usually 18 to 20, and by having those credits distributed over the traditional subject areas (English, Mathematics, Social Studies, Science, Languages, Fine Arts, and Physical Education), the student is considered ready to receive his or her diploma. Because of this, students can be graduated with barely passing grades as long as they stay in school long enough to amass their required credits. Other students, however, may exceed the number of credits required for graduation by the end of their Junior year, but lack "four years of English." This deficiency in their distribution requirement means they will need to attend another year of school to pick up that one particular credit.

 THAT PARENTHICAL H

If you've taken the Advanced Placement exam in a particular subject area and have been awarded a grade of 3, 4, or 5, you should certainly indicate your honors level work with an (H) next to the course name on your transcript. However, many homeschoolers do honors level work that is not verified by an exam. If you feel you have done honors level work and can support your contention with documentation from your portfolio, place an (H) next to the name of that coursework, too.

Should homeschoolers want to show colleges or employers that they have met the same basic course requirements as their schooled peers, they also can fulfill distribution requirements—but on their own timetable. Again, let me emphasize that what is entered on a traditional transcript are course names. By arranging course names thematically rather than chronologically you can avoid explaining how you acquired four credits in English in only three years.

This is a quantitative display of information, and people who find this type of transcript useful will count your credits. Make sure your figures add up!

CONTENT STANDARDS TRANSCRIPT

Content-based transcripts answer the questions:

- *What did the teacher cover in class?*

- *How much of it does he or she think you knew by the end of the course?*

Rather than being based only on course titles and seat time, a content standards transcript is more specific about the material in the curriculum. It is still an *input variable* transcript with the amount of content covered as its focal point. Content-based transcripts describe the material the student was taught, the text that was used, or the experiences he or she had. This model helps the reader understand the breadth of the curriculum and the extent of the program. The norm is teacher evaluation rather than self-evaluation, and grades are usually given, telling the reader of the transcript the relative amount of content that the teacher felt the student understood. So long as a teacher feels a student has "passed" the course Carnegie credit is awarded. Acquisition of enough credits is usually the criterion for graduation.

Homeschoolers who use a textbook-based approach will find this type of transcript useful, explaining to colleges what English IV, U.S. History I, or French III entailed. Homeschoolers who engage in a more eclectic program can still use this model, renaming their experiences to fit the classic subject headings, deciding whether they want to add grades next to the course names.

However, there is always a difference between what was taught and what was learned. While this type of transcript may accurately describe what was in the book or what the student experienced, it doesn't necessarily clarify what the student learned or what he or she can do with the learning. For that you need clear performance standards.

PERFORMANCE STANDARDS TRANSCRIPTS

If content standards describe the written test for a learner's permit, performance standards describe the road test. This is a skills-based model for a transcript. The key question that the reviewer asks and that the transcript should answer is:

- *What can you do?*

Rather than defining learning as input, either time spent in class or a list of content to be taught, performance standards focus on output: Can the student demonstrate in practice the knowledge he or she has learned? Also called mastery learning, evaluation by performance standards tells far more about a student's learning than letter grades. A performance standards transcript is descriptive and relies on qualitative evaluation, usually by rubric. This means that the assessment could be carried out by someone other than the instructor, perhaps even by the student.

Performance standards ask the student to display higher-level thinking and performance skills (see Appendix C for "Bloom's Taxonomy of Learning") instead of simply passing a test that assesses knowledge or comprehension. Knowledge described by curriculum content may be a necessary starting point, but performance assessments ask the student to go beyond the mere acquisition of content and to apply, interpret, analyze, theorize, and evaluate it. This is complex, integrated learning that is best assessed by performance tasks that mimic (or are part of) the real world.

 SHOW WHAT YOU KNOW

Businesses find it difficult to use conventional high school grades to compare applicants nowadays, since a B from one school is rarely equivalent to a B from another. They want to know what applicants can do. Use a performance standards transcript to enumerate demonstrable skills in:

- Communications
- Mathematics
- Technology
- Problem-solving

When schools become involved in mastery learning, they usually devise a comprehensive list of demonstrable complex skills, each of which needs to be accomplished at a level of proficiency before graduation. Students in schools based on the Hudson Institute's Modern Red Schoolhouse model, for example, acquire "Hudson units." These reflect accomplishment, as opposed to Carnegie units that calculate time spent in class. Because much of homeschooling is based on the real world application of skills, and because time spent learning is often irrelevant, performance standards are an especially appropriate vehicle for describing a homeschooler's learning. If your family has expectations of what a young adult should be able to accomplish, then you have already established your homeschool graduation standards. Once listed, they become the foundation of your transcript.

THE RESUME TRANSCRIPT: THE COURSE OF YOUR LIFE

This model might be more accurately termed a "curriculum vitae" (literally, "the course of one's life"), which is similar to a resume but details line by line precisely what you have done in the past few years. Like the traditional model, the resume transcript notes only your course names, plus a grade if you have one. However, it sidesteps the issue of credits entirely, allowing the reader to see broad areas in which the student has had experiences throughout adolescence. Within those large divisions, the layout is in a rough chronological order, although similar activities are grouped together whenever possible to give a sense of thematic unity.

Because homeschoolers tend to regard activities that schools term co- or extracurricular as integral to their learning, the resume transcript is an ideal vehicle for giving equal weight to formative experiences in work, volunteerism, travel, athletics, and the arts. It is the one transcript format that allows for learning beyond the home to be specified and tallied. It answers three questions:

- *What have you done with all of your time spent homeschooling?*

- *Who are you?*

- *How well rounded are you?*

Even though it has a clean, streamlined format, the resume tells an incredible amount about the student's interests and aspirations. It has a design that permits the student to devote line after line to activities that would never show up on a traditional course-based transcript, while still allowing the reader to calculate dates to ascertain that the student has had four years of American and World Literature.

It is also an excellent format to use when job hunting. Although not technically a resume, it does organize and display information in a similar fashion. Because employers read and analyze resumes on a regular basis, your transcript will have a familiar look and feel to them, making it a

 RESUME TRANSCRIPTS

Resume transcripts are useful not only with employers, but also with alumni interviewers, many of whom have business backgrounds and may be unfamiliar with homeschooling. Just as job seekers keep an updated resume on hand, homeschoolers should have a resume *transcript* readily available.

useful way to describe what you've done and how well rounded you are. The implication of the resume transcript is that you are a competent and capable young adult and that had you been schooled traditionally you *surely* would have been granted a diploma!

A Narrative Transcript: The Exhibition Model

The Coalition of Essential Schools is a network of contemporary high schools where an Exit Exhibition is required for graduation. An Exit Exhibition is a holistic evaluation, where the student must present and defend a major interdisciplinary project to a panel of reviewers from the school and community. The reviewers assess the presentation and then, if warranted, accept it as evidence of mature, sophisticated learning that qualifies the student for graduation. An Exit Exhibition answers these questions:

- *What have you learned in depth?*

- *Can you integrate your knowledge and skills?*

- *Can you present your information effectively?*

- *What new knowledge did you construct?*

Exhibitions encompass theorizing, research, analysis, writing, graphic displays of data, and oral presentation skills, all with the support of a mentor. They are the high school equivalent of a university's defense of thesis or oral comprehension exams. Exhibitions ask a student to engage in far more than recall of factual information. They expect that the student will not only be a consumer of knowledge but a producer of it as well.

 EXHIBIT YOU LEARNING

Exhibitions can identify mature, reflective learners who do more than just receive and repeat information. These students can:

- Construct a sophisticated learning project

- Deconstruct the project into a narrative transcript

By engaging in a project of this magnitude, a student will be constructing knowledge. At the conclusion of the project, he or she should be able to deconstruct it to recognize the learning in both content and skills that occurred along the way. This analysis would be the basis for a reflective transcript tightly written either as a report or in narrative format.

THE PARENTS' ROLE

Even though the student should be the author of his or her transcript, parental support is crucial. Think of it as a team effort, an exercise in cooperation and collaboration working toward a common goal. Parents can begin to store information in an easily retrievable format, modeling for their children how to keep records and gradually handing that responsibility over to them.

Parents can help with the memory work. Using the techniques described in Chapter 4, "Creating Your Portfolio," and in the next chapter, "Creating Your Transcript," parents can help their son or

PARENTS AS PARTNERS

Does your son or daughter seem overwhelmed? Try:

- Listening to concerns

- Brainstorming

- Breaking the process into manageable tasks

daughter remember past learning. They can also fill in details their child may have overlooked or add their own reminiscences, not just as Mom or Dad but as the their child's educational facilitator. Parents who have been observant as educators can add information and perspective while still respecting their adolescent's ownership of his or her learning. Finally, parents can find artifacts that are stored away, things that their child may not even know had been saved.

When their child begins the writing phase of the process, parents can offer feedback on the drafts. Their role would be that of coach, asking questions and offering strategies while letting their child do the work and make the decisions. They can offer guidance and advice from their adult perspective, supporting and encouraging often, prodding when necessary.

Parents will need to keep abreast of deadlines and timelines, and to write their own transcript attachments: the student and school profiles. The student profile is a one-page document that addresses overall student competency, personal as well as academic. It may be thought of as a homeschool guidance department report. The school profile clarifies the "why" and "how" of your homeschool program so that the school or employer better understands your educational philosophy, curriculum, practices, and methods of assessment. Both profiles are routine inclusions in a college application packet, and instructions for writing them are detailed in Chapter 10, "A Homeschooler's Comprehensive College Application."

A SPECIAL NOTE FOR PARENTS . . .

My last piece of advice for parents is to remember that though your personal educational philosophy was a critical factor in the decision to homeschool, your adolescent has developed his or her own definition of meaningful learning. This emerging philosophy will become clearer as he or she assumes ownership of the transcript process, making decisions about what to include and for whom the transcript is intended. As the transcript moves toward completion, parents and children are bringing closure to a longstanding educational and personal relationship. Parents need to respect their sons' and daughters' independent thinking, while adolescents need to acknowledge the interdependent nature of this project.

 FAMILY TIES

Creating a homeschool transcript or a portfolio is not an individual endeavor. Use the memories of your entire family as a resource.

CHAPTER 8

Creating Your
Transcript

Now that you've noted, recorded, saved, archived, and probably even portfolioed your homeschooling experiences, how are you going to mold your experiences into a comprehensive transcript? This chapter will walk you through the steps of building a transcript:

- Remembering

- Recognizing

- Framing

- Fitting

- Writing

- Formatting

- Proofreading, polishing, and printing

 A ONCE-IN-A-LIFETIME OCCURRENCE

You'll probably write many resumes in the course of your life, but only one homeschool transcript. Give it the time and attention it deserves!

Sound intimidating? Don't worry. As I describe each step in the sequence, I will share what the experience was like for my own son so that you can envision what the process looks like in practice. Your experience will differ, of course, but it should be helpful to watch someone work through the tasks knowing that he eventually arrived at a finished product that served him well.

HANDLING THE RAW MATERIAL

RECORD-KEEPING

Homeschoolers need to keep record-keeping in perspective. Because a homeschool transcript reflects the student's ownership of his or her learning, record-keeping should eventually become the student's responsibility. Parents can help their children develop a record-keeping and filing

A THREE-STEP PROCESS

When you create your transcript you'll:

- **Claim it:** Recognize the learning in your experience.

- **Frame it:** Organize your learning and give it a context.

- **Name it:** Put your learning into words.

system that will be easy to work with by the time college application and job hunting comes around. Unfortunately, if it is nearing the end of adolescence and your family hasn't been disciplined about keeping records, you will need to reconstruct events from memory. In either case, relax and take a realistic perspective: This will be an intense but short-term project, whereas spending time with your family and pursuing your specialized interests were long-term homeschool goals.

If you have developed homeschool portfolios using the techniques in this book, you know that once you recall a learning experience to include in your portfolio you need to find (or construct) an artifact to represent it. In the transcript process, the reverse is true: You look through your artifacts in order to resurrect memories.

Your memory is your most important resource in the transcript process, and good record-keeping makes remembering easier. Homeschoolers need a simple, non-intrusive system of record-keeping so that memories and the information they contain will be easy to retrieve. Appendix B, "The Discovery Process," contains a wide variety of forms to use for jotting down brief explanatory notes about homeschool events. As simple as they are, the worksheets give you a place to put information before it gets forgotten. But rather than adopt an entirely new system, adapt the suggestions you find here to the system you already use.

TRACKING DATES

Your record-keeping system may not look like that of a conventional school, but date your artifacts and information with the same care schools do. Eventually, you may decide that you want to develop a traditional-looking transcript that emphasizes dates and grades. If so, you will need to have that information available. Keep track of time, even if you intend to create a more open-ended transcript model. Dates can be associative, helping you remember what else you were doing during a particular phase of adolescence or when you reached certain benchmarks in your learning.

In trying to reconstruct the past, it is more important to have a record of what you actually did, rather than what you planned to do. This is why a log is more valuable than a plan book or family calendar. A student's diaries or personal journals, while excellent tools for reflection, are usually written in a style that makes simple recall of events difficult. A separate, inexpensive pocket calendar makes an ideal logbook. Rather than using it at the end of the day to plan what you intend to do next, simply record five things you actually did. These do not need to be academic activities or learning experiences, just things that you want to remember. Be assured that many of these "unimportant" details of daily life will appear in your transcript several years later.

Keeping a log is appropriately the student's responsibility. But I would urge parents to write a two- or three-page narrative on a semester basis throughout their sons' and daughters' high school years. Reading through these narratives at the end of adolescence will be an extraordinary experience. Progress and the patterns that went unnoticed on a daily basis will be evident from these semester records. They will be helpful no matter which type of transcript you create, but they will be especially useful if you decide to develop a performance standard transcript or a reflective one.

COLLECTING ARTIFACTS AND INFORMATION

What should you save? When your child is twelve years old how do you know what he or she will find useful and important at age seventeen? What about artifacts that represent experiences done "just for fun"? Might they later be indicative of a pattern, representing the early stages of serious, focused, intensely personal learning?

Earlier in Chapter 3, "Portfolio Basics," I gave three guidelines for saving "stuff":

- If you talked about it, save it.

- If it looks interesting, save it.

- If you can't get another one, save it.

If an artifact meets any of the above three criteria, don't discard it! You never know what will be important later, or if an item will represent early phases of more complex learning.

You will also need to collect information. Unlike artifacts, information is not easily visible. The "Memory Archives" worksheets in Appendix B provide a way for you to list and access a wide variety of information about learning experiences. These can be the basis for any type of transcript, but if you are constructing a traditional or content-based model, they can prove especially useful. Some of the worksheets will be more reflective of the way you homeschool than others, but it is likely that you will have several entries for each worksheet by the time you are ready to develop a comprehensive transcript.

Check the list of artifacts in Appendix B for a glimpse at the variety of items that can either refresh your memory or serve as documentation. If you are just beginning to use the "Memory Archives" worksheets you may find that they suggest ways to build a strong, multifaceted learning package by exploring a variety of life experiences. Toward the end of adolescence, the data you have recorded will help you to recognize how you learned a particular "subject" in a multitude of ways, through:

- Direct instruction

- Independent study and research

- Books read, films viewed, and performances attended

- Projects, exhibitions, and demonstrations

- Extra- and cocurricular activities

- Employment, internships, apprenticeships, and volunteer and service activities

- Travel and day trips

TWO TYPES OF DOCUMENTATION

Primary: Material created or written by you

Secondary: Material written about you and your work.

Reviewing lists from several years ago will give you plenty of raw material for creating courses retroactively when you sit down to write your transcript.

SECONDARY SOURCE MATERIAL

All the products and memories of your homeschool experience that were created *by* you are your primary source material. Your secondary source materials are those things that have been written *about* you. The latter are the materials that verify your self-evaluations, adding weight, credibility and a sense of professional detachment.

Secondary source material close to home would be parent narratives written on a semester basis and any notes, plan books, calendars, and computer files relating to homeschooling that have been kept by parents. Once you move beyond your household and into the community, you should be able to acquire a variety of paperwork that will support your contention that you are a capable learner and a competent young adult. There are scores of these listed in "Artifacts and Evidence" in Appendix B, but for starters try collecting:

- References

- Recommendations

- Commendations and awards

- Number and letter grades

- Certificates of attendance

- Thank-you notes

- Newspaper and magazine articles about you

Although you might not use number or letter grades in your homeschool program, you may have taken courses or classes where grades were given. While it is important to keep the copy of the transcript or grade report that was mailed to you, you can extend the evaluation by requesting that the instructor write a letter detailing the course content and your level of participation. These will be useful if you write a content-based transcript or design one in resume format.

Even if a grade or certificate of attendance was not awarded for an outside course, request verification of your participation from the instructor anyhow. I always had my sons ask their teachers for written feedback. Early in adolescence they felt awkward making the request, but they warmed up to the practice and eventually each had a file of solid documentation backing up their transcript entries. You can use the following suggestions when requesting verification and feedback from mentors, employers, and volunteer coordinators, too:

- First, ask for the letter several weeks before the course ends. This helps the instructor put a name to your face and gives him or her time to compose a letter by the end of the course. When making the request, always let the instructor know that you are a home-schooler, that you need a one page letter as external verification for your transcript and portfolio, and that you would like it written on letterhead stationery to add credibility to the documentation. Since you will be using the letter to build your transcript, it will be given to you rather than sent to a school or college. Give your instructor a stamped, self-addressed envelope so that he or she can mail it to your home after the course ends.

- Be specific about what you would like your instructor to say. If you want verification that you can demonstrate a particular skill—for example, using a telescope to identify certain celestial objects—say so. Whenever possible, ask the instructor to note processes such as group participation, or personal traits such as organization or perseverance. It is also useful to ask him or her to comment on the foundational knowledge you brought to the course. For example, my son took a physics course he needed to utilize algebraic equations to solve the problem sets. Although he never had taken a formal algebra class, his ability to apply the mathematics implied that he had, indeed, mastered the content of Algebra II. Thus, the verification letter that was ostensibly about his performance in a physics course actually signed off on his competency in mathematics, as well.

- I strongly suggest that you make copies of these letters to keep at home and that you save the originals in a safe deposit box along with other important paperwork relating to homeschooling such as any transcripts sent to you by a correspondence school, umbrella school, distance learning organization, or college or university. While official copies of these will be sent directly from the issuing school to the college you want to attend, you still should attach one of your unofficial copies to your homeschool transcript.

REMEMBERING AND RETRIEVING

The techniques in this section are designed to help you retrieve whatever information you have hidden away in your home and in your memories so you can begin to assemble your transcript with confidence.

RECOLLECTION TECHNIQUES

In Chapter 4, "Creating Your Portfolio," I enumerated a number of techniques that could be used to help recall activities and events that shaped your learning. They are described briefly here in order to give you a quick overview of the strategies that are available to you. There are a couple of additional suggestions, more attuned to the transcript process than the portfolio process, that are included toward the end of this section, too. Because each technique is geared to a particular learning style, experiment with all of them to see which will give you the best results.

 RECOLLECT AND COLLECT

The raw material for your transcript resides in your memory. Use the "Memory Archives" worksheets to help you recollect. Then collect those memories by writing them down.

Visualizations use a question and answer format to take the listener back in time to an event he or she wants to remember in greater detail. The questions move from the external setting, to the activity, and then finally to the identification of what was learned from the experience. This type of memory work is well suited to recalling experiential learning that was rich and detailed, such as performances, fairs, day trips, etc.

Mind maps are a type of graphic organizer that helps recall learning that was interdisciplinary and highly associative. Mind maps make the connections between various aspects of learning visible on paper. They are excellent for showing how learning that at first appears full of vaguely connected loose ends is indeed part of a pattern.

Look-arounds help you inventory the memories that are right in front of you. A simple technique that requires only pencil and paper, it helps you recognize past learning in the everyday items you have collected over time.

Box and folder sorting has you rifle through storage areas for the things you cared about enough to save. Because a transcript is a comprehensive document that covers several years of learning, make a quick run through everything, pulling out anything that grabs your attention. Even if your selections do not seem like academic transcript material, don't worry. Chances are that if you took notice of them, they point toward something you ought to remember.

When you did something may be important for your transcript, so try to reconstruct the past few years from the refrigerator calendar, photographs, your diary or log, even the family checkbook. Even if the dates themselves are not going to be used on your transcript, a *timeline* may help you remember other events that you had forgotten that happened around the same time.

Internet bookmarks can help you reconstruct subjects you explored during adolescence. Bookmarks can either reflect associative interdisciplinary investigations or document how you delved into a particular subject in depth. Either way, use them to refresh your memory.

Highlighted books hold hints to what you thought. Homeschoolers tend not to produce as much writing in literature and the other subject areas as their schooled peers. They produce discourse rather then essays. Highlighted and annotated books can help you to recall discussions and track your intellectual growth.

TECHNIQUES FOR THE TIME CRUNCHED

When organizing materials for college, deadlines come faster than you ever anticipated. You know that you should have developed a transcript at the end of your Junior year and finalized it during the summer, but here it is November and you're just getting started. The feeling of frenzy as deadlines approach can overwhelm and immobilize you. Since you can't work harder, and there's no time to work longer, you need to work smarter. Here are some strategies we've used in a crunch.

"How do you know about . . . ? Whadda ya know about . . . ?"

These are our family's versions of brainstorming. In *"How do you know about . . . ?"* my son would name an area where he felt a level of competency, and then together we would generate as long a list as possible of activities and experiences that led to that mastery.

In *"Whadda ya know about . . . ?"* the initial response was usually, "Well, not much." This happened, for example when I queried my son Tad on Russia and the former Soviet Union. He first stated that he really didn't know all that much about it. Then he recited a few standard bits of information and all of a sudden began to laugh. "Remember the little bear?" The little bear, Misha, was the logo of a children's book club we had joined when Tad was in the sixth grade. Each month we would get English translations of Russian children's books along with a note from Misha, the little bear. Remembering Misha helped Tad relax and remember Marx and Lenin, Faberge eggs, Catherine the Great, Sputnik, the Cuban missile crisis, the Baltic republics, and more. He had a wealth of information about the subject; he just needed a bit of prodding to bring it to the surface. Notice also that I said he *relaxed* and then remembered. Over and over again, I have found that to be the sequence. Once the tension breaks, memories start flooding in.

The Double Dozen

Similar to a graphic organizer, this is a literal spreadsheet. You will need two sheets of paper as large as you can find. One of the papers, which will be labeled *Who I Am*, is for the student to complete. The other, *What I've Done*, is for the student and family to work on together.

With a crayon or marker divide each sheet into twelve boxes or "puzzle pieces" and label each section as described on the following pages.

The student can keep the *Who I Am* sheet in his or her room. The *What I've Done* sheet should be left in a high traffic area of the home. For the next two or three days, whenever a memory surfaces that seems to have a specific place in the emerging schema, write it on the sheet in an appropriate place. If a memory's placement seems ambiguous, write it on a sticky paper and place it in a temporary location until you can decide where you think it belongs. As the page starts to fill, some areas will become cluttered with ideas and memories. Add more paper, use more sticky notes, keep the ideas coming. In just a few days, your spreadsheet will have gotten you ready to move to the next step: recognizing the knowledge, skills, traits, and growth in all of the experiences that you and your family have remembered.

RECOGNIZING YOUR LEARNING AND ACCOMPLISHMENTS

Once you have remembered all the wonderful experiences you have had during your life as a homeschooler, you need to discern the learning hidden in those events. This can be frustrating for unschoolers and for those who homeschool more flexibly. To them the term "experiential learning" is a redundancy! I know I felt that way when an elementary school principal asked what my son had *learned* by laying his ear to the ground and listening for sounds during a unit we had done on Native Americans. I presume he wanted to hear that Tad, at six years of age, understood that sound travels faster through a solid (the ground) than through a gas (the air). I, on the other hand, figured that Tad was smart enough to come to that conclusion himself at some point in the future when he had stored up more of these varied and interesting experiences. In fact, what appeared at the time to have been an isolated experience with no "learning" evident may well have been a small but critical piece of Tad's understanding of physics that he had constructed by the end of adolescence.

Viewing your knowledge and skills as a product of *all* your life experiences is important in the transcript process. Nothing should be considered as trivial, meaningless or done "just for fun." However, the persons reading your transcript, like the principal I described above, will want to know more than the fact that you have led an interesting life. They will want to discover if you

Who I Am

My Beliefs	My Interests	My Roles
My Personal Traits	**My Skills**	**My Learning Style**
My Problem-Solving Style	**My Gifts and Talents**	**My Struggles and Challenges**
My Next Step	**My Short-Term Goals**	**My Long-Term Goals**

acquired knowledge and skills as the result of it. And in order for *them* to see what you've learned *you* have to see it first.

Although the word "recognition" literally means to "know again," you may be labeling your knowledge and skills formally for the first time. That labeling is what this recognition phase is all about.

CLAIMING YOUR LEARNING

In order to help recognize learning, look at one of your experiences and ask if it involved one of the following concepts. If it does, claim your learning!

- Questioning, hypothesizing

- Problem creation, problem-solving

- Analysis, reasoning

What I've Done

For Fun!	Employment, Internships, and Apprenticeships	Travel
Museums, Historic Sites, Parks and Nature Reserves	Volunteer and Service Activities	Community Activities
Religious Activities	Hobbies	Group Memberships
Family Responsibilities	Independent Study	Classes and Courses

- Evaluation, assessment, critique

- Collecting and organizing data

- Experimenting, risk-taking

- Writing, speaking, discussing

- Using technology skills

- Teamwork, leadership

- Perseverance, discipline

- Time management

- Creativity, passion, humor

Check Appendix C, "Helpful Words and Terms," for both "Bloom's Taxonomy of Learning" for a host of other skills you display as a learner, and the "Department of Labor's Dictionary of

WHICH IS WHICH?

Knowledge is information-based.

Skills are action-based.

Occupational Titles" to find words that describe your employability skills. Test your experiences against these terms.

What you are doing here is taking the specifics of your learning out of the vast context that surrounds them. You are *extracting your learning.* For the reader of your transcript, the kaleidoscopic details of your experience would only obscure the streamlined and powerful learning that lies underneath. You cannot simply show the readers of your transcript your experiences and expect them to extract the learning out of it. It is simply too confusing and distracting, and they don't have the time. *You* need to do it for them.

Sorting It Out

If you have artifacts, lay them out on the floor. See which ones evoke the strongest words to describe learning. Notice if a number of heretofore unimportant items, perhaps souvenirs, look as if they are actually components of a larger package of learning. If you are using the spread sheets from the previous activities, use a marker to join seemingly disparate experiences where you see a link. Your eyes will see connections and patterns, a literal web forming on the sheet as you draw the lines.

Often your artifacts or web will deliver your learning right to you, causing you to wonder how you could have missed something so obvious. When my son Tad did this exercise, he noticed that he had been to just about every National Seashore on the Eastern seaboard, from Acadia in Maine where he had explored tide pools to Pennekamp Coral Reef in Key Largo, Florida where he first went snorkeling. The New England Aquarium is nearby, as is rocky Cape Ann and sandy Cape Cod. He had participated in Dr. Robert Ballard's *Jason Project* from the program's start, looking at tube worms in the volcanic vents off the coast of Sicily. Books with titles like *At the Sea's Edge* and *The Shoreline Naturalist* were always shelved within easy reach. Furthermore, Tad was aware of applied oceanography: the political aspects of shoreline property ownership, the clean-up of Boston Harbor, and the economic impact of an organism called "red tide" that periodically threatens the shellfish beds along the New England coast. Did all this constitute learning? You bet! He had a solid foundation in oceanography even though he had never taken a formal course in the subject.

TRUST YOUR EYE

When you lay things out in front of you, your eye will detect patterns that your thoughts had missed.

Now that you've recognized your learning, your next task is to discern "chunks" of learning, much like Tad did with oceanography. These may be activities that were separated from each other in time, but which now can be combined to describe a deeper, more complex type of learning. On the other hand, you may have had a broad, multifaceted experience, such as running a home-based business, that required you to learn a variety of things in a great many areas. The

WHERE DOES CURRICULUM COME FROM?

Who creates curriculum? Human beings.

How do they create it? By organizing their prior experiences.

important thing is to identify the knowledge and skills you now possess and to locate them in the experiences that you have had.

For the time being, do not limit your definition of learning to what you think should go on your final transcript. That will come later. Right now, just spend time identifying where learning exists, hidden among your wealth of homeschool experiences.

CREATING COURSES AND CURRICULA

It's important to realize that courses and curriculum do not spring to life spontaneously. *People* create curriculum. You need to stop thinking of yourself as a learner, or *consumer,* of someone else's curriculum and instead, start thinking of yourself as a *producer* of your own curriculum. You have acquired, or "banked," a lifetime of experiences. Now you need to remember them, reflect on them, organize them, and write them down to share with others.

In the last activity you claimed your learning; now you get to frame it, using accurate but descriptive language. This is a challenge in both curriculum development and marketing. It may help to think of your transcript as a brochure that both describes your homeschool learning *and* piques the interest of the reader. Although you need to approach it from both angles, you will handle it one step at a time.

Before you get down to the brass tacks of writing your curriculum, acquire a copy of a high school course selection handbook. This should be a public document available through your state's Department of Education, your Superintendent's office, or your local high school's guidance department. This will give you some idea of what your district offers its students. It also will let you see the educational phrasing used to describe the traditional English, Math, Social Studies, Science, and Foreign Language programs that are found in comprehensive high schools. The handbook will act as your primer to understanding the school-based language familiar to employers and college admissions officials.

You should also acquire course catalogs from the colleges you want to attend. It is important to get the course *catalog,* not just the viewbook. The catalog lists the actual course descriptions, while

FINDING ANSWERS TO BASIC QUESTIONS ABOUT A COLLEGE

1. What do they do here?

   Read the college's course catalogs; do not just flip through the viewbooks

2. What do they usually see in applicants?

   Read through your local high school's course selection booklet to see what traditionally educated students will have on their transcripts

3. What is this college looking for?

   Study the questions on their application to intuit what type of student interests them.

the viewbook is simply promotional literature that is sent out to prospective students. Your goal in reading through the course catalog is to see what no viewbook can adequately show: the academic inner workings of the school. Your district's high school handbook tells you where local students are coming from, academically. The college's course catalog tells you where they are going. This information is important for several reasons:

- The sheer number of courses in a particular area will tell you much about the school—high school or college—and what it thinks is important. The course descriptions themselves can give you a feel for the school's curriculum.

- Course descriptions can also indicate if you might have "taken" certain of the college or high school's basic courses (often called "distribution requirements") simply by the way you and your family configured homeschooling during adolescence.

- The way college course descriptions are written tells something about the person who is reading the catalog, a person already accepted, a person *you* would like to be few years from now. Course descriptions can serve as a model and a guide for what a college expects of its students . . . and of you, the applicant.

- Finally, the course catalog tells you something about the culture of the college or university, in much the same way that a telephone book gives clues to the community it represents. Careful reading between the lines of the course catalog is one more strategy to help you get a window on the school, to know your audience a bit better as you move through the college selection process.

Right now, you are going to develop a variety of different courses. Don't worry about how "good" they are or if they will eventually go on your transcript. You can determine quality and appropriateness later. You don't even need to write them up formally at this point. Just get your skeletal course outlines set.

Here are five course and curriculum development strategies. I have included highlights of how each worked in our family so you can get a feel for how the technique looks in practice.

COURSE TITLING

Course titling is the simplest of the techniques. Analytical in nature, it goes from the whole (the overall title) to its parts. In this method of course development you actually "deconstruct" the main topic by breaking it into its components. In 1-2-3 order you:

1. Start with an area you know a great deal about.

2. Give it a title.

3. List everything you know about it.

Starting with a favorite area is important. This allows you to work the technique on familiar ground, guaranteeing that the ideas will come thick and fast. One of my son's "safe" areas was the Civil War. Just creating the course title "The American Civil War" and putting quotes around it brought back an enormous list of content Tad had learned . . . somehow. States' rights and slavery; Harper's Ferry; Lee's being asked to head the *Union* army; the siege of Petersburg; the slaughter at Gettysburg; Andersonville Prison; Appomattox; and more. All in some sort of context, all with higher level thinking skills. It was a single unified package of learning.

WHAT DOES A COURSE DESCRIPTION LOOK LIKE?

United States History: The War Between the States. This course investigated remote and immediate causes of the Civil War, the rise of the abolitionists, the economic environment, pivotal political events, and the impact of the war on everyday life. Discussions of military strategy were supplemented by visits to Gettysburg, Manassas, Fredericksburg, and Petersburg. The war in the West, the use of naval warfare, and an overview of Reconstruction were also presented.

CLUSTER FORMATION

This type of phenomenon, described above for oceanography, happens when seemingly isolated incidents form themselves into clusters of related learning. This process, which takes the parts (the separate events) and creates the whole (the course name), is synthetic in nature. You are building a course from all its component parts, taking a batch of discrete experiences and organizing them under one heading. This was the method used in the exercise called "Create-a-Course," in Chapter 2, "Assessment Basics." Again, the instructions can be simply stated:

1. Note a group of learning experiences with a common theme.

2. "Bundle" them together into a curriculum unit.

3. Give your course a name that is both accurate and interesting.

This method is excellent for packaging your literature into something more descriptive than English III. If you have spent a great deal of time reading 20th Century Women Poets or Chicano Fiction, write it up as a course description.

LEARNING BY ASSOCIATION

Interdisciplinary learning happens when associations are made between traditional subject areas. What is quilting? Art, home economics, mathematics, women's studies? It's *all* these things! Because quilting is not confined to just one area of the high school curriculum it needs its own interdisciplinary "frame" to describe its unique knowledge and skills. Try calling it *Quilting: Pioneer Women's Perspectives.* This may sound more like a college course than a high school one, but homeschoolers have the time, flexibility, and freedom to delve into a subject and "take" more of these specialized "courses" during adolescence.

Once you've identified the associations and connections in your interdisciplinary learning, think about how you might organize it as a course and write it up for your own "course catalog" or marketing brochure. Remember, most courses that cross subject area boundaries have skills involved. Make sure to include those skills in your course description, too.

 PACKAGING LEARNING

Both my sons studied the history, literature, music, religion, and public health issues of England in the 1500s. We called it Elizabethan England: Politics, Playwrights, and Plague.

DISTRIBUTING YOUR LEARNING

How could my son put a month in Ireland, two weeks in Sicily, or repeated visits to Washington, D.C., on his transcript? These experiences were rich and multifaceted, similar to the interdisciplinary ones mentioned above. However, they can be easily dissociated and their parts distributed to other curriculum areas, offering an Irish, Italian, or governmental "flavor" to more conventionally framed courses. Celtic fiddling, for example, went under music, Liam O'Flahery's short stories were part of literature, the border raid we witnessed went under politics, and a visit to Dysert O'Dea, a castle in County Claire, was considered both European history and family genealogy.

You may or may not want to create a course titled *Tracing My Roots: A Journey Through the West of Ireland*, but do have confidence that just about everything eventually finds its proper place in the grand scheme of things. The point is, nothing you've learned and experienced is ever really lost. Distributing your homeschool learning lets you enrich, enliven, and enhance more traditional subject areas.

FILLING IN THE GAPS

Missing something? My son Tad hadn't studied mathematics systematically in a schoolish sequence. But that didn't mean he didn't *know* it or that he couldn't extend his knowledge quickly. Because of this, we decided to treat mathematics as an overall skill rather than as bits and pieces of knowledge. If Tad was able to apply required mathematics in other coursework, should it matter that he hadn't done hundreds of problem sets? Of course not. The key was to think in terms of skill mastery. If he had mastered the skill, he passed the course and could legitimately include it on his transcript. This would be true for other skill-based courses such as Expository Writing, Public Speaking, or Technology.

For traditional areas where you feel you lack content, check out your local district's high school handbook. You will probably discover that you have already met the minimum standards for graduation. In fact, just by living a low-key but rich homeschool experience my younger son Jed had almost *double* the number of credits required for graduation! You will probably find you aren't *really* missing anything at all!

 NO SECOND LANGUAGE?

Worried because you haven't studied a second language? Most colleges have an undergraduate language requirement that you will need to fulfill once you are admitted, but discuss with an admissions counselor how you might waive any requirement for high school language study.

Finally, remember that we *all* have gaps in our learning. Schooled students do, too! Most of them haven't studied astronomy by stargazing, or done yoga for physical education, or experienced Shakespeare's plays the way he intended: in performance. Accept the fact that in four short years you couldn't do everything. Instead, concentrate on what you *have* done and the things that you have done well. Use your transcript to describe and draw attention to all the marvelous things you managed to do during your homeschooled adolescence.

MATCHING YOUR TRANSCRIPT TO YOUR AUDIENCE

The key to creating your transcript is to design it for a specific college. It is not enough simply to demonstrate that your homeschool experience matches or exceeds that of your schooled peers. You need to show the school that you're the type of student they'd like to accept.

At this point in the transcript process, you should have plenty of homeschool course ideas. In the portfolio process, this was the point where you had some decision making to do. You needed to weed out artifacts that were inappropriate, duplicate, extraneous, of lesser quality, or of low credibility. The same is true in the transcript process. As you do your weeding, you will decide which courses stay and deserve the full written treatment.

COURSE EVALUATION

Your courses can be evaluated like portfolio artifacts, using four basic criteria:

- Purpose
- Quality
- Credibility
- Clarity

When you evaluate your course ideas, however, remember that it is not enough for you to feel that they are appropriate, good, believable, and clear. You need to discover how purpose, quality, credibility, and clarity are defined by *your audience*. This means you need to discover what the person reading your transcript wants to see.

By now you should have already checked with prospective schools to find out if there are courses that need to appear on your transcript. Make sure you find a way to include them. Is there course content or skills that your readers will be looking for? If so, make sure they can find them on your transcript. Be attentive to how you name your courses in order to make it clear to the readers that you have the knowledge and skills they want in a candidate.

You will also need to determine the quality of your courses. You probably already know which are your strongest ones and which are less developed. You'll also need to determine what quality looks like to your audience. Is it high grades? Good written communication skills? Different answers to this question can help you decide which transcript prototype will best present your learning.

 OUR FAMILY'S CRITERIA

Our sons could put it on their transcripts if they:

- Felt it was significant
- Could describe what they learned, not just what they experienced
- Could discuss it with a knowledgeable adult after only a minimal review

---

What does your audience consider to be credible evidence? For some schools it is *quantifiable information:* dates, grades, and credits. If you find this to be true, name your

THE HALO EFFECT

Have you taken a course outside the home for which you received a grade? The readers of your transcript may conclude that your at-home learning in that subject area is of equal quality.

learning traditionally and format it using a traditional transcript model that includes the expected numerical information. If you feel the reviewers are looking for *qualitative evidence* make sure your transcript is backed up by your portfolio and letters of recommendation.

FORMAT

Of the five transcript prototypes described in the previous chapter (Carnegie units, content standards, performance standards, resume, or narrative) you will need to decide which would best showcase your work in the eyes of the reader. This may mean that you will need to utilize different transcript models for different schools. Before you move to the next phase and start writing and formatting your transcript, check out the transcripts in Appendix A, "A Portfolio and Transcript Sampler," to see how the same information fits into each of the prototypes. Which feels most comfortable to you? Which would fit the type of learning you have done most? And if you haven't already done so, telephone each of the schools to which you want to apply and ask if they prefer homeschool transcript information to be presented in any particular way.

Regardless of the model you choose, you will need to experiment to see how your learning will fit into the display. You may decide to use conventional subject headings or create new interdisciplinary ones. Perhaps you will put most of your courses in a traditional format but add a resume to round out experiential learning. You may find a school that would accept a narrative if it is supplemented by test scores and other quantifiable information. If your external coursework is limited to only one or two courses or none at all, a performance standard transcript may be your best bet.

Think this step through carefully, but don't become immobilized by the decision-making process. Pick a prototype and get ready to write!

WRITING YOUR TRANSCRIPT

When you identified your learning, you claimed it; when you turned it into course outlines, you framed it. Now it is time to name it, using words to describe your knowledge and skills.

Like portfolio development, creation of a transcript should be a collaborative effort between homeschooled adolescents and their parents. Student ownership of the content is critical. However, families may differ in their view of who should do the actual writing of the transcript. Some transcript types lend themselves to personal writing that should be done by the student, whereas others maintain such a level of distance that personal authorship hardly matters.

Because each transcript type will hold your learning in a different way, your writing will need to fit your knowledge and skills into your chosen "container." In fact, if you intend to create a Carnegie-unit transcript you might feel that you don't need to do any writing, that all you need to do is identify the names of your courses and get them down on paper. However, do not skip this step! Naming your learning is not just for the transcript. It will ultimately affect all the other components of your application package: how your parents write the student and school profiles, how you acknowledge co- and extracurricular learning, your portfolio of supporting artifacts, and your application essay. Furthermore, naming your learning now will help you during the college interview process when you are asked about what you know and how you learned it. Regardless of which prototype you eventually use for your transcript, remember that the writing phase is as much for *you* as it is for others.

ORGANIZING YOUR TRANSCRIPT

When you begin writing, you will need to determine how you will organize your courses. Think again about how you would arrange and sequence them in a booklet or brochure. You will need to come up with organizational headings that gather similar courses in one place. Experiment with these techniques:

- Use the major high school subject areas as separate and discrete divisions of learning: English, Mathematics, History and Social Sciences, Biological and Physical Sciences, World Languages, Fine Arts, and Physical Education.

- Combine subjects that you feel were connected to each other in your learning. My son patterned his organization after the Coalition of Essential Schools model: Arts/Literature, History/Philosophy, Mathematics/Science.

- Create your own new interdisciplinary headings that reflect the way you configured learning. You may find Women's Studies; Justice, Law, and Society; or simply the word Mexico are far more descriptive of what you have done than conventional divisions of learning. For suggestions, look in college course catalogs for the names of the majors they offer. Many majors, especially in the humanities and social sciences, have titles reflective of complex, interdisciplinary study that homeschoolers may have pursued during their high school years.

- Organize your learning into core subjects and electives. Since your definition of core learning may differ from that of high schools, this type of organization would help clarify the subjects you value and the emphasis you placed on them. Religious Studies would certainly fall into this category, as would areas such as Computer Science, Theater, or Business.

- Focus on the application of knowledge by using skills rather than content as an organizing device. This would be especially appropriate for a performance standards transcript that divided learning into Communication Skills, Research Skills, Applied Mathematics, Teamwork and Leadership Skills, and Personal Management Skills.

WRITING IT DOWN

This is where you will begin to use the high school handbooks and college catalogs. Study them to get a feel for the language they use to describe and discuss the courses they offer. At times it will seem as if you are reading in a new language. Persevere. Your goal is to use this educational language and line of thinking to clarify and communicate what you have done as a homeschooler.

WHICH QUESTION IS YOUR TRANSCRIPT ANSWERING?

- What grade did you get?

- What content was covered?

- What can you do?

- How well-rounded are you?

For each course that you envisioned, write a descriptive paragraph of no more than four sentences. Keep in mind the prototype you have decided to use. To focus your writing, go back to the previous chapter and review the questions that each particular type of transcript was designed to answer. *Your paragraph should answer those key questions.* Depending on your focus, your transcript will stress either input (time, credits, course content) or output (performance standards, applied knowledge.) Do this activity even if all you eventually do is give your homeschool learning brief course names on a Carnegie unit transcript. Remember, you are doing this reflective writing as part of your whole employment or college application process. It is not done just to create the transcript itself.

When writing course descriptions for your transcript look through the high school handbook, locate a similar course and try to model your description on theirs. Think of this as an exercise in translation. This modeling strategy using a high school handbook can be especially useful if you are developing a traditional or content standards transcript. If you are designing a narrative transcript or one that includes a great deal of interdisciplinary learning try this same exercise using a college catalog as your guide.

Every course needs a name. While high schools usually name their courses in broad generalities, colleges tend to title theirs more descriptively. If your course content warrants it, be specific when you title your course for your transcript. On the other hand, if you feel that your learning in a particular subject covered a great deal of ground but did not go into much depth, label it as a survey course. This lets the reader know that there is breadth to your learning in that area.

Be forthright about your strengths. While you don't want to be boastful, this is not the time to be shy, humble, or self-effacing. If you think you have done honors level work, put that H in parentheses next to the name of the course! If you are not philosophically opposed to using alphanumerics, you can always slip in grades, GPA (grade point average), credits, units, and test scores (SAT, AP, CLEP). Remember, colleges are looking for rigor in coursework. If your homeschool program fits that description, you should make it clear in the way you write up your courses.

MASTERY LEARNING: GRADE-A WORK

Homeschoolers find it easy to work toward mastery learning since they can:

- Cover material in their dominant learning style

- Study on a personal timetable rather than the school calendar

- Acquire individualized feedback to improve performance

- Engage in career-relevant, interest-driven studies

Because homeschoolers configure time differently from schools, you will need to decide if you want to assign dates to your learning. Some courses, whether taken at home or elsewhere, have clear beginning and ending dates. Others will be much more difficult to pin down to a specific timeframe since learning occurred over several years. You may want to avoid dates entirely if much of your homeschool learning was shaped in this fashion. Or, you may decide to organize your courses thematically rather than chronologically to show a continuum of learning without specifying dates. This strategy is useful for awarding credit for learning that occurred early in adolescence, since middle school coursework is usually not considered credit-worthy even if the content (often in mathematics and languages) is equivalent to that offered at the high school level. Thematic organization also can be used to describe learning that occurred during a "year off," either during high school or after homeschool "graduation." Finally, it permits you to award credit for learning that happened during non-standard time units such as summer programs, intensive workshops, etc.

If you have taken courses for which you received a transcript, include the information for that course on your homeschool transcript, too. If possible, write the course description exactly as it appeared in the school's catalog. In this way, the reader will have a comprehensive document that presents an overall picture of your experience, both schooled and homeschooled. To verify this information, include a photocopy of the school's transcript made from the copy in your records. Acknowledge that it is an unofficial version but that an official one is on order from the issuing school and will be mailed directly to the admissions office.

A Writing Rubric

Make no mistake about it, if you are a homeschooler, your transcript is a writing sample. Take a look at how your writing might be evaluated.

- Is it dynamic and interesting? If you were writing your course descriptions as advertising copy, would prospective students find them informative and engaging?

- Does it use vocabulary that is mature for an adolescent but not pompous? Does it avoid homeschool jargon? When appropriate, does it use educational terminology that will help the reader interpret and translate your homeschool experience? Does it explain learning using descriptive words such as those found in "Bloom's Taxonomy of Learning" and the "Department of Labor's Dictionary of Occupational Titles"?

- How does your writing meet the four overall criteria: purpose, quality, credibility, and clarity? Have you avoided being unfocused, sloppy, exaggerated, and vague?

Getting an Objective Opinion

Once you have chosen and filled in your template you will need to line up a reader. This might be someone familiar with your family, a veteran homeschooler, or a person with expertise in either

 REVISION AND EDITING

You need a reader to **preview** your transcript before you send it off for a college or employer to **review.**

higher education or the field you aspire to enter. The reader's job will be to suggest areas for revision and editing. (Proofreading is quite different and will come later, after all the revising and editing are finished.) Your reader should be able to tell you if something obvious has been omitted. Or if you have said something that might be misinterpreted by a reviewer unfamiliar with homeschooling. Or if there is just too much material. Or a lack of focus. Or . . . .

Remember that your transcript is going to be one of many sheets of paper before the persons reviewing your file. It is imperative that somewhere on the page you *tell them it's a transcript!* Because your transcript may not look like a conventional one, the persons reviewing your application folder may assume it is simply another piece of supplementary information. It is important to label it clearly by including the word "transcript" prominently on its first page. If your transcript is part of a portfolio with a table of contents identifying each item, you might assume that this is sufficient clarification. However, paperwork inevitably get shuffled and separated. Unless your transcript is properly labeled, the reviewers may be searching for something that looks like a traditional transcript and may assume you neglected to submit one.

Style

Writers and editors use a stylebook to add consistency to a work. We don't usually notice when a style is rigorously followed, but it certainly grabs our attention when it's not! *Style* refers to the choices that every writer must make about spelling, capitalization, punctuation, word division, and so on. In the traditional transcript where I elected to organize learning into credits, for example, I needed to decide whether I was going to spell out the word "credits," or use an abbreviation such as "cr," "cr.," or "crs." I decided to spell out the whole word in each subheading, but to use an abbreviation in the entries. In this case, even though I made a conscious decision to use two different styles, I was consistent in my use of each. If you create a heading in straight capitals, don't mix capitals and lowercase letters the next time around. And if you underline the first subheading, make sure you underline each and every subheading that follows. Numbered and bulleted lists are another area where improper alignment sticks out like a sore thumb. The basic rule here is to avoid skipping around. Choose a style you like as your standard and stick with it.

Layout

A variety of visual effects can add a delightful touch to a portfolio, but a transcript and its supporting documentation will benefit from continuity and a clean professional look. One way to add a sense of unity to your paperwork is to use a consistent font for your printed material. Select a font that is contemporary, uncluttered, and easy to read. If you find that you are running a few lines too long, rather than changing the font's size to shorten the text, adjust the top and bottom margins, adding a tenth of an inch to each.

Similarly, if you decide to organize your transcript by writing course descriptions, which are usually only three or four sentences long, be careful as you get toward the end of the page. You want to avoid splitting such a short paragraph in half. This is another situation when you can adjust the margins to create a more organized visual presentation.

 UNITY AND SIMPLICITY

Your transcript should have a unified appearance. You can use your word-processing program to add a border to your transcript, but limit the use of other "bells and whistles."

GRAMMAR AND USAGE

Your proofreader should detect any lapse in grammar or usage. He or she should check for:

- Parallel construction

- Consistent verb tenses

- Proper pronoun antecedents

- Correct comma usage

If you are giving letter grades, arrange the line breaks so that the grade is at the extreme left or right. Watch out for using the initials of a person whose name begins with A, B, C, D, or F. In one instance, I shortened the name of an official that had overseen my son's work to D. Noonan. Unfortunately, the line break left the "D" at the far right. When I scanned the hard copy quickly the "D" caught my eye, and I wondered for an instant what course my son had taken in which he had earned a "D." If my eye could be tricked, if only for that instant, imagine a college admissions officer, who is accustomed to seeing letter grades. In quickly scanning the page he or she would interpret that "D" as an almost-failing grade!

Use the print preview feature of your word-processing program to "eyeball" the look of your transcript. Is there a column of dates that looks misaligned? Is the print too dense on the page? Do you need more white space? Is there consistent spacing between sections? Use principles of good graphic design to make your transcript unified and pleasing to the eye.

PROOFREADING, PRINTING, AND ASSEMBLING

Final Proofreading

Proofread, proofread, proofread! Do not depend on the spell checker! It will not differentiate between an "its" and an "it's." It will not catch that you wrote "car" for "care." Or that you changed the syntax of the sentence and still have the participle "studying" where you ought to have substituted the infinitive "to study." Nor will it notice omitted words. Watch for proper names. Make sure that the name of the school or the official to whom you will send your transcript is spelled correctly. Rather than being a help here, a spell checker can actually trip you up. On one occasion when writing a narrative regarding an art school my son had visited, I did a final spell check and mistakenly accepted the computer's suggestion to respell Montserrat College of Art. Imagine my horror when I saw that the printed copy read "*Monster* College of Art"!

This goes to show that when you are absolutely convinced that all the revising, editing, and self-proofreading is finished, you need to print out a hard copy and hand it to someone else. Ideally your proofreader should be someone who is uninvolved with the content of the transcript and can focus on the format and details instead.

Allow plenty of time for your documents to be proofread. Inevitably there will be changes that you will need to make in your word-processing document, which then needs to be printed, which then needs to be proofread again, which then needs to be photocopied! I cannot stress this strongly enough: Leave enough time!

Printing

Aesthetics are important. Your transcript, like your portfolio, represents you and projects an image. As a homeschooler you cannot hide behind a school's unattractive or nondescript transcript. Realize that your hand-crafted version will make an impression on the reviewer even before he or she begins to read through it. Know the image you want to project, and then make sure your transcript is aligned with it.

If you want to add an air of professionalism and maturity, use heavyweight resume quality paper for printing your transcript. You can buy a small amount of this paper in a packet designed for home offices if you plan to print your transcript at home. Or, you can print out a plain paper copy at home and take it to your local copy center where it can be printed on resume quality paper. Remember, too, that your parents will be writing the school and student profiles that will accompany the transcript in your college application packet. These profiles should be printed on professional quality paper, too.

If you have decided to use one consistent transcript format for all your prospective schools or employers, it is sensible to make multiple copies so you will have extras easily available at home. If you intend to create several types of transcripts to send to different kinds of colleges, make sure you have at least two extra copies for your files: one as your original in secure storage, and the other to serve as a convenient master copy to be duplicated should you need extra copies in the future.

Signature

Colleges always make it clear that they will not accept photocopies of transcripts, that they want only "official" ones that are signed by and sent out directly from the issuing school. Homeschooling parents should feel comfortable adding this touch of formality to the transcripts created under their supervision. In addition to being their child's primary educators and facilitators, homeschooling parents are the principals and guidance directors of their child's school. Thus, their signatures ought to appear on the transcript. They literally "sign off" on the fact that their child has accomplished the things listed on the document.

For more traditionally formatted transcripts, the parents can add their signatures at the bottom of the page. If the transcript runs to a second page they can initial it as they would a legal document. In order to formally certify our son's reflective Exit Exhibition transcript, which was several pages long, my husband and I wrote a separate cover letter which we then signed in blue ink. Another approach, similar to that used for letters of recommendation, would be to place the folded transcript in a business-sized envelope, seal it, then sign it across the flap.

 WHY BLUE?

Colleges and employers expect that you will submit a signed-by-the-school original transcript. Your parents' signatures in blue ink indicates that the document is your official homeschool transcript, not a photocopy.

FINAL THOUGHTS

Finished? Soon your audience will be looking at your transcript, using it to evaluate you. But right now, take a look at it yourself. Here's a one question quiz to evaluate your transcript:

Does it describe you to your own satisfaction?

If so, congratulations! Remember, the whole purpose of alternative assessment was for you to engage in thoughtful and mature self-evaluation. As you developed your comprehensive transcript you reflected on the growth and change that occurred over the past few years. May that self-knowledge serve you well as you move toward your next stage of learning.

C H A P T E R   9

Preparing for
College Admissions

Most of what you need in order to develop your final transcript and high-stakes portfolio is contained in the book's earlier chapters. Chapter 10, " A Homeschooler's Comprehensive College Application," will give you the specific information you need to create your own application packet and portfolio, and this chapter will give you an overview of the college admissions process and how you can best position yourself to gain admission to the college of your choice. You'll learn how to:

- Understand the college application and admissions process

- Identify your audience

- Learn to identify your niche and market yourself

APPLICATION AND ADMISSIONS

Ten years ago, if you were a homeschooled college applicant you'd be a rarity. Some schools would appreciate you for the diversity you'd bring to their campus, while others would find you too odd to admit. Fortunately, times have changed, and homeschooled applicants have become more common. They are still interesting, still puzzling, and they still add a bit of novelty to the freshman class, but they're not all that unusual. Because you probably won't be the school's first homeschooled applicant, you'll be able to get feedback about how it handles homeschooled students. Armed with this information, you will be better positioned to give the admissions committee what *they* want so that, in turn, they will give you what *you* want: a letter of acceptance.

The college application process is a daunting sequence of procedures, but homeschoolers need not feel alone as they contemplate creating their admissions packet. Remember that *every* college applicant has to assemble an admissions packet. A student who attends a traditional high school probably doesn't call the packet a portfolio, but nonetheless his or her guidance counselor bundles up a packet of paperwork to accompany the completed application form and sends it off on the student's behalf. Typically, the paperwork will consist of letters of recommendation, an essay, and an official transcript noting the student's grade point average (GPA) and rank in class. The student's high school may also add other items to the packet that are not mentioned in the

YOUR ADMISSIONS PACKET IS YOU!

Your admissions packet is YOU! It is your alter ego, your proxy, your parallel self. It has to stand in for you, support you, answer questions about you, and make the admissions committee like you enough to ask you to come to their campus for the next four years.

application booklet. Chief among these is a document called a school profile, which describes the high school—its mission statement, its programs, the demographics of its student body, the school's average SAT scores, etc.

Your homeschool admissions packet will include the same standard application materials as the schooled student: routine forms, school and student profiles, recommendations, even a transcript. However, because the admissions staff sees only a handful of homeschoolers each year, your packet needs to go beyond that of the average high schooler. Your portfolio needs to demonstrate that you have academic and personal potential even though you engaged in a novel approach to learning during your high school years.

As a homeschooler, you are used to acquiring knowledge from many different sources, and learning about college admissions should be no exception. If you haven't already, I suggest you get a copy of Cafi Cohen's book, *And What About College?: How Homeschooling Can Lead to Admissions to the Best Colleges & Universities*. Cafi covers the admissions process for homeschoolers in great detail and reveals the steps that have proven successful for her family.

POSITIONING YOURSELF FOR ADMISSION

Unfortunately, filling out a stack of papers, writing a couple of essays, and sitting through several interviews doesn't necessarily grant you the right to pack your bags and enroll in classes in the fall. The papers, essays, and interviews are part of the *application* process; but the *admissions* process is yet another thing altogether. Once you (and all of the other students hoping to go to college next fall) have submitted the required paperwork, the college admissions committee will make decisions about which of the applicants they will admit and which ones they won't. This chapter will prepare you for the admissions process by showing you how to determine a college's expectations, find your niche, and market yourself in a way that will make you irresistible!

KNOW YOUR AUDIENCE

Knowing your audience and their expectations is the first key to being accepted by the college of your choice. You need to realize that your college admissions audience is actually made up of two parts: the institution you are applying to (with all of its rules, regulations, and requirements that must be met) and the individuals—the human beings—who sit on the admissions committee and review your file.

WHEN WILL YOU GRADUATE?

Will you finish your high school by the end of your 11th grade year? This may be the case if you homeschooled on a flexible schedule that allowed for acceleration. This means you need to begin your college investigations early if you intend to apply for admission as a "graduating junior."

THE HOMESCHOOL ALTERNATIVE

Some colleges have policies that waive traditional requirements in order to accept graduates of new models of secondary education. An example of this would be students from the Coalition of Essential Schools, secondary schools where graduation is determined by what is termed an "Exit Exhibition." As a homeschooler, it is sensible for you to look into schools that are already comfortable with alternative documentation.

WORKING WITH THE INSTITUTION

In order to receive favorable consideration from colleges and universities, you will need to view homeschooling and documentation more dispassionately than you might have in the past. If you feel panicked because you were educated nontraditionally, you need to keep in mind how much you have learned and not become self-effacing and apologetic because you lack traditional credentials. On the other hand, if you view homeschooling from only a value-added perspective and believe that credentials are superfluous, you will need to accept that the university expects to see some credible and quantitative documentation.

CREDENTIALS CONCERNS

The admissions policy section of most college viewbooks will most likely state that the school considers every student on an individual basis. It usually continues, however, by listing a standard menu of required academic units in English, Social Studies, Mathematics, Science, and Fine Arts. The words "units," "years," and "grades" (concepts most homeschooling programs don't subscribe to) are mentioned early in the text—suggesting that they are a priority—while the words "recommendations," "essays," and "interviews" (tools homeschooled students know and use well) appear toward the end, if at all. Homeschoolers need to ask just how rigid or flexible these published guidelines are. It is critical to know what is nonnegotiable and what is open for discussion. If you find the guidelines are flexible, you can tailor your experiences to fit the university's requirements.

A state college or university may pose a unique problem for homeschoolers if the school is required by legislation to use a numerical formula—involving class rank, GPA, and SAT scores—to rank applicants in the admission pool. Homeschoolers need to ask how they and other nontraditionally educated students can be exempted from this particular filtering formula and how they can show student competency in another way.

Traditional high schools vary dramatically in their philosophy, standards, curriculum, teaching, facilities, and overall quality, so colleges and universities want to know whether or not the applicant is enrolled in an accredited high school program, Usually, the high school guidance counselor will submit a school profile describing the school's mission statement, programs, demographics, average SAT scores, etc. with a traditionally schooled applicant's packet. You will need to ask how you can answer the college or university's questions about the high school (homeschool) you "attended." Your homeschool profile, which will address these concerns, is described fully in the next chapter.

As you're creating your high school transcript, don't forget to look into any records you may have lingering at traditional schools. If you attended traditional high school in the past and decided to homeschool your last several years, you may be listed on your local school's records as a dropout.

This may be simply a matter of record-keeping, but it will raise eyebrows. It is critical that you know what is on your school record and are ready to defuse it if necessary.

You may be concerned that not having a diploma will hinder your chances for admission, but remember that traditionally schooled students don't have diplomas at the time of application either. Schools ask them for information about courses in progress and require first semester and final grades. As a homeschooler, you must also provide documentation of your progress. If your homeschool program does not give grades or does not organize learning into courses, read through Chapters 7 and 8 on creating transcripts to determine how you can provide the information colleges need in a format familiar to them.

HOMESCHOOLER-SPECIFIC REQUIREMENTS

Realize that while some colleges have informal homeschool admissions policies that you can only learn about through conversations with admissions representatives, others have outlined their policies on an addenda sheet that you can request. Still others have homeschool admissions information included on their website. Do your research. It is a waste of time to create an admissions packet that doesn't meet the demands of the school to which you're applying.

> "I wrote to about two dozen schools. I asked if the particular school had any recommendations about submitting a nontraditional transcript, alternative methods, parental letters as teacher recommendations, etc. Some schools, like Stanford, Amherst, Columbia and Cornell, wrote detailed letters outlining what they thought was necessary for them to evaluate my application. Other schools sent several successive form letters, some even professing their willingness to help in any way if I had questions about the admissions process. I found this a bit puzzling since my letter was extremely straightforward."
>
> —Tad Heuer

When contacting schools to learn about their homeschool admissions policies, it is wise to find your way to the person who is responsible for implementing those procedures. Speak to that specific person about your interest in the school and the concerns that you have as a homeschooler. Do not get your information from the general office staff who may not be fully aware of how homeschoolers are dealt with during the admissions process.

The following two questionnaires should help you discover more about a school's attitude toward and expectations of homeschoolers. The first one assumes the school has had experience with homeschoolers and is ready to answer your questions. The second questionnaire is designed to get information from a school that doesn't have clear homeschool guidelines. In that case, you will want to ask about their procedures for *non-traditionally educated students*. This is the catch-all phrase that colleges use to describe a whole spectrum of students including homeschoolers, grandmothers who are starting college with forty-year old diplomas, and high school dropouts with GEDs.

THE INITIAL PHONE CALL

1. Introduce yourself as a homeschooler.

2. Ask to speak to the person who deals with homeschooled applicants.

3. Write that person's name down!

4. Ask questions from the master list. Write down the answers.

5. Thank the admissions officer and recheck the spelling of his or her name.

QUESTIONNAIRE #1
Colleges Experienced Working with Homeschoolers

Admissions Official_____ College_____

Address_____

Telephone_____ E-mail_____

- How do you handle the admissions process for homeschoolers?

- Approximately how many homeschoolers apply to your school each year?

- Do you know how many homeschoolers you accepted last year?

- What kind of alternative documentation have students submitted that you found useful?

- Have homeschoolers requested admission based on a portfolio?

- Who evaluates portfolios at your school?

- Which items would you suggest including in a homeschool portfolio?

- How and when should I submit portfolio material?

- Do I need a homeschool transcript? If so, what format would you suggest?

- Which of the usual requirements (e.g., 2 years of foreign language) are negotiable?

- Could you make an admissions decision based on the following package?

  - A profile of the homeschool's philosophy and practice written by the parents

  - A profile of the student written by the parents and/or significant mentors

  - Narrative descriptions of areas where learning has been achieved and/or mastery has been displayed

  - A portfolio of artifacts to document the student's learning experiences

  - The student's resume

  - The student's reflective essay

- Is there anything you would suggest omitting? Adding?

- How much weight does the interview carry for nontraditional students?

QUESTIONNAIRE #2
Colleges Less Familiar with Homeschoolers

Admissions Official_____ College____ _____

Address_____

Telephone_____ E-mail_____

- How do you handle the admissions process for nontraditional students:

  - Homeschoolers

  - Students from nontraditional private schools

  - Students from restructured secondary schools (e.g., Coalition or Paideia Schools)

  - International students

  - Dropouts from traditional high school settings

  - Mature students

- How many nontraditionally educated apply to your school each year?

- How many of these students do you usually admit?

- If students go to a nontraditional school, what form do their transcripts and documentation packages usually take?

- What kind of alternative documentation have students submitted that you found useful?

- How do you deal with nontraditional documentation?

- Do you convert nontraditional courses to Carnegie credits?

- What importance do you give to a nontraditional student's taking CLEP exams or community college courses?

- Which of the usual requirements (e.g., 2 years of foreign language) are negotiable?

- Do nontraditional students request admission based on a portfolio?

- Who evaluates portfolios at your school?

- Could you make an admissions decision based on following package?

  - A profile of the homeschool's philosophy and practice written by the parents

  - A profile of the student written by the parents and/or significant mentors

  - Narrative descriptions of areas where learning has been achieved and/or mastery has been displayed

  - A portfolio of artifacts to document the student's learning experiences

  - A student's resume

  - The student's reflective essay

continues

Colleges Less Familiar with Homeschoolers (cont.)

- Is this too much, too cumbersome?

- What else might you want to know about:

  - The student?

  - The curriculum?

  - The assessments?

  - The family's homeschooling approach and philosophy?

- How much weight does the interview carry for nontraditional students?

- When does an alternative approach create a positive impression? A negative one?

WORKING WITH THE ADMISSIONS STAFF

Although you're applying to an institution, the committee that ultimately decides if you're granted admission is made up of individual human beings. This committee of men and women must always respect the mission and goals of the college or university, but they are also charged with recognizing an applicant's personal achievements. Given the large number of applications a school receives, no one admissions official reviews each and every student's folder personally. In most cases, prospective students are assigned to a specific admissions counselor who then shepherds that student's application through the process. As you can imagine, as a homeschooler it will be important for you to make this person your advocate. Some schools have specific staff members and committees assigned to deal with nontraditionally educated students, and you'll want those individuals in your corner when decision-making time comes around.

THE ADVOCATE

In looking for an advocate, you want to find someone who can not only answer your homeschool specific questions, but who can also guide you through the intricacies of the homeschooler's application process. Your contact can tell you how best to format your information and present it convincingly. If you can meet your contact personally, either informally at a college fair or more formally at an on-campus interview, so much the better. By doing so, you are demystifying who you are as a homeschooler—becoming less of a stereotype and more of an individual. At this point, having learned more about you, your resource person can be candid about your chances of acceptance. With any luck, he or she will be in a position to act as an advocate, supporting your acceptance when the admissions committee meets.

 THE FOLLOW-UP LETTER

Did you forget to ask something? Think of new question a day later? Send a follow-up letter asking whatever you need to have answered. Don't delay! You want your letter to arrive while your conversation is fresh in the admissions officer's mind.

WHO WORKS FOR ADMISSIONS?

Each college or university has a mix of admissions personnel:

- Veteran administrators who bring a sense of history to the process

- Younger staff, often new alumni in touch with campus trends

- Alumni who interview students off-campus

- Long-term office staff who know and understand student concerns

- Students who act as receptionists, tour guides, or hosts for overnight visits

Communication is vitally important for building rapport with your advocate. Telephone calls, written notes, and personal contact are each important in order to establish a relationship with your contact. Your telephone calls give an indication of your poise and oral presentation skills. A letter showcases your written communication (and is retained in your application folder for future reference). A handshake at a college fair displays your sociability and friendliness. The on-site interview allows your contact to know you in greater depth and to review your portfolio. And of course, after the interview, a thank-you note shows you have follow-up skills (and good manners!).

The Interview

Before attending an interview, you would be wise to read up on the subject both in college admissions guidebooks and here in Chapter 5, "Presenting the Portfolio." Notes of these meetings are added to your folder and discussed at the admissions committee meeting, so it's important you attend your interview prepared.

During your interview, you will have a chance to answer questions, both specific and general, about homeschooling. Don't fret. You are well prepared to answer them. You've probably responded to the most predictable ones many times before! However, it may help to engage in some role playing to give yourself a feel for answering those same questions comfortably in a high-stakes situation . . . and with a smile on your face. This time, the questions are being asked for genuine educational reasons, neither out of idle curiosity nor for school board accountability. The college wants to know how homeschooling has prepared you to be part of their community, both socially and academically. Have answers ready for questions about leadership, teamwork, and outside

 SHOW OFF YOUR COMMUNICATION SKILLS

Don't overlook these opportunities to demonstrate your communication skills:

- A letter (writing skills)

- A phone call (oral presentation skills)

- A personal interview (conversational skills)

- A thank-you note!

interests. If you have done nongraded homeschooling, know how you will respond to questions that will attempt to clarify how you would fit in academically at the school.

INTERVIEW TYPES

There are three types of interviews, each corresponding to where you are in the admissions process:

- **Informational interviews** that acquaint you with the college, its programs, and its policies toward homeschoolers.

- **Feedback interviews** where you discuss your goals, present your initial portfolio, and ask for specifics on how to strengthen your application.

- **Summary interviews** that occur after your application has been submitted. You may submit your portfolio at the same time, or the interview may be held off-campus with an alumnus.

Whenever possible, try to arrange for an interview with a senior admissions official or the staff member responsible for homeschoolers. This is an opportunity to acquire an influential advocate who can champion your case when the admissions committee meets. Make the most of it.

Many colleges also have alumni who interview students during the application process, particularly if the student lives at a distance from the college and would not otherwise have an opportunity to interview with a college official. Remember that alumni are going to be very concerned about how a homeschooler would fit in at their alma mater. They may be wonderfully open toward your nontraditional learning, but still hesitant to believe that you are now ready to tackle more formalized schooling. All the maturity and poise you have acquired are going to be on display at that meeting. Be honest, enthusiastic, engaging, and informative as you explain how your unique opportunity to homeschool has prepared you for college life.

TRY TO RELAX

Your interview will go more smoothly if you are prepared and relaxed. Write out four or five of your questions so that you'll have them ready should the conversation lag. Remember, too, that your portfolio can act as a prop should you need a bit of prompting.

FINDING YOUR MATCH AND YOUR NICHE

The media knows a niche when it sees one. When Grant Colfax, a bright Californian, became one of the first homeschoolers to be accepted by Harvard, a local newspaper announced the event with the headline, *Goat Boy Goes To Harvard.* Grant was not your generic student. He was a homeschooler . . . who raised goats! As you prepare to market yourself to colleges and universities, it's important that you develop your own niche. Although you may not have a niche as unique as Grant Colfax's, you can surely find something in your homeschool experience that sets you apart from the crowd.

MARKETING YOURSELF

You are an unknown quantity at the college of your choice. Don't be shy! If you know you and the school are a good match, mention it in:

- Correspondence with the school

- Your essay

- An interview

When you apply to a college you are marketing yourself—you are selling an image of yourself and your accomplishments. Your goal is to convince the college or university that you and the school are a good match, and that you would make a welcome addition to their freshman class. You can increase the chance that a school will "buy" what you have to offer by marketing your unique talents, interests, and competencies.

The admissions office is bound to take note of you just for being a homeschooler, and if you're a capable homeschooling student, most colleges would probably like to admit you. However, homeschooling *just by itself* is not enough of a niche to make you marketable. When you're preparing to present yourself to a school, you need to think of yourself as a "homeschooler who . . . ." That "who . . ." is the part that distinguishes you from the rest of the applicant pool. It is the aspect of yourself that makes you memorable for all the right reasons and highlights why you and the school are a good match for each other.

On the other hand, you may not want the college to think of you *primarily* as a homeschooler. Instead, you might prefer to describe yourself as "a . . . who's been homeschooled." Whatever your preferred emphasis, realize that the background of every student, homeschooled or not, is an item on the admissions committee's agenda. You must rely on something beyond academics to truly set you apart.

Showcasing Your Special Interests

Admissions officers see top-notch candidates with impeccable credentials all the time. Consequently, applicants must rely on their own unique characteristics to set themselves above the crowd. Luckily, individualization has been integrated into your homeschool curriculum.

 A QUESTION OF EMPHASIS

Would you rather be thought of as:

- "A homeschooler who . . . "? or

- "A . . . who was homeschooled"?

My older son feels he was a homeschooler who was active in politics. My younger son considers himself an artist who was homeschooled. Decide how you want to emphasize your homeschooling to colleges and employers.

MARKET YOUR HOMESCHOOL ANGLE

How has homeschooling allowed you to maximize your learning? Has it contributed to:

- Academic enrichment or acceleration?

- The pursuit of a subject in depth?

- Learning about a diverse range of people?

Schooled students are often quite limited in their experiences and activities, primarily because they need to schedule their extracurricular interests on weekends, during school vacations, or after school hours. Not so for homeschoolers! Because you were not bound by the schedule of the school day or school year, you have had the luxury of time—time to pursue interests *and excel* at them. Colleges will want and expect to hear about how you used that time.

Homeschoolers' lives are *substantively* different from that of an applicant with a 4.3 GPA and a host of extracurricular activities. Rather than compete for admission on the same terms as schooled students (after all, there is no way you are going to demonstrate leadership by serving as vice-president of the junior class!), you need to concentrate on marketing yourself as a unique commodity ("a homeschooler who . . . ") that will be an asset to the incoming freshman class. Again, the more the school sees that you and it are a good match for each other, the more likely your chance of acceptance.

Imagine being part of an admissions committee and receiving information on these three students. One participates in Revolutionary War reenactments and has apprenticed with a violin maker. Another went to China as an Operation Smile volunteer and sings folk songs in a coffee-house on weekends. And another created a documentary on the territorial behaviors of Canada geese and presented it to the land use committee responsible for managing town playgrounds.

Homeschooling has allowed each of these teenagers to engage in intriguing *combinations* of activities. These kids are interesting people! They are not telling college officials something boring or forgettable, such as that they'd "like to do something with computers" or that they'd "really like to work with children." They already have *demonstrable* special interests that have flourished in the flexible atmosphere that homeschooling permits.

As a homeschooler, you were probably able to pursue and do well in a variety of activities. If you have developed several very different sets of interests, you may want to tailor your portfolio and application packet for each college on your list. This is not so much a matter of having a split personality as it is highlighting the part of yourself that is most attractive to a particular institution. My older son, for example, had an interest in both public policy and music. When he applied to American University in Washington, D.C., he stressed his internship at the Massachusetts State House and his gubernatorial campaign work, stating that he hoped to use the cultural assets of our nation's capital to support his musical interests. When applying to the Rome School of Music at Catholic University, which is also in D.C., he showcased his musical skills while letting the school know that its location would afford him the possibility of governmental internships. This was smart positioning. By showing how he and each school were a match for each other, he was accepted by both.

MULTIFACTED HOMESCHOOLERS

If you have varied interests, you may find yourself applying to several very different colleges. Think how you can market yourself to each one by highlighting aspects of yourself that are aligned with each school's program.

ASSESSING YOUR SKILLS

If you have engaged in the portfolio process throughout your high school years you probably have a good idea of where your unique strengths lie. If you haven't, take this quick inventory now. The questions are designed not to show your overall capabilities, but to highlight the less conventional aspects of yourself that you may have overlooked.

EXERCISE: This is a homeschooler who has . . .

Unusual skills for an adolescent:

_____

_____

Skills taken to a sophisticated level:

_____

_____

Unique service opportunities:

_____

_____

Mature leadership responsibilities:

_____

_____

Offbeat travel experiences:

_____

_____

Employment in a specialized field:

_____

_____

Unusual hobbies or interests:

_____

_____

Interaction with specialized groups or individuals:

_____

_____

Unusual artistic or athletic talent:

_____

_____

Membership in interesting, offbeat groups:

_____

_____

Independent projects:

_____

_____

Collaborative projects:

_____

_____

Areas of in-depth research:

_____

_____

Now that you have an overview of the admissions process, it's time to take a look at each individual item in your application packet. In the next chapter, you'll discover how to create each of these components and develop a rich and complex portrait of you and your homeschooling.

CHAPTER 10

A Homeschooler's Comprehensive
College Application

Your portfolio and transcript are only two components of your high-stakes college application packet. They will be accompanied by an array of materials that, taken as a whole, portray you and your achievements. This chapter will help you round out your admissions folder by discussing all the items you need to include:

- A cover letter

- The completed application form

- The personal essay

- Letters of recommendation

- Information on extracurricular activities

- Your portfolio with its cover letter, table of contents, and reflective writing

- Your transcript, signed by your parents

- A student profile and/or guidance department form

- Your school/homeschool profile

- Your resume with information not included elsewhere

Each of these will be explained below, using examples from my older son's college application packet.

 PACKET CRITERIA: THE CLASSIC FOUR

Each of your artifacts needs to be:

- Of high quality

- Criteria-referenced—according to what the reviewers want to see

- Credible—something the reviewer will consider to be solid evidence of learning

- Clear as to what the item is and why it's been included

THE ADMISSIONS PACKAGE RUBRIC

In Chapter 2, "Assessment Basics," I discussed the term "rubric." As you'll remember, a rubric is an evaluation tool for situations where you need to consider many interrelated variables. Surely creating a college admissions packet is such a situation! You need to decide which criteria are important, and then evaluate how well you've met those criteria on a scale from poor through excellent.

As you develop your college admissions packet and select items for your portfolio, keep the following two rubrics' criteria in mind. Then, after you think the packet is complete, run through the list again. How would you rate yourself? (Remember, each school will have its own set of criteria, so you may need to consider each application packet separately.) We will come back to these rubrics as the chapter ends, but right now keep them in mind as you select portfolio items, design your transcript, and write your first drafts.

RUBRIC #1
Things to Emphasize

Have I included *clear* and *credible* material that shows:

Academic Excellence:

Achievement (breadth)

Expertise (depth)

Personal Traits:

Leadership

Maturity

Curiosity

Resourcefulness

Uniqueness and Individuality

Community Involvement

Other traits this school seems to value:

1. _____

2. _____

3. _____

4. _____

Have I demonstrated how the school and I are " a good match"?

Have I shown that I am "a homeschooler who . . ."?

RUBRIC #2
Things to Avoid

Have I avoided:

Sloppiness and disorganization

A bulging, overloaded folder

Dullness

Repetition

A one-dimensional image

Arrogance or self-deprecation

Cuteness

Feeble attempts at humor

Other traits this school might dislike:

1. _____

2. _____

3. _____

4. _____

KEEPING THINGS ORGANIZED

Remember, each college has its own list of requirements. It is imperative not only to know the requirements of each school, but to keep them straight! This is no small task when you are applying to several schools. Things get even more complicated when you are fine-tuning your submissions to highlight the good match that you perceive between yourself and each college. Our family found that the best way to deal with the organization and management of paperwork was

---

 QUESTIONS YOUR APPLICATION PACKET ANSWERS

Like a good news story, your application should answer the following questions about you and your education:

Who?: Your student and personal profile

What?: The course content; what you studied and learned

When?: Learning in a four- to six-year block

Where?: In the home and beyond

Why?: Your family's educational philosophy

How?: The educational practices you employed

What story would your packet tell? What do you need to do to tell your story more effectively?

to create a folder for each school. We also determined which items would be sent to schools as standard issue, and which would be tailored to each institution.

THE INTRODUCTORY LETTER

This letter, addressed to your contact in the admissions office, should be a natural follow-up to the conversations and correspondence you have already had. In it you will re-introduce yourself and highlight why you believe that you and the school are a good match.

 CREATING A MATCH

Sometimes this "matchmaking" is better positioned in the essay. In fact, some schools require that one of your essays detail why you want to attend their institution.

The following sample introductory letter shows the admissions office that you are knowledgeable about the college and explains how you see your interests reflected in its programs. The letter mentions not only the college's academic majors but also any co- and extracurricular activities that you have investigated. It details how your current homeschool activities are tied to your future studies, which this institution is uniquely positioned to offer. The letter also touches on the interdisciplinary nature of major programs offered at the college and shows how homeschooling prepared you to think beyond the traditional high school disciplines. Any admissions officer reading this letter would know that you had done your research and found a school well aligned with your personal experience and goals.

Mr. William Marsden
Office of Admissions
Boston College
Chestnut Hill, MA 02167-3809

Dear Mr. Marsden:

I am applying to Boston College as a homeschooled student with a nontraditional education. Although I have taken several courses at my local high school and at Framingham State College, most of my education has been done at home in a program designed by my parents and myself.

We have completed the preliminary application as thoroughly as possible and are submitting it along with my homeschool transcript, a profile of our family's homeschool, a student profile compiled by my parents, and a sample portfolio that includes letters of recommendation and other documentation.

I am especially interested in Boston College because it is one of the few schools in the country that offers an integrated program in Irish studies. Although I am primarily interested in political science, I also play the violin and am interested in Celtic music. Short stories, especially those by Irish authors, are my favorite type of literature. A month-long trip to Ireland and visits from Irish friends convinced me that Irish studies is something I want to pursue. Your junior year abroad program at University College, Cork is something I hope to experience.

Because we live in the Boston area I am familiar with programs put on by your music department. I am currently a violist in the New England Conservatory Youth Symphony Orchestra and a member of the choir at St. Mary's, Holliston. If accepted by BC I hope to join one of your string or vocal ensembles.

I am very impressed by the courses offered in your political science department. I am interested in local and national politics and plan to attend the Washington Seminar this spring. I also had the opportunity to intern at the Massachusetts State House last summer in the office of Representative Barbara Gardner.

Of all the colleges that I investigated, BC is the only one that offers programs in everything important to me: Irish studies, history, political science, and music.

My parents and I would be glad to answer any questions you have about our homeschool program. I will be contacting your office soon to schedule an interview.

Thank you for taking the time to read this letter and look through the accompanying package.

Sincerely,

Tad Heuer

THE APPLICATION

Although colleges differ in the materials they require from homeschoolers, I can all but guarantee that every college you are interested in will require you to fill out an application. I have found that each school's essay questions are very revealing of its mission and the type of student it is seeking. Answering the essay questions well can help you prove that you're a good fit for their mission.

Alternatively, some applicants prefer to fill out what is called the "Common Application," which is a single admissions form that is accepted by a large number of colleges and universities

THE ESSAY QUESTION

A school's essay questions can be most revealing as to the type of student they are seeking.

- Tell us about a tradition that is honored by your family, your friends, or your culture and discuss why it is important.

- Having observed the recent success of television shows about young people, our school has decided to pitch a pilot to the networks. We are taking this opportunity to get help from the intended audience: you.

- You have just completed a 300-page autobiography. Please submit page 217.

nationwide. Although the Common Application offers an efficient way of applying to schools, you may prefer to utilize the individual application of each school to ensure you supply them with the precise information they want. If you send in the Common Application you may not be able to showcase the range of interests you have or write a second essay that would add life and energy to your application. The choice is up to you, but I personally think it's worth the time to complete the college's own form.

THE COMMON APPLICATION

For more information on the "Common App" check out the website at www.comonapp.org.

Each school's application is different, but without fail every one will have a section that is difficult for homeschoolers to complete. Try to fill out the application to the best of your ability, but in places where you are unsure of an appropriate response, call your contact in the admissions office and ask for specific directions. When you write the introductory letter for your admissions packet, mention that you filled out the form according to (insert name of person)'s suggestions.

In sections that are meaningless for homeschooled students, do not simply write the initials "N A" or the words "None Available." Remember that in all probability you *do* have relevant information, but not in the form the college expects to see. In the space provided, you can add a line or two directing the reader to other parts of the admissions packet where you feel the question can be better answered. For example, most schools will inquire about extracurricular interests. For homeschoolers, activities termed "extra" curricular may well be the mainstays of their homeschool program. For traditionally schooled students, being engaged in an archaeology dig, flying a plane, or working for an architect might be diversions or opportunities for career exploration. But these activities shouldn't be considered "extra" for you if they are integral components of your homeschool learning. In such instances, you should direct the reader to your resume or the appropriate parts of your portfolio or transcript for fuller details. If your participation in the activity is the subject of your personal essay, you could make a note of that, too.

THE PERSONAL ESSAY

Some schools tell you precisely what the subject of your personal essay should be. Others will provide you with a more open-ended question. Still others will leave the topic up to you. Whichever route they choose, *follow their directions!* You may have written a dynamic essay for school #1, but

FILLING IN THE BLANKS

In the space where the college asks for your high school's name, do not simply write in your family's pet name for your homeschool, such as our Heueristics. If a school name appears in that blank, the college will assume you are indicating a correspondence school or umbrella school that you attended. After spending time searching for its profile or other descriptive information, the admissions office staff will not be amused to discover that you were being coy. If you use a school-like name to refer to your family's homeschool program, by all means make that fact clear!

if it doesn't match the requirements of school #2, don't include it in both packets. It's tempting to think of writing a generic essay that could be submitted to a number of schools. *Don't.* If you have something to say that you strongly feel is important but that doesn't meet the criteria laid down by the school, include it as an additional essay in your portfolio—perhaps as an opinion piece that highlights your alignment with the school or your unique capabilities—but don't "substitute" it for one of the required essays. The committee could deem your application "unacceptable" for not following their guidelines.

POLISHING YOUR ESSAY

I would strongly suggest that you have a reader for your essay during the writing process and a proofreader at the end of it. Your essay will still be your work, but it will be a polished piece, not a hastily printed second draft. The essay's content tells the college something about you, but so does its form and its mechanics (grammar and syntax, punctuation and spelling). When you're writing your essay—and as you're editing it—keep going back to the rubrics earlier in this section. The essay is a valuable tool to express your opinions, maturity, and personality, and you want to put your best piece of writing in front of the admissions committee.

 DON'T MAKE THEM YAWN!

Admissions officers read hundreds of applications each year. Will yours stand out from the crowd? Yes, simply because you're a homeschooler. But that's not enough. You still need to avoid being:

- Trite
- Dull
- Boring

ADDRESSING HOMESCHOOLING IN YOUR ESSAY

Where does homeschooling itself fit into the essay? That depends. You could easily make it the topic of your essay, describing to the college what the word "homeschooling" means for you and your family. Or, you could write about things that you were able to experience only because of homeschooling's flexible nature. Or, you could take an opposite view and tell about challenges you faced (and met) as a homeschooler and an educational outsider.

> While you want to avoid your essay's being perceived as dull, boring, or forgettable, do not try to be funny. Writing humor is an art. Unless you have spent your high school years refining this craft, do not attempt it in a high-stakes essay. Sounding highfalutin and pseudo-intellectual is also a mistake. In short, try to sound neither funny nor phony.

Some students want information about homeschooling to come from other parts of the package rather than the essay. They prefer to use the essay to create a richer, fuller portrait of themselves by addressing aspects of their personality not evident from other artifacts. Check to see if you repeat in your essay what is shown elsewhere in your admissions packet (through your portfolio, transcript, application, etc.). If you have the opportunity, use the essay to add something new about yourself and to demonstrate that you and the school are a good match.

SAMPLE ESSAYS

Here are three application essays that were written by my son Tad. Each essay was tailored to a particular school's mission and personality. And each one is short! By all means, try to pare down your prose to one page. This first essay is focused on homeschooling and was used to apply to Brown, where Tad was accepted and from which he later was graduated.

I didn't choose to be taught at home; my parents decided for me. I was four, and my toddler priorities lay elsewhere. Little did I know that I was volunteering for an educational experiment. Every September my parents and I had our annual discussion about continuing homeschooling versus sending me to "regular" school. I don't know if I thought school would be a bit boring or if I was afraid of change, but I always chose to stay home. I did go to school for a few classes and for violin lessons, but much of my time there was spent explaining my sporadic attendance to teachers and classmates. I grew accustomed to giving both rote and wry answers to questions like, "Do you watch TV all day?" The rote answer was "No, of course not. I do the same things you do in school." The wry answer was "Yes, from nine to noon," watching their faces form expressions of disbelief. I didn't tell them I was watching Massachusetts Educational Television on PBS.

When discussing homeschooling with strangers or skeptical parents, the first question usually concerns "socialization," often posed bluntly as "Do you have any friends?" Sports and orchestra brought me into contact with kids my age, but even then it was a common interest rather than a common age that drew us together. Over the years, I found wonderful friends in Mendelssohn, O. Henry, a German woman on my paper route who was a World War II refugee, *Newsweek*, a paralyzed basketball coach who couldn't walk but still coached me as if he could, history books, and a range of musical instruments from viola to tin whistle. People are always relieved to discover that I'm not a hermit.

Homeschooling gave me the freedom to explore and experiment. We traded houses with an Irish family and lived in Galway for a month. I was never given actual lessons on "how to write a sentence"; I learned as I wrote history essays. Few schools would have allowed me to research the sinking of the Titanic, but my parents let me read about it, build models of it, and learn about watertight bulkheads. (I even managed to finish my math book that year, too.)

As I got older, people started to ask if being taught at home was going to hinder me in college. After all, they said, you don't know what it's like to work for grades or take classroom tests. Maybe I did start to second-guess myself, so I took some college courses. My grades indicated what I learned from the professors, but not what I learned from the students. Many of them were older, juggling full-time jobs and their education, but they really wanted to be in class. One 47-year-old man who was in China during the Cultural Revolution said he was taking biology so "when my son asks why the grass is green, I can tell him."

Homeschooling was the right choice for me. It taught me to learn outside the classroom, inside the classroom, from other people, and from my own mistakes. Above all, home-schooling has given me the desire to continue learning for the rest of my life.

The second essay was on an assigned theme: a significant experience. Tad framed the experience as a challenge he had faced and overcome, and then he focused the content of the essay on music. This essay was sent to Catholic University's Rome School of Music, where he also was accepted. When Tad wrote this, he was considering a musical performance major with a concentration in viola. Again, note the match and the niche that he achieved in this essay.

Topic: Evaluate a significant experience or achievement that has special meaning to you.

Playing the viola allows my emotions to weave their way into my music. Shaping a discordant sound into expressive music has been a lengthy, laborious, but ultimately rewarding process.

I was switched from violin to viola by Melba Sandberg, a brusque, no-nonsense conductor at the New England

continues

Conservatory. During my violin seating audition, in what I thought was polite conversation, she remarked that my hands were large enough to play viola; had I ever thought of doing so? I replied that I hadn't, smiled, and played my piece. The following Saturday, nervous but excited, I brought my violin to the first rehearsal. When I walked in the door, Mrs. Sandberg accosted me and demanded, "Where's your viola?"

Under her pressure I switched, but the challenges of reading a new clef and adjusting my fingers were frustrating. It had taken me six years playing the violin to get into this orchestra. Now I was expected to play a new instrument at high performance standards. This created enormous tension at home over the next few months. I would avoid practicing and complain about my "insensitive conductor" all week. This displeasure reached its climax every Saturday morning as my mother drove me into Boston for rehearsal.

During the ride home, however, a marked change was often evident. After playing the viola for three hours in the company of other musicians and discovering how wonderfully the viola combined with the entire spectrum of orchestral sound, I would soften. I wouldn't admit it, but I was beginning to like the viola.

The next spring I auditioned for and won a seat in the NEC Youth Symphony. Comfortable with my instrument and my place in the orchestra, I started to play with confidence. I also discovered the advantages of the viola. The viola doesn't need the pyrotechnical passages given to the violins; instead, it has resonance and depth. I began to enjoy the indispensable role of the viola in string quartets. Now, I love the viola.

Without Melba Sandberg's prodding I never would have risked playing the viola. Her persistence, which upset my comfortable world, was really a challenge to believe in myself. Before this experience I had often shrouded myself in the security of the familiar. Mrs. Sandberg's enduring, sometimes obstinate confidence forced me to confront the boundaries I had placed on myself. She taught me to embrace a challenge rather than shrink from it. I learned to trust those who believe in me, and I learned to trust myself.

Finally, the third essay, and probably our family's favorite. The essay was written for American University, a school located in Washington, D.C., with strong programs in public policy and government. They gave applicants a number of essay topics from which to choose, and Tad thought that this one looked like the most fun. This topic allowed him to demonstrate his knowledge and understanding of politics in a unique way, without being pseudo-intellectual or boring.

Topic: Write the headline newspaper article for January 1, 2015.

Still the *United* States?

In 1995, Pete Wilson, governor of a unified California, said, "We declare to Washington that California is a proud and sovereign state, not a colony of the federal government." What sounded then like political rhetoric is quickly becoming reality. Nationally, the United States has been weakened in the past few years by increased regional loyalty. The recent split of California into three separate states is possibly just the beginning of a bitter "cold war" between regions. John Engle, an expert on Western American affairs, believes this strife began in earnest after the 1996 election, when the GOP took control of all three branches of government. "As states started to fight for federal deregulation and for control over programs like AFDC, Social Security and Medicare, the autonomy they received emboldened them. Now they'd like to extend their control into areas like the Department of Defense, which could literally prove explosive."

Sarah Reinhart, a public policy consultant with the Institute for Unity, agrees. "The irony of this entire situation is that none of our elected officials are thinking for the benefit of the nation as a whole," she said. "Each representative and senator naturally wants the most money and prestige for his or her district, and we essentially have a fifty-seven state bidding war." There are those who feel this new state power is good, however. "Texas is bigger than most European countries," said Sen. Jim Houlihan, R-TX. "Why should we get only two votes in the Senate and then be forced to accept all these Mexican immigrants? I say keep the power in Texas and keep the people from Rhode Island out of our business."

States in the Northeast, already worried about how their geographical size may affect future developments, have banded together in a "Federal Unity Alliance." While the

continues

Northeast FUA (and the one created by several Midwestern states lacking large populations) appears to support the federal government, state officials speaking on the condition of anonymity said the Alliances were actually created to ward off possible arable land shortages in the Northeast and military manpower shortages in the Midwest. "I'll stand by the federal government," one FUA governor said, "but I don't know if I can trust my colleagues to do the same."

Some Democratic legislators are working to halt the wave of power and money to the states. "What happens if there's a forest fire in Wyoming, or an earthquake in Oregon, or a flood in Missouri?" asked Sen. David Wilbraham, D-PA. "There won't be a Federal Emergency Management Agency to bail out these states, no pool of money to rebuild them." Rep. Cleopatra Kifamo, D-BR, ranking minority member on the House Working Americans Committee, fears environmental and labor laws are already being undermined.

"States used to welcome federal control in these areas because it prevented other states from setting lower standards and luring business away," she noted. "Now with state control of those areas, environmental protection laws and workers' rights are being eroded for profit."

In a search for a historical precedent some point to "Democracy in America", written 180 years ago in 1830. Author Alexis de Tocqueville felt that the keys to America's success were western expansion, decentralized government, and personal responsibility. But with allegiance to a too large, too impersonal United States waning no one foresees a rebirth of that free and unifying spirit. "Why should the United States be any different?" asked one Angolan diplomat. "Britain was once the ruler of the world. Now with the loss of Scotland and Northern Ireland, they're nobody. America's time has come and gone."

RECOMMENDATIONS

For schooled students, extra outside recommendations are likely to be viewed as padding for a weak candidate. For homeschoolers, however, they are critical components of the college application packet. They take the homeschooler out of the home and offer an outsider's perspective. As such, they provide college admissions officials with clear, credible documentation on which to base a decision.

"TEACHER" RECOMMENDATIONS

Schooled students usually are advised not to look beyond their school for recommendations unless there are unusual circumstances. By definition, homeschooling is an unusual circumstance! Can you think of three references who can comment on your academic achievement? This is one more reason to cultivate mentor relationships during your teenage years.

There are two types of recommendations that you can send to a college: academic and personal. Academic ones are usually termed "teacher recommendations" (since high school teachers usually fill them out for traditionally schooled students) and seek to gain objective information about your academic integrity and abilities. Personal recommendations attest to your unique individual, or personal, qualities. Essentially, recommendations seek to verify through a credible, third-party source that you possess the characteristics the school thinks are important.

Some colleges provide forms to be ripped out of the application booklet for recommendations. If the school you're applying to has its own forms and you have appropriate teachers to fill them in, use them. However, remember that many of your homeschool "teachers" probably are not certified secondary school teachers. That means that while they are attempting to validate your credibility, they need to verify their own! One way to deal with the issue is to suggest they fill out the school's form as best they can and also attach a short note written on their letterhead stationery describing their qualifications and relationship to you (music instructor, math tutor, family friend, etc.).

CHOOSING A RECOMMENDER

Because these letters go into your folder to enhance your image, it goes without saying that the persons you choose to write your recommendations should have good written communication skills. In addition, they should know you well enough both to write convincingly about your academic or personal traits, and to discuss why you are a good match for the school. If you are looking to major in biology, for example, get a recommendation from someone who has supervised your work in a lab. If you're positioning yourself for a concentration in American history, have the head of your local historical association write about the first-person living-history presentation you created as a homeschool community service project for the town's schools. While these people may not be teachers in the conventional sense, they surely can address all the traits listed on the teacher recommendation form: creativity, independence, work habits, and potential for growth.

ACADEMIC RECOMMENDATIONS

If you are reading this chapter in the fall of your senior year, it may be too late for you to implement the following strategy, but if you're getting a jump on the process earlier, you can use this classic portfolio archiving tactic. During your teenage years ask for a note from every "teacher" in every "course" you take. For example, if you took a course at a local college or university get a letter from the professor *at the end of the course*. Do not wait until the fall of your senior year to request a recommendation. By then your professor may well have forgotten you and have nothing specific to say, or worse, may no longer be at the school or easily accessible. My son's biology professor at the local state college, for example, was a research scientist who worked in Africa collecting data on the vocalizations of hippopotami for much of the year. Even if he could remember my son and offer specific feedback on Tad's personal and academic skills, there would have been no easy way to get in touch with him in the field. My son requested that letter as soon as his grades were posted. Letters such as these verify not just that you have the *potential* to do college work, but that you've *already* done it. While this example is from academia, you can ask for recommendations from many other places during your teenage years. Build your file as you go; don't wait until the end.

In most high schools, a teacher fills in the recommendation form and routes it to a guidance counselor, who then organizes the application packet and sends it to the university on the student's behalf. This gives an aura of internal security—the student hasn't seen the recommendation and hasn't had the ability to tamper with it. In order to replicate this security safeguard, homeschoolers can ask that the person writing the recommendation place the materials in an envelope, seal it, write his or her signature across the flap, and cover the signature with a piece of cellophane tape. Then you can include it, still sealed, when you assemble your application packet at home. Of course, many high school teachers feel comfortable giving students a signed original of the recommendation letter to keep in their files. Ask your recommenders if they are willing to do this, too. Then, should you ever need an extra copy, you'll have one available.

 RECOMMENDATION LETTERS: SPECIFIC, NOT GENERIC

Explain to your recommenders the niche you are trying to cultivate and have them address their comments to it. Also, make sure you give each of them the following two things:

- A stamped envelope appropriately addressed—either to the admissions office if the letter is being mailed directly to the school, or to your home address if you will be including it in your application packet.

- Adequate time to compose their letter!

PERSONAL RECOMMENDATIONS

When gathering your recommendations, make sure the personal ones aren't actually *impersonal* ones. Padding your recommendations with nice generic notes from community leaders who know your parents is not going to impress the admissions committee. If your priest, pastor, or rabbi knows you well enough to speak about your personality and your specific service achievements, great! If he or she only knows you as someone's son or daughter, seek a recommendation elsewhere.

PARENT EVALUATIONS

Finally, we come to Mom and Dad. They, of course, are your faculty, facilitators, and guidance counselors. They can address their teacher role by filling out a recommendation form for a specific academic discipline, much as a high school English teacher would. It may be useful to have them do this in an area where either they have expertise or you lack outside verification. On the other hand, they might write a brief note on the teacher recommendation form stating that their

PARENT/COUNSELOR EVALUATIONS

Most high school students never see their guidance counselor's report, but you may see the one your parents write. Will their comments reflect your own self-evaluation? Probably. But don't be surprised if there are areas where you and your parents don't see eye to eye.

fuller academic evaluation is contained in the transcript or in the student profile, both of which are discussed below.

EXTRA- OR COCURRICULAR ACTIVITIES

As mentioned earlier, what schools term "*extra*-curricular activities" may be quite curricular for homeschoolers. Because homeschoolers can pursue and research personal interests in depth you can develop expertise in areas where most schooled students cannot. This is another place where a homeschooler can exploit the niche factor. However, you need to decide which activities are extracurricular for *you*, and not be limited by conventional expectations.

EXTRA- OR COCURRICULAR ACTIVITIES

You're in luck! Homeschoolers tend to have demonstrable interests. Rather than talking about pursuing your dream "someday," chances are you've already started. Check Chapter 8, "Creating Your Transcript," to see how to show that your consuming interest is not just an "extra" but really something "curricular."

Another term that schools use is "cocurricular." This refers to activities that are more closely related to the traditional academic disciplines. Thus, a high school would most likely consider French Club and field trips to the state legislature cocurricular activities while chorus, alas, would fall into the extracurricular category. For you as a homeschooler the word "cocurricular" may be useful in organizing a list of experiences that you feel are closely aligned with what you were learning but which may appear to be marginal or "fluff" to an outsider. This is especially true of travel, museum visits, theatrical and musical performances, etc. Whenever possible, try to describe these activities, which may well be the foundation of your homeschooling program, as both legitimate learning experiences (cocurricular) *and* personal interests or passions (extracurricular). Enumerate them on the activities form but add an asterisk with a note saying that these items will be more fully addressed on your transcript.

Remember, too, that while college officials are familiar with most traditional high school activities, awards, and achievements—such as earning a letter in varsity football or induction into the National Honor Society—they may be less aware of awards given outside the confines of a school. For example, if you won an agriculture award, either in a youth organization such as 4-H or in an exhibition where you were competing against adults, you will need to give the reviewers some sort of context for your achievement. No matter how familiar and important it is to you, you must assume that the college officials know nothing of the award or the organization granting it. It is worth remembering that if someone on the committee asks, *What does this mean?* then you haven't explained your activity or achievement adequately.

ORGANIZING YOUR ACTIVITIES

Once you've categorized your activities to your own satisfaction, you need to organize them under a few topical headings. This is important—giving each activity on the list a place in the overall scheme shows that you consider them thematically linked, not just a catch-all of interesting experiences. The key here is to avoid the laundry list. So often, students who have engaged in many activities put them all down in one long list, hoping that quantity alone will impress the college admissions committee. In fact, the reverse is true. The long list approach gives the impression of a dilettante who was cursory and shallow, someone who never discovered an area of interest or explored it in any depth.

 SEE ATTACHED

Rather than squeeze the information into the space allotted on the application, note whether the school says you can use additional sheets to describe your activities, community involvement, and hobbies. Many schools do. Also, if your award is truly important in its field, chances are it will surface in your essay, on your resume, or as a portfolio artifact where you can give it the extra treatment it deserves. Simply put an asterisk next to it on the list of honors and awards and note where the reviewers will find additional information.

When organizing your lists of extra- and cocurricular activities, think of sequencing them in levels of importance. Let's say that you have won eight music awards in the last three years, and they make a long, impressive list. However, you want to major in environmental studies, and it takes only one line of type to mention your three years of part-time employment at a nature center. The way you present your materials should emphasize the match you are trying to highlight. Do not lead the reviewers' attention away from environmental studies just because you are proud of your music awards. Put science first, using key words from the "Bloom's Taxonomy of Learning" or the "Department of Labor's Dictionary of Occupational Titles" found in Appendix C to describe the responsibilities you had at the nature center. *Then* you can note your musical achievements.

CREATING AN EXTRACURRICULAR RESUME

One way to draw attention to depth of achievement in a particular area is to create a resume devoted to it. Be sure to note the existence of this additional sheet somewhere on the extracurricular activity form. For example, when my son wanted to inform a conservatory about his performing arts background he shaped his list into resume format and printed it out on a separate piece of resume-quality bond paper. He then placed the sheet inside the application so the reviewers would not have to hunt for it. Here's his example. Notice how he sequenced his experience for this resume, with his most recent (and most prestigious) orchestral experience first. Also note how he developed a service component, rather than simply including these activities under the more general category of "Music." Had he wanted to major in drama, on the other hand, he certainly would have named the plays in which he had acted rather than simply naming the theater groups in which he participated.

TAD HEUER
164 NORFOLK STREET
HOLLISTON, MA 01746
(508) 555-1436

Performing Arts Resume

MUSIC

1993-94	New England Conservatory Youth Symphony Orchestra (viola)
1992-93	New England Conservatory Youth Repertory Orchestra (viola)
1990-91	Performing Arts Youth Symphony Orchestra (violin)
1990-93	Massachusetts Junior/Senior Central District Orchestra (violin)
1989-93	Holliston High School Orchestra (violin)
1993	Violinist, Holliston High School: "Fiddler on the Roof," Ashland Youth Theater: "The Boyfriend"
1993	Apprentice luthier, emphasis on stringed instrument repair
1991-	Drummer/Fifer, Tenth Massachusetts Regiment reenactment group
1992	Member, Boston Scottish Fiddle Society

DRAMA

1990-93	Member, Holliston High School Drama Club
1991-92	Member, Ashland Youth Theater

MEDIA

1992	WMTW (Maine) Radio Internship

SERVICE

1993	Audio Cataloger, Holliston Public Library
1992-	Violin Soloist, St. Mary's Church, Holliston Public Library
1992-	Member, St. Mary's Adult Choir

YOUR PORTFOLIO AND ITS TABLE OF CONTENTS

Because portfolios are more fully examined and explained elsewhere, this chapter will touch on only a few additional points. If you haven't read the earlier chapters, let me briefly define what a portfolio is: a small but representative collection of artifacts, thoughtfully selected, which describes you, your interests, and your abilities. For your college application it should describe—as everything in the packet should—a unique individual compatible with the school's vision and mission.

DETERMINING YOUR CONTENT

Recognize that colleges may be justifiably weary of students who "pad" weak applications with extraneous materials. However, homeschoolers *need* to show what they know through artifacts. For homeschoolers the portfolio is an essential rather than supplemental component of the application packet. How do you handle this dilemma?

First, get feedback from your admissions office contact early in the application process. He or she should be able to suggest the most appropriate way to configure a portfolio, how many items to include, the areas the reviewers would need to see addressed, etc.

Also, check the instructions in the application booklet. Often there are notes that tell how supplementary materials should be submitted. While these, of course, are intended to apply to schooled students' supplements, the format and packaging suggestions may be useful since they describe what this particular school's admissions officials expect to see. Understanding the school's definition of a portfolio can help you discuss *your* vision of a portfolio with your contact in the admissions office. He or she will be better able to act as your advocate if you can describe in advance how (and why) your portfolio may look different from those of schooled students.

 FAT FOLDER SYNDROME

A bulging admissions packet for a traditionally schooled student can mean that he or she is literally padding the application—adding loads of supplementary materials to shore up a weak candidacy. Not so for homeschoolers! You need to include more materials to explain how you spent the past four years. Still, leaner is better. Use the suggestions in Chapters 3 and 4 to create a packet that is both streamlined and comprehensive.

When it comes to the number of artifacts to include, my advice is to keep it lean and streamlined. Your judgment and selectivity are being evaluated here. If you throw in too much material you will appear indecisive, disorganized, and nonreflective. Remember the definition: a *small* but representative collection . . . .

For your college admissions portfolio which by its very nature is a high-stakes portfolio, it is important that you follow the suggestions in Chapter 4, "Creating Your Portfolio," regarding balance, color, use of graphic images, sequencing of artifacts, etc. A portfolio's visual impact is important; you want to use it to your advantage, making it reflect positively on you.

COMPILING A TABLE OF CONTENTS

Remember that once you've assembled your portfolio you will need to create a table of contents for it. The table of contents is your reviewer's introduction to this parallel self, this proxy that you've created. Realize that you need to help the reviewer both anticipate *what* is in the portfolio and understand *why* it's there. For this reason, an annotated table of contents, which provides clarification and context, can be a useful device. On the other hand, you may wish to write a brief table of contents like the one below and add clarifying comments to each artifact separately.

This second method, individual annotation, is effective when a longer, more descriptive note is necessary to justify or clarify an item's inclusion. Notice that this portfolio was designed to showcase three areas: writing, politics, and music. Science is touched on only briefly and mathematics doesn't appear at all. Other components of the packet were used to address those areas. Note, too, that there was an audio (cassette) and a visual (photographic) artifact included along with the written ones.

```
Thaddeus Heuer
164 Norfolk Street
Holliston, MA 01746
(508) 555-1436
```

Homeschool Portfolio

This portfolio contains supporting documentation from my homeschool program. Each item is accompanied by descriptive or reflective comments:

1. Essay on gender identity and toys

2. Cover sheet and introduction of a report on magnetic res onance imaging, teacher's comments included

3. Handwritten response to an examination question on Woodrow Wilson and the League of Nations written for a course taken at Framingham State College

4. Review of the book *Seven Days in May*

5. An opinion piece on term limits published in *The Middlesex News*

6. Photo of myself in reenactment regalia as a regimental musician

7. Tape of Handel violin sonatas and Irish fiddle music

YOUR TRANSCRIPT AND ITS COVER LETTER

The development of transcripts is covered in Chapter 7, "Transcript Basics," and Chapter 8, "Creating Your Transcript," but I will add a few comments here about your transcript's role in your college application packet. The college or university to which you apply will be looking for something that looks like a high school transcript. Chances are, yours will look quite different. If you haven't done so already, discuss with your contact in the admissions office how the college would like to see your homeschool learning displayed on a transcript. Then you can determine which of the various formats discussed in Chapter 7 is most appropriate.

SEVERAL KINDS OF TRANSCRIPTS

Your transcript might describe:

- The names of your courses

- The content of your coursework

- What you know

- What you can actually do with what you know

Study the types of transcripts you can create and select wisely. You want what it tells about you to match what the school of your choice wants to know.

After you've decided on your transcript format and created its final draft, you still need someone to officially witness or "sign off" on it. This could be one or both of your parents, your mentor, a guidance counselor at a school you attended, etc. The goal is to add formality, credibility, and an outsider's verification to the transcript you and your family have developed. If you decided to use a one-page, form-like transcript, it should be signed at the bottom with the name of the person and, if you like, his or her title typed beneath the signature. Parents can legitimately claim to be "Head of School" as long as it is abundantly clear that the school is a homeschool. If you developed a narrative transcript, such as the one referred to below, have your designated witness write a short cover letter, print it on bond paper, and sign it in blue or black ink. If you need more than one copy of your transcript because you are applying to several schools, you may photocopy the transcript itself, but each should have its own cover letter, printed on bond paper and signed in ink. See the sample letter on page 209.

Of course, if you have attended high school or college or have taken other coursework for which you received grades, you will need the guidance department of those schools to send official copies of your transcripts to the college of your choice. It is useful, however, to include a photocopies of the transcripts in your college application packet, noting that you realize that these are *unofficial* documentation and that official transcripts have been already requested. This gives college officials an advance view of you and your grades as well as alerting them as to material they should be receiving.

STUDENT PROFILE AND/OR GUIDANCE DEPARTMENT REPORT

In addition to teacher recommendation forms, your college application booklet probably includes a guidance counselor report form. This is where the high school attempts to describe overall student competency. If you decide to use the counselor's form, your parents will be the most likely candidates to complete it. Again, it is not in your best interests to portray your mother as a school employee who is writing as a disinterested third party. If family members complete these records, you should make that clear from the outset.

Bill and Loretta Heuer   Re: Tad Heuer
Heueristics
164 Norfolk Street
Holliston, MA 01746
(508) 555-1436

The following transcript is divided into three parts:
Literature and Composition; Science and Mathematics; and
History, Politics, and Social Science. Most of Tad's learning has been done at home; exceptions (courses taken either
at our local high school or at a college) have been marked
with an asterisk. Descriptions of these courses have been
taken directly from school catalogs, and the grade earned in
each is noted. Official transcripts from these institutions
will be forwarded to your office.

The remainder of the transcript has been crafted collaboratively between Tad and ourselves. It reflects not only content covered but areas where mastery has been displayed. Our
criteria for the inclusion of any item was Tad's being comfortable discussing the topic with only minimal review.

Because of the comprehensive, collaborative, and public
nature of this transcript my husband and I consider it Tad's
Exit Exhibition. Accordingly, we consider him to be graduated from our homeschool program.

(Parent Signatures)

An alternative to completing the form itself is to have your parents note on the form that they
have written a student profile that appears on a separate sheet of paper. If you feel it is warranted, paper clip the counselor form and the profile to each other. In writing a student profile, your
parents can use their own ideas as well as the criteria listed on the school's form, the items in
Rubric #1 (see above), or the list of descriptive words listed in Appendix C, "Helpful Words and
Terms." Whichever format they use, whatever descriptive terms they employ, their report should

 CLARITY REGARDING AUTHORSHIP

In the area of authorship you need to be clear to the point of transparency:

- What in the packet is yours?

- What is your parent's?

- What is an outsider's?

Make sure there is no confusion as to who wrote what!

show balance. No matter how smart or delightful you are, you have flaws that render you less than perfect. Your parents will need to mention some of them. However, your profile can always frame these characteristics in terms of how you've learned to recognize them in yourself and how you're striving to overcome them.

Here's how we described our older son, organizing our student profile by using some of the categories that appeared on the guidance counselor's form.

William and Loretta Heuer   Re: Tad Heuer
Heueristics
164 Norfolk Street
Holliston, MA 01746
(508) 555-1436

STUDENT PROFILE

Learning Style

Tad has excellent study skills. He knows how to access human, print, and electronic resources and is able to approach learning in a variety of ways: independent reading and investigations, study groups, classroom lecture, laboratory work, etc. Although he can become immersed in a subject, he also dabbles in areas that look potentially interesting. He is excited about learning and sets high standards for himself.

Academic Mastery

Because we do not give grades in our homeschool program, Tad's transcript is composed of areas in which we feel he has demonstrated mastery. Our criteria for mastery are twofold. Tad should be able to:

- hold his own during a conversation on the subject with an interested adult, asking meaningful questions about what he doesn't know

- notice interdisciplinary links between subjects and take multiple perspectives on a topic

Work in Progress

Tad is a fast and flexible learner who can approach knowledge gaps on an as-needed or just-in-time basis. Future areas for investigation include: music theory and composition, art appreciation, foreign language using accelerated learning techniques, mathematical applications, poetry and drama.

Personal Traits/Maturity

In addition to displaying a seriousness of purpose and a dry
sense of humor, Tad is:

self-directed	motivated	coachable	loyal
disciplined	confident	trustworthy	mature
responsible	reflective	independent	

Tad is not the world's biggest risk taker, but he can recognize opportunity and take advantage of it.

Evaluation

We believe that Tad is ready to begin study at the college
level. In addition to his wide store of general knowledge,
he has specialized knowledge in areas pursued through independent study. He is at the edge of adult learning, ready to
grow. Not only do we love Tad as a son but we also like him
as a person, respect him as a learner, and admire him as a
competent young adult.

 FAST AND FLEXIBLE LEARNERS

Just-in-time learning (or JIT), mentioned in Tad's profile, is a contemporary learning model that is well suited to our information age, when knowledge is expanding so rapidly that we can't learn all we need to know ahead of time. A JIT learner is able to learn at precisely the right time whatever is necessary to solve a problem.

Finally, read the guidance counselor's form *carefully*! There may be a schoolish item or two that you'll need to address such as rank in class or graduation date. Do not skip over them! Perhaps they could be handled in the student profile, or perhaps in the school profile, which is explained in the next section. Attempt to answer these questions as best as you can, again looking to your contact in the admissions office for advice. For example, certain high schools are doing away with class rank. Because of this, one college states on its counselor evaluation form: "Nongraded/unranked school systems must provide some type of academic assessment of the individual in relation to peers." In a situation such as this, ask the admissions office for examples of documentation that nongraded schools are currently submitting for comparison.

HOMESCHOOL PROGRAM PROFILE

Everyone knows that high schools differ from one another. A "B" in one school may be an "A–" or a "C+" in another. Even schools within the same city or town can be radically different in philosophy, demographics, expectations, and student achievement. Because of this, a college wants to

PARENTS' ROLE

All parents have a role in the college admissions process. They need to:

- Offer their perspectives on various schools and programs

- Keep a master calendar for the myriad of dates and deadlines

- Discuss the financial realities of college attendance with their child

In addition, homeschool parents need to:

- Continue to mentor their son or daughter

- Complete forms as teacher, guidance counselor, and head of school

- Create student and school profiles

- Explain whatever facets of their homeschool program need clarification

know what kind of school an applicant is coming from. What was the program like in the school he or she attended? This is where a college tries to evaluate program competency. If a certain high school has already sent a number of students to a particular college, the college will have a "feel" for that secondary school. In other words, the high school will have built up some sort of track record. When a college admissions official sees an "A" on the transcript of a student from that school, he or she will be able to evaluate its worth. If a college is unfamiliar with a secondary school, it attempts to evaluate the school's program by using what is called a school profile. This is a sheet of paper that states the school's mission statement, describes its geographic setting and socioeconomic level, notes its average SAT scores, its graduation policy, etc.

Your homeschool has its own educational philosophy and mission. This explains *why* you homeschool. Furthermore, you engage in educational practices that make your family's homeschooling different from that of other homeschoolers. This is *how* you homeschool. Because homeschooling is such a decentralized phenomenon, the college has no way of knowing what your "school" was like unless you tell them. Worse, the college may make stereotypical assumptions about homeschooling that are far removed from your family's experience. This is why a profile that clarifies your homeschool program—how and why you homeschool—is necessary.

Who should write the school profile? That depends. If a family has been homeschooling since pre-Kindergarten days, chances are the parents have a well-developed educational philosophy that has had a powerful impact on their children's learning. Moreover, they are probably practiced at discussing it. On the other hand, if a student decided to leave school at an older age and design his or her own homeschool program, a student-written profile may be more authentic and appropriate. Ideally, of course, the school profile should be a collaborative effort. However, because we homeschoolers tend to use our own jargon to describe our philosophy and practices, it is wise to have a nonhomeschooling friend critique the school profile for clarity. The goal of the school profile is to make your family's homeschooling clear, not more confusing.

When you begin writing your homeschool profile, think of it as a descriptive document—one that could be used as advertising copy, a press release, or the text on the homepage of your family's website. The profile should be crisp, clear, organized, and brief. Keep it to a page or less. Avoid rambling philosophical treatises. If you feel you have to write a homeschool manifesto, fine. But send it to your local newspaper, not the college admissions office. If you do submit a long prose piece to a college, realize that an overworked admissions officer will scan it rather then read it. You are not trying to convince the admissions committee members to homeschool their own children but to accept yours into their freshman class.

In the following school profile written by my husband and myself, note that we included information about our philosophy, our graduation standards, the content to which our son was exposed, the educational practices used in our homeschool, and how evaluation was accomplished. This is an organization model familiar to most educators: mission statement, goals (graduation or performance standards), curriculum (content standards), methodology, and, finally, assessment.

Bill and Loretta Heuer   Re: Tad Heuer
Heueristics
164 Norfolk Street
Holliston, MA 01746
(508) 555-1436

Homeschool Profile

Thirteen years ago when we decided not to enroll our son in preschool, we called our home alternative *La Famille*. The name aptly described our educational philosophy. Since then our family, society, and technology have changed. We now consider our family's homeschool *Heueristics*, a play on the word "heuristic," learning through investigation, discovery and feedback.

We define learning neither as input (course content and time on task) nor output (observable products or behaviors) but as a dynamic, flexible relationship of both. We believe learning is constructed, iterative, recursive . . . heuristic.

In order to be graduated from our home education program, we expect our children to display levels of competence through excellence in classical and contemporary learning: literature, oral and written communication, mathematics, U.S. and European history, cultural studies, political science, theology, the behavioral sciences, the natural sciences, computer science, creative self-expression in the arts, critical/analytical thinking, and personal/academic management.

While we expect a level of mastery in these areas, we acknowledge that the content and sequence of our children's learning may differ from that found in more traditional settings.

continues

In creating individualized educational plans for our children we have utilized not only home tutorials and self-directed learning, but also classes at the local high school, coursework at a nearby college, internships, travel, computer assisted learning, individual and group instruction in the performing arts, museum studies, and multiage experiences.

In general, evaluation has been based on performance assessments rather than on conventional testing. While grades are available for formal coursework, the children also have portfolios that document other learning experiences. Included in these are anecdotal reports and narratives, artifacts that document and display learning, and reflective self-assessments.

Signed,

Bill and Loretta Heuer

RESUME

By the time a college official has read this deeply into the application packet, he or she should have a good idea of the type of student you are. So, is a resume needed? Take a look at the items you have already assembled. Did you use a resume format somewhere already? Perhaps to showcase your extra- or cocurricular activities? Did you decide to use a resume format for your transcript? Has your work experience already been fully discussed in your essay? In other words, what will a formal resume add besides one more sheet of paper?

A separate resume will be useful only when it presents information that can strengthen your candidacy and for which there was no other place in the packet. For example, suppose you intend to major in shoreline ecology at college, and in the past six years you acquired most of your scientific learning by traveling extensively with your family from Maine to the Florida Keys, camping in National Parks, and visiting local aquariums. A travel resume would be an ideal supplement to add verification and credibility to your interest. Similarly, if you started and are running a home-based business, a copy of your professional resume would add a nice touch to your application packet. However, rather than thinking of these as stand-alone resumes, consider how they might be included as part of your portfolio.

Again, do not include a resume simply to add more bulk to your folder. Colleges won't necessarily be expecting one, and they won't miss it if it's not there. The rule of thumb: If it enhances you, by all means use it. If it is simply repeating in short form what has been said better elsewhere, consider leaving it out.

WAIT, THEN MAIL IT; MAIL IT AND WAIT

Whew! Time to catch your breath! But don't go to the post office just yet. Ideally, once an application packet is complete, you should set it aside for a several days. During that time, give it to a reader who will critique it for you. You want to choose a person who is both caring and ruthlessly honest. Your reader can use the criteria from the two rubrics given earlier in this chapter, but you especially want feedback regarding:

- Clarity

- Credibility of documentation

- Organization

- Tone

- Grammar, syntax, and spelling errors that the computer missed

TIME TO DECIDE

Admissions committees usually will accept you or reject you based on a five to ten minute discussion of your folder's contents. How does this affect the way you have constructed your packet as your parallel self?

Once you've incorporated your reader's suggestions, I suggest that you photocopy each and every piece of paper in the packet. In fact, if you are applying to several colleges it is wise to photocopy in bulk all the pieces that are going to be sent to more than one college. It is wearisome to locate originals for another application packet and duplicate them one by one later. While much of your written work probably resides on your hard drive or individual diskettes, it is often easier and more practical to pull a hard copy from a file folder whenever you need a particular document for reference or follow-up.

EVALUATE EACH PIECE

First, look at every individual artifact. Then assess your portfolio overall. Ask yourself:

- Does it sound like me?

- Does it sound like what I know about this particular school?

- How credible is this piece of documentation?

- How clear is it?

- Can anything be misinterpreted or misunderstood?

- Is every word spelled correctly?

- Are all the required pieces included?

- Have I followed the suggestions of my advocate?

When you finally are ready to let the packet go, do one last run-through. Check and double-check to make sure that:

- All required submissions are included
- You have at least one copy of everything you're sending away

Finally, rather than writing simply "Admissions Office" on your envelope, address your packet to the specific staff member who has been your contact throughout the application process. Remember to *check the spelling of his or her name* one last time! It is a difficult task, handing that manila envelope across the counter to the postal clerk. You've put so much time, energy, and attention to detail into that packet—that parallel self you've created. But remember, all that effort wasn't just for *them*. Look at what *you've* discovered about yourself in the process!

APPENDIX A

A Portfolio and
Transcript Sampler

This section contains the tables of contents from sample portfolios as well as actual transcripts similar to those discussed earlier in this book. Read through each example, noting the scope and variety of artifacts and information that each one contains.

PORTFOLIOS

The following table of contents samples are provided to give you an overview of each portfolio style.

TRAIT-BASED PORTFOLIO

Here you are presenting "evidence that shows . . ." a particular trait or level of competency. In this case, the trait is responsibility, but others that you might want to display, especially for an employer or a volunteer coordinator, could be teamwork, leadership, organization, tolerance, or creativity. Your goal is to take a trait, which is intangible, and find evidence that shows you possess that particular quality.

This list of artifacts relates to my son Jed's responsible management and customer service for a 30-customer newspaper route.

Responsibility

- Letter from District Manager Donna Hendricks complimenting me on dealing with delinquent customers

- Spreadsheets for the past two months showing accounting practices

- Thank-you note from a satisfied customer

- *Middlesex News Carrier Newsletter* showing my being named Carrier of the Month

- Picture of me in the January 6 blizzard ready to deliver my papers

- *Middlesex News* clipping thanking carriers for delivery during the storm

- Customer survey I developed to show satisfaction for: promptness, friendly service, always delivering a dry paper, always delivering it where they want it

- Route list from the start showing 18 customers, one from now showing that the route grew to 30 customers

SHOWCASE PORTFOLIO

Showcase portfolios give you a place to show off your best work. Especially appropriate when reporting to your school system, they are also used in other high-stakes situations such as applying for a job or college admission. This is the place to show polished work, not rough drafts or work in progress. Remember, you are not bound to show only your most recent work. Even if you are presenting your portfolio at the end of the school year, its artifacts need not be end-of-the-year work. Showcase your *best* work, regardless of when it was completed.

The following artifacts are an eclectic mix and display samples of best work from several curricular areas. Your showcase portfolio, however, could be built around a single theme—best work in mathematics, for example.

11th Grade Showcase

Poetry

- Poem selected from each chapter of the anthology, *Western Wind*

- Creative writing from the project, *Poetry, People and Plagues*

- Clipping from *The Middlesex News*: Jed's presentation at a poetry reading

- Lyrics and audiotape of Jed's song, "Christmas Theory"

- William Blake's "Tyger" project: websites, Blake's painting, Jed's painting

Algebra 2

- Work samples: quadratic equations and related graphs

- Annotated texts

US History: Bill of Rights

- Second Amendment project: articles displaying range of views on gun ownership, gun control

Fine Arts: Photography

- Transcript from Massachusetts College of Art

- Work samples: landscape, portrait, still life

Fine Arts: Figure Drawing

- Letter from instructor

- Work samples: charcoal, pastel, pencil drawings

Health and Physical Education

- CPR certificate

- Course outline and verification letter from yoga instructor

THEMATIC PORTFOLIO

These portfolios contain artifacts that come from different academic subject areas but share a common theme. Since themes tend to cross the boundaries between academic disciplines, these portfolios are considered interdisciplinary in nature. In order to make sure your theme is clear to the reviewer, your annotations should indicate the artifacts' rationale for inclusion and their connection to one another.

This portfolio shows how reading, drama, film, song, and museum visits were used to link literature and history. This selection focuses only on one history play and one comedy even though several more plays were read, watched, discussed, and written about during the unit.

Shakespearean Drama, British History

- Family tree for Houses of Lancaster and York

- *Richard III,* acting edition of the play with stage directions

- *Boston Globe* review of the film *Looking For Richard*

- Revised, edited, and proofread critique of the three film versions of *Richard III*

- First draft of essay on Henry VIII and the problem of succession

- Receipt for the videos, *The Six Wives of Henry VIII*

- Annotated book, *Men and Women in Revolution and War 1600–1815*

- Playbill: *The Complete Works of William Shakespeare, (Abridged)*

- Written materials from the Folger Shakespeare Library, Washington D.C.

- Performance schedule for Shakespeare's 433rd birthday at the Folger Library

- A list of Elizabethan compliments and insults

- Excerpt from *A Midsummer Night's Dream* used for Spontaneous Shakespeare, an audience participation activity

- Audiotape of the Broadside Band's, *Songs and Dances from Shakespeare*

SKILL-BASED PORTFOLIO

Your skill-based portfolio might focus on writing, public speaking, problem solving, technology use, the visual and performing arts, athletics, or unique manual skills. Consider using technology to show your skill in action if your skill does not result in a tangible product. Your artifacts might indicate mastery, but they also can be used to establish your novice baseline. Used this way, a skill-based portfolio can show growth over time when you review it at some point in the future.

This portfolio was developed to show not only my son's current skill level as a fiddler, but the level of performance he was aspiring to. It displays the various ways he acquired knowledge about Celtic music and includes a written evaluation from his teacher. This was included to inform a reviewer about aspects of Tad's musicianship that were not evident from the taped performance pieces that were chosen for this particular portfolio.

Celtic Music

- Tape of Tad's fiddle music and that of a master fiddler playing the same pieces

- Transcript of Tad's interview with the master fiddler

- Evaluation letter from Tad's music teacher

- Selection of sheet music that indicates both early and current skill levels

- Calendar showing attendance at Celtic music events

- Autographed programs from festivals and events

- Discography of music Tad listened to and/or had purchased for his collection

---

PROJECT PORTFOLIO

Because a portfolio's collection of artifacts can show how a project moves from start to finish, it is an ideal tool for documenting project-based learning. Since projects are often publicly presented, these portfolios may be filled with photos, video clips, publicity items, and newspaper articles. These types of artifacts may be difficult to find after the project is over, so make sure you save and archive artifacts every step of the way.

Both individual and group projects can be shaped into a portfolio. For this portfolio, which refers to acting in a stage play, the annotations and reflections should indicate the level of participation.

The Diary of Anne Frank

- Annotated script of the play

- Calendar of rehearsal dates

- Photo of set under construction

- Brochure and "passport" from the Holocaust Museum, Washington, D.C.

- Photo of Jed with the show's consultant, Holocaust survivor Misha Defonseca

- Dust jacket from *Misha: A Mémoire of the Holocaust Years*, which was read by all cast members

- Newspaper article previewing the play

- Publicity photo of Jed in costume

- Poster advertising the play

- Program

- Video clip of one of Jed's scenes

- Written reflection: how acting in this particular show affected him

---

TRANSCRIPTS

The following pages contain five different transcripts, all based on the same information: my son Tad's three years of high school homeschooling, after which we considered him graduated from our homeschool program. The transcripts range from cool and detached to warm and witty.

CARNEGIE UNIT TRANSCRIPT

This is a familiar-looking Carnegie unit transcript with grades, course names, and credits earned. No explanation of course content is given. The transcript asks the reader to assume what was learned based on the titles of the courses. Rather than being organized chronologically as is usual, this version is arranged thematically according to the basic high school subject divisions: English, Mathematics, Social Studies, Science, Arts, Physical Education, and Business electives. This was done to show a progression of learning in each of the subject areas and to display the even distribution of Tad's learning.

Transcript For: Thaddeus Alan Heuer   Year of Graduation: 1993   Credits: 22.25

Grade   Course   Carnegie Credits

ENGLISH: 4.5 CREDITS

Grade	Course	Credits	Grade	Course	Credits
A	117 Freshman English	1.0	A	*†132 College Freshman English (Syracuse University: 6 credits)	1.0
A	127 Sophomore English	1.0			
A	177 Junior English	1.0			
A	153 Twentieth Century Authors	.5			

SOCIAL STUDIES: 4.5 CREDITS

Grade	Course	Credits	Grade	Course	Credits
A	200 Survey of World Civilization	1.0	A	241 World Geography	.5
A	†212 U.S. History, 1865–present (Framingham State College: 4 credits)	1.0	A	242 Global Studies	.5
			A	243 World Perspectives	.5
			A	247 U.S. Government	.5
A+	*229 Modern European History	.5			

SCIENCE : 3.5 CREDITS

Grade	Course	Credits	Grade	Course	Credits
A	* Introduction to Physical Science	NC	A	†314 Accelerated Biology (Framingham State College: 4 credits)	1.0
A	*306 Physical Science II	1.0			
			A	*324 Accelerated Chemistry	1.0
			A	*334 Accelerated Physics	.5

MATHEMATICS: 3 CREDITS

Grade	Course	Credits	Grade	Course	Credits
A–	416 Accelerated Algebra	1.0	B+	434 Geometry	1.0
B+	426 Algebra II	1.0			

FOREIGN LANGUAGE: 1 CREDIT

Grade	Course	Credits
A	972 Latin I	1.0

BUSINESS AND COMMUNICATIONS: 1.5 CREDITS

Grade	Course	Credits	Grade	Course	Credits
A	605 Word Processing	.5	A	831 Public Speaking	.5
A	608 Advanced Word Processing	.5			

MUSIC: 3 CREDITS

Grade	Course	Credits	Grade	Course	Credits
A	827 History of Music	1.0	A	*852 Chamber Orchestra (2 years @ .5 credit)	1.0
A	861 Music Theory/Composition I	1.0			

HEALTH/PHYSICAL EDUCATION: 1.25 CREDITS

Grade	Course	Credits	Grade	Course	Credits
A	901, 902, 905, 906 Physical Education	1.0	P	*913 CPR	NC
			P	914 Making Choices	NC
A	*911 Health Education	.25			

* Course taken at Holliston High School
† Course taken for college credit
NC course taken for no credit
P Course given Pass/Fail

CONTENTS STANDARD OR COURSE EQUIVALENCY TRANSCRIPT

This is a contents standard or course equivalency transcript that aligns homeschool learning with traditional high school courses. The content of each course, whether unschooled at home or taken in a more formal setting, is described so that the reader has a general idea of the scope of material covered. An artifact available for review is noted for each entry. Grades and credits are also given.

Content Standards: Course Equivalency

We believe that Tad has met standards for competency through mastery in the following areas which are presented as courses in the Holliston High School Program of Studies, 1993–1994. Other courses for which Holliston does not appear to have an equivalent this year are noted at the end. A (*) signifies a course taken at Holliston High School; a (+) denotes an equivalent course taken at Framingham State College.

Each course title is followed by a representative artifact that might be used to help document Tad's off-campus learning.

English Equivalent: 4.5 credits

117 Freshman English (1 cr)

Year-end anecdotal report on literature and composition submitted to S. Kadra for review.

127 Sophomore English (1 cr)

Reports written on Alan Paton's *Cry the Beloved Country* and Edith Wharton's *Ethan Frome*.

177 Junior English: Writing and Literature Requirement: Advanced Writing/Survey of English Literature (1 cr)

Essay on term limits published in *The Middlesex News*.

Ten-page parody newsletter based on Shakespeare's *Macbeth*.

153 Twentieth Century Authors (.5 cr) (material covered during grades 9, 10, 11)

Reports written on Sinclair Lewis' *Main Street*, F. Scott Fitzgerald's *The Great Gatsby,* and Ernest Hemingway's *The Sun Also Rises.*

*132 College Freshman English (1 cr)

Holliston High School/Syracuse University course taught by S. Kadra. First semester grade: A-; Second semester grade: pending.

<u>Social Studies Equivalent: 4.5 credits</u>

200 Survey of World Civilization (1 cr)

Answers to essay questions on the fall of Rome, medieval life, and the Reformation.

+212 Survey U.S. History, 1865-present (1 cr)

Framingham State College course, taught by Dr. Grozier. Grade for course: A

*229 Modern European History (.5 cr)

Holliston High School course, taught by L. Provencher. Grade for course: A+

241 World Geography (.5 cr)

A variety of updated atlases (political, environmental, and sociological) and a packet of recent news articles on physical and political geography on which Tad can be interviewed.

242 Global Studies (.5 cr)

Materials packet containing articles on the politics, history, economy, religions, and cultural expressions of various nation states on which Tad can be interviewed.

243 World Perspectives (.5 cr)

Three years of *Scholastic Update,* a secondary school magazine dealing with domestic and international current events on which Tad can be interviewed.

Documentation of family membership in organizations such as Greenpeace (hazardous waste), Technoserve (poverty and third world agricultural development), Amnesty International (human rights), and Bread for the World (hunger) that take an international perspective on contemporary issues.

continues

247 U.S. Government (.5 cr)

Essay describing Tad's summer internship with Rep. Barbara Gardner.

Science Equivalent: 3.5 credits

* Introduction to Physical Science (NC)

Holliston High School course, taught by D. Hardy. Grade for course: A

*306 Physical Science II (1 cr)

Holliston High School course, taught by P. Amati. Grade for course: A

+314 Accelerated Biology (1 cr)

Framingham State College course, taught by Dr. Barklow. Grade for course: A

*324 Accelerated Chemistry (1 cr)

Holliston High School course, taught by G. Page. Grade for course: A

*334 Accelerated Physics (.5 cr)

Holliston High School course, taught by J. Maloof. First semester grade: A

Mathematics Equivalent: 4 credits

401 Consumer Mathematics (1 cr)

Copy of Tad's checkbook ledger showing management of discretionary purchases, instructional costs, and business expenses.

416 Accelerated Algebra (1 cr)

Performance level accepted as a prerequisite for Holliston High School science courses.

426 Algebra II (1 cr)

Performance level accepted as a prerequisite for Holliston High School science courses.

434 Geometry (1 cr)

Text, notebooks of problem sets.

SAT score of 640 in Math (88th percentile).

Foreign Language Equivalent: 1 credit

972 Latin I (1 cr)

Copy of an end-of-the-year translation from Latin to English.

Business Equivalent: 1 credit

605 Word Processing (.5 cr)

Copies of content area coursework written with Professional Write software.

608 Information Management (.5 cr)

Copy of spreadsheet done on Microsoft Excel.

Communications Equivalent: .5 credit

831 Public Speaking (.5 cr)

Text of speech given to Confirmation candidates at St. Mary's. Letter from program coordinator commenting on his presentation.

Music Equivalent: 3 credits

827 History of Music (1 cr)

Discography of personal recordings from Medieval, Renaissance, Baroque, Classical, Romantic, and Contemporary periods used for home listening.

861 Music Theory/Composition I (1 cr)

Written and taped copies of Tad's Irish fiddle compositions.

Performance level of sight reading accepted as prerequisite for New England Conservatory Youth Symphony.

continues

*852 Chamber Orchestra (2 years at .5 cr = 1 cr)

Holliston High School course, taught by A. Finstein.
Grade for each year: A

Physical Education Equivalent: 1 credit

901, 902, 905, 906 Physical Education

Sailing. Since neither of Tad's parents sail, they
arranged for him to take several seasons of sailing
instruction.

Skiing. Since neither of Tad's parents ski, they
arranged for him to take several seasons of skiing
instruction.

Basketball Officiating and Coaching. Tad attended the
IAABO (International Association of Approved Basketball
Officials) course that is used to prepare officials for
certification. Verification of Tad's refereeing experience and an evaluation of his performance can be made
by D. McCann, director of referees for Holliston CYO
Basketball.

Baseball Officiating. Copy of Tad's essay on the unique
problems of teenage umpires. Verification of Tad's
umpiring experience and an evaluation of his performance can be made by Holliston Youth Baseball directors
of umpires, L. Mosher and B. Tuohey.

Health Education Equivalent: .25 credit

*911 Health Education (.25 cr)

Holliston High School course, taught by P. Rowles.
Grade for course: A

*913 CPR (NC)

Holliston High School course, taught by P. Rowles.
Grade for course: P

Making Choices (NC)

Verification by health professionals and civic leaders
that Tad has displayed wise individual and social decision-making with regard to contemporary issues.

Total Equivalent Credits: 23.25

Addenda:

Although not listed in the 1993–1994 program of studies, other courses that may have been offered in previous years and for which artifacts are available are:

Survey of U.S. History (1620–1850)

United States History: The Civil War

World War II: The European Theater and the Holocaust

Chamber Orchestra

PERFORMANCE STANDARDS TRANSCRIPT

This is a performance standards transcript that describes our family's graduation criteria and how Tad demonstrated that he met them. Rather than being based on numerical grades, time spent learning a subject, or other *quantitative* ways to assess learning, this transcript takes a *qualitative* approach. Evaluation was based on informal observation of Tad's skill in applying what he had learned. No grades were given. Instead, he needed to show that he could perform the tasks at what we determined to be a level of competency through mastery.

Performance Standards Transcript

We have observed that Tad can:

- Read, analyze, discuss, and write about significant literary works, both historical and contemporary

- Use correct grammar in oral and written presentations

- Write well-structured expository and persuasive essays

- Write a short story

- Conduct an interview

- Write clear and succinct business letters, memoranda, and press releases

- Defend his views on various subjects, contemporary and historical

- Discuss important American documents

- Deliver prepared and extemporaneous oral presentations

- Discuss current events in their historical and intellectual contexts

- Display and utilize cultural, historic, scientific, and mathematical literacy

- Write a scientific research paper

- Devise, execute, and evaluate a scientific project and present the results in writing

- Apply mathematical concepts in the physical and social sciences

- Utilize arithmetic, geometry, statistics, economics, and probability in daily life

- Earn and manage discretionary funds

- Use computer technology for word processing, spread-sheets, databases, simulations, instruction, research, and interactive communication

- Maintain physical fitness through regular exercise, sound nutrition, and adherence to principles of healthy living

- Cycle, swim, ski, and sail

- Officiate and coach youth basketball

- Officiate youth baseball

- Demonstrate an advanced skill in the performing arts

- Perform community service projects

- Participate in the political life of the community

- Complete a supervised internship

- Complete a comprehensive and reflective Exit Exhibition

RESUME TRANSCRIPT

Below is a resume transcript that includes not only course names but extra- and cocurricular activities. No formal descriptions of course content are included, but each subject area is expanded by describing the type of allied activities in which Tad participated. This transcript explains how he spent time learning outside the home and what his interests were. It effectively portrays the breadth of his homeschool learning and offers insights into his personality.

```
                        TAD HEUER
                   164 NORFOLK STREET
                   HOLLISTON, MA 01746
                     (508) 555-1436
```

English

1989-94   Comprehensive American and World Literature

1990-92   Town Editor, Holliston High School Newspaper

1993   Short story submitted to *Merlyn's Pen*, request-
               ed to revise for publication

1993   Syracuse University Project Advance, Freshman
               English: Writing Studio (3 semester credits,
               course grade A-)

1994   Syracuse University Project Advance, Freshman
               English: Reading and Interpretation: From
               Language to Discourse (3 semester credits,
               course in progress)

Sciences

1990-91   Introduction to Physical Science (course
               grade: A)

1991-92   Physical Science II (course grade: A)

1992-93   Accelerated Chemistry, papers written on quan-
               tum electrodynamics and nuclear magnetic reso-
               nance (course grade: A)

1993-94   Accelerated Physics (course in progress)

1993   Framingham State College, General Biology (4
               semester credits, course grade: A)

Mathematics, Computers, Economics, Business

1990-91   Algebra I

1991-92   Algebra II

1992-93   Geometry

1994-   Trigonometry

1990-   Keyboarding, word processing, spreadsheet and
               database use, beginning BASIC programming

1987-   Personal Finance Management: savings and
               checking

1987-   Management of a 35-customer newspaper route

Social Studies

1988-93   Integrated World Civilization, American
               History, Contemporary Events

1992   Modern European History (Course grade: A)

1993   Aide to Massachusetts State Representative
               Barbara Gardner, D-8th Middlesex District

1993   Framingham State College, U.S. History: After
               Reconstruction (4 semester credits, course
               grade: A)

1992-93   First-person Revolutionary War presentations at
               elementary schools and historic sites

Language

1991-92   Latin

Music

1989-93   Member, Holliston High School Orchestra
               (violin)

1993-94   Member, New England Conservatory Youth Symphony
               Orchestra (viola)

continues

1992–93	Member, New England Conservatory Youth Repertory Orchestra (viola)
1990–91	Member, Performing Arts Youth Symphony Orchestra (violin)
1990–93	Member, Massachusetts Junior/Senior Central District Orchestra (violin)
1992–	Violin Soloist, St. Mary's Church, Holliston Public Library
1993	Principal Violinist, Holliston High School: "Fiddler on the Roof," Ashland Youth Theater: "The Boyfriend"
1993	Apprentice luthier, emphasis on stringed instrument repair
1991–	Drummer and Fifer, Tenth Massachusetts Regiment reenactment group
1992	Member, Boston Scottish Fiddle Society
1992–	Member, St. Mary's Adult Choir

Performing and Visual Arts

1990–93	Member, Holliston High School Drama Club
1991–92	Member, Ashland Youth Theater
1992	WMTW (Maine) Radio Internship
1986–93	Museum visits (Boston Museum of Fine Arts, Isabella Stewart Gardner Museum, Rodin Museum, Carnegie Institute, Smithsonian Museums, etc.)

Physical Education

1992–93	Letter, Holliston J.V. Basketball
1991	Assistant Coach, Holliston Grade 6 CYO Basketball Travel Team

1992	Passed IAABO Basketball Referee Test
1992–	Referee, Holliston CYO Basketball
1991–	Umpire, Holliston Little League
1991–	Member, Charles River Community Boat Club
1990	Red Cross Advanced Swimmer
1988–	Recreational Skiing
1992	Certified to administer CPR

Travel

1985–	Extensive travel in eastern U.S.
1989	Republic of Ireland
1990–91	Toronto and Montreal, Canada
1994	Sicily

Service

1992–93	Aide, Kindergarten religious education program
1986–92	Altarserver, St. Mary's Church
1993–	Eucharistic Minister, St. Mary's Church
1991	Historical Interpreter, Holliston Historical Society's 18th Century Program
1993	Audio Cataloger, Holliston Public Library
1989	Transcriber, Holliston Gravestone Documentation Project
1990–	Gardening work for neighborhood elderly

Reflective Transcript

The following is a reflective transcript, the centerpiece of Tad's Exit Exhibition. Constructed and written in the winter of his Junior year, it integrates knowledge, skills, critical analysis, and self-reflection, all with a sense of humor! Used as a transcript, it comes with a cover letter signed by myself and my husband as very proud parent-educators.

Bill and Loretta Heuer
Re: Tad Heuer
Heueristics
164 Norfolk Street
Holliston, MA 01746
(508) 555-1436

The following transcript is divided into three parts: Literature and Composition; Science and Mathematics; and History, Politics, and Social Science. Most of Tad's learning has been done at home; exceptions (courses taken either at our local high school or at a college) have been marked with an asterisk. Descriptions of these courses have been taken from school catalogs, and the grade earned in each is noted. Official transcripts from these institutions will be forwarded to your office.

The remainder of the transcript has been crafted collaboratively between Tad and ourselves. It reflects not only content covered, but also areas where mastery has been displayed. Our criterion for the inclusion of any item was Tad's being comfortable discussing the topic with only minimal review.

Because of the comprehensive, collaborative, and public nature of this transcript project, we consider it Tad's Exit Exhibition. Accordingly, we consider him to be graduated from our homeschool program.

Bill and Loretta Heuer

Literature, Composition, and Communication

* Writer's Studio (WRT 105). College freshman writing course in which daily journal writing, longer reflective essays, an ethnography, and a literary analysis were required. Peer critique and group discussion were important components of the process. (One-semester course taken through Syracuse University's SUPA extension program, 3 undergraduate credits. Course grade: A-)

* Reading and Interpretation: From Language to Discourse (ETS 141). An introduction to contemporary literary analysis. Class discussion and written reports focused on textual studies and the writings of critical theorists such as Saussure, Derrida, and Barthes. (One-semester course taken through Syracuse University's SUPA extension program, 3 undergraduate credits. Course grade: pending)

Creative and Practical Writing. A variety of writing experiences have been a component of my homeschool program: news and feature articles for the school newspaper, research and technical writing for science courses, and short stories for personal expression. Writing press releases and responses to constituents was part of my political internship.

Short Stories of the World. "Why did you write a novel?" "Because I didn't have time to write a short story." So goes a joke between two writers. The short story is indeed one of the most intricate forms of writing, fitting introduction, development, and conclusion into ten or twenty pages and still expressing a powerful moral theme. How this is done effectively was the focus of this course. I also was expected to identify each author's style and to draw parallels among various authors and stories. Writers studied included Hemingway, Saki, Chekov, Steinbeck, Henry, O'Flaherty, Conrad, DeMauppasant, Jackson, Bradbury, Poe, Kipling, and London.

Gothic and Dickensian Literature. Prosperity and penury, infatuation and enmity, richly textured characters and the immortal "dark and stormy night" are all combined masterfully to produce the Gothic era of literature. In this course, the writings of the Brontë sisters and Henry James were discussed, with emphasis on the use of extensive detail and secondary meanings. Charles Dickens' *A Tale of Two Cities*,

continues

Great Expectations, David Copperfield, A Christmas Carol,
and *Oliver Twist* were read, watched in performance, and
discussed.

Twentieth Century American Writers. A change in social values and customs at the beginning of the twentieth century
triggered a change in the style of writing that continues to
this day. Authors read for this course include Fitzgerald,
Lewis, Angelou, Hemingway, Wharton, and Steinbeck, each of
whom left a unique impression on the world of literature.

Shakespearean and Modern Drama. Plays read include *Macbeth,*
The Merchant of Venice, Romeo and Juliet, Twelfth Night,
Julius Caesar, Our Town, The Crucible, The Andersonville
Trial, and *A Raisin in the Sun.* Live performances and tele-
vised productions supplemented the readings. A project
related to each play was required.

The World Wars in Literature. In this course, works written
during and about the First and Second World Wars were read
and discussed. Contrasts between Allied and Axis/Central
authors were explored, and firsthand accounts in diaries,
journals, and newspapers were used. Some authors include:
Hersey, Remarque, Frank, Ten-Boom, Fitzgerald, Hemingway,
and Ryan.

Metaphors for Reality: Science Fiction. This course used the
writings of Shute, LeGuin, L'Engle, Tolkien, Azimov, and
Bradbury to explore why writers choose to work in this
genre. It also investigated how to understand and enjoy the
metaphoric and analogical meanings employed.

The Genre of Mystery and Horror. Humans have always relished
the chill that runs up the spine while reading scary stories. In this course, the works of E. A. Poe, A. C. Doyle,
Agatha Christie, Shirley Jackson, and Henry James were read.
Each author has a distinctive style, yet they all share a
common trait: the ability to frighten the reader while working the mind.

The Movie or the Book? For this course, we explored differences and similarities between written and cinematic versions of *A Tale of Two Cities, The Longest Day, Ethan Frome,*
Of Mice and Men, I Am the Cheese, etc. Focus was on the
director's interpretation of the book and the effectiveness
of the presentation.

Young Adults in Literature. Often merely vehicles for larger themes or introducing older characters, young adults rarely play the leading roles in major works. In this course, I read works which feature adolescents, their problems, and their fears. Authors include Golding, Knowles, Cormier, Townsend, Salinger, and Gunther. The ability of adults to write with an adolescent voice was explored, as well as the reasons authors use teenager characters instead of adults to communicate ideas.

International Children's Literature. Works written for children must get their message across simply yet powerfully. This course discussed children's books from the United States, Ireland, France, and Russia. Cultural differences in writing style were discussed as were stories that crossed national boundaries. Other topics included criteria for writing for a young audience, the role of illustrations, and metaphor in children's literature.

History, Politics, and Social Science

World Civilizations. Survey course covering ancient Egypt and Greece, Medieval and Renaissance Europe, the Reformation, the Aztecs, the age of Exploration, and the Enlightenment.

The Romans. Course constructed from the cultural segment of Latin language study. Learning included the social, scientific, military, political, and legal aspects of Roman culture.

British History. Survey course covering the breakdown of the Roman Empire, the Norman invasion, the Magna Carta, the parliamentary system, and the monarchy through the reign of William and Mary.

* Topics in Modern European History. Mastery of survey course material covering the French Revolution, the Age of Napoleon and the Congress of Vienna, and World War I. (One-semester course taken at Holliston High School. Grade for course: A+)

United States History: Colonial, Revolutionary, and Federal Periods. Interdisciplinary course covering both political and social history. Constructed from textbook material, readings in literature and nonfiction, participation in Revolutionary War reenactments, and visits to historic sites in the New England and Mid-Atlantic states.

United States History: The Civil War. This course investigated remote and immediate causes of the war, the economic environment, the rise of the abolitionists, pivotal political events, and the impact of the war on everyday life. Discussions of military strategy were supplemented by visits to Gettysburg, Manassas, Fredericksburg, and Petersburg. The war in the West, the use of naval warfare, and an overview of Reconstruction were also presented.

* United States History: 1870–present. Content focused on industrialization, the rise of trade unions, immigration, World War I, the Great Depression, World War II, and the Korean and Vietnamese conflicts. (One-semester course taken at Framingham State College, 4 undergraduate credits. Grade for course: A)

World War II: The European Theater and the Holocaust. Course constructed from independent study of texts, nonfiction, literature, news accounts, film footage, museum visits, first-person sources, interviews with emigrants and veterans, etc. Learning covered military, political, social, and religious areas.

Russian/Soviet History and Civilization. A survey course covering Russian humanities and politics. The humanities segment focused on writers, artisans, and composers, concluding with a study of everyday life in the former USSR using contemporary young adult literature. The political portion traced Russian history from Peter the Great to the overthrow of Nicholas II during the Bolshevik Revolution. The influence of Marx, Engels, Lenin, and Stalin on world affairs from 1917 to 1945 was discussed. Also included were postwar issues such as the Cold War, the space race, the Cuban Missile Crisis, and the recent collapse of the Soviet Union/Eastern Bloc.

Ireland: An Interdisciplinary Survey. Course material mastered includes Irish pre-history, geography, and natural resources; Celtic art and music; contemporary Irish short stories; and Irish-British relations from the sixteenth century to the present.

Italy: An Interdisciplinary Survey. Material covered includes Italian history since unification; current political issues; topography; vulcanism; Italian music, dance, cuisine, and cultural customs; emigration; religion; and an introduction to the Italian language. Visits to Greco-Roman ruins, archaeological sites, and prehistoric catacombs were also included.

U.S. Constitution. Working knowledge of the document acquired by reading the Constitution and its amendments and by studying its application in selected court cases from both the nineteenth and twentieth centuries.

Contemporary American Issues: Foreign and Domestic. A family discussion course constructed daily from print and electronic media with attention given to relationships among current issues. Critique of the media's selection and presentation of material was expected. Recent topics include American military involvement abroad, free trade and emerging isolationism,

continues

feminist perspectives on social issues, race relations, gun control, national health care, and unemployment.

Practical Politics: Domestic and Foreign. Material covered state and federal governmental systems and the American electoral process. An internship with a legislator at the Massachusetts State House was also a component. Foreign governmental systems and their effect on historical events were also examined, and participation at a week-long Washington Workshop Seminar was included.

From Portraits to Snapshots: Life in America, Seventeenth Century to the Present. This course focused on everyday life in America rather than on military and political issues. Materials included *American Heritage* magazine, eyewitness accounts, diaries, newspaper articles, art, music, and visits to living history sites such as Sturbridge Village, Plimoth Plantation, Strawbery Banke, Williamsburg, the Lowell and Fall River mills, and forts on the Appalachian frontier. Town records were used to research local history.

The Modern American Educational System. This course utilized newspaper and magazine articles, books, and essays written about the past and current state of American education. Different types of systems (public, private, religious, and alternative) were analyzed. The writings of Holt, Sizer, Adler, Llywellyn, Hailey, Colfax, and Owen were discussed. The authors' novel solutions and possible biases were explored. One project was reviewing textbooks from the past twenty years to investigate changes in the style, social attitudes, and information threshold of the American educational system.

Science and Mathematics

* Introduction to Physical Science. IPS is a laboratory-oriented course in which 65 percent of the time is spent performing laboratory experiments. In this course, students acquire skills in setting up and carrying out experiments, collecting and analyzing data, and drawing conclusions from experiences. Mastery of skills and concepts is derived through the inquiry approach and mastery is measured by the application of what is learned through experimentation and word problems. Students must be able to demonstrate skills in reading and the application of mathematics. (Two-semester course taken at Holliston High School. Grade for course: A)

* Physical Science II. An inquiry-approach, lab-oriented course aimed at establishing a sound foundation for what energy is, the various forms of energy, and the various laws dealing with energy, with the ultimate goal being their immediate application to chemistry, biology, and physics. The student will enhance his skills at setting up, carrying out, and analyzing experiments. The degree of mastery of concepts and skills learned in this course will be measured by application of what is learned through experimentation and the solution of copious word problems. The student must be able to demonstrate skills in reading and the application of mathematical skills and graphing techniques. (Two-semester course taken at Holliston High School. Grade for course: A)

* Accelerated Chemistry. This course is laboratory oriented. Concepts will be learned through laboratory activities, lectures, demonstrations, and discussions. The atmosphere is directed toward independent student activity which will require student initiative and self-motivation. Students will be required to conduct experiments, collect and interpret data, and draw conclusions in formal laboratory reports. The nature of the subject matter includes behavior of atoms, behavior of substances in solutions, behavior of nuclear particles, and the family of elements. (Two-semester course taken at Holliston High School. Grade for course: A)

* Accelerated Physics. The major topics of the course include a study of motion and its causes, gravitational force, work, and energy in its various forms. The student will study these topics in depth through an approach utilizing laboratory

continues

investigations, class lecture, and group discussion of problems. Mathematical, graphic, and descriptive interpretation of collected data will receive heavy emphasis in this course. It is recommended for students who have a strong interest in science-related fields and who been successful in mathematics. (First semester of course taken at Holliston High School. Grade at end of semester: A)

* Biological Concepts. This approach to the study of life will emphasize how conceptual thinking is involved in understanding the problems encountered in each of four major areas of biology. These will include evolution and origin of life, cellular processes and genetics, environmental and behavioral science, and basic physiological systems. The interrelationship of these areas and their effects on human biology will be stressed. (One-semester course taken at Framingham State College, 4 undergraduate credits. Grade for course: A)

Earth and Environmental Science. Course constructed from a variety of resources and experiences. Content included the study of rocks, metals, and minerals; location of mineral resources; radioactive dating; fossil records; the water cycle; water and wind erosion; stream and riverbed geology; geothermal energy; glaciers; earthquakes; volcanoes; meteorology; and ecological concerns.

Oceanography. Course constructed from a variety of resources and experiences. Physical aspects of the oceans such as plate tectonics, Ewing cores, ocean floor geography, and mapping techniques were covered. Materials from the JASON Project, sponsored by Hole Oceanographic Institution under Dr. Robert Ballard, were used. Content covered Lake Ontario shipwrecks, sea life, and underwater volcanoes in the Mediterranean, and the ecology of the Galapagos Islands. In-depth studies of the *Titanic, Bismarck,* and *Isis* shipwrecks were also included. Technological aspects of oceanography such as sonar, satellites, depth finding, and reading oceanographic charts were studied. Visits to marine science museums and aquariums emphasized the aquatic food chain and the diversity of life in both fresh and salt water. Several whale watches and follow-up studies were also included in the curriculum.

Sequential Mathematics. Material covered a college prepara-
tory algebra (I and II) and geometry curricula during a
three-year span. Emphasis was on the concept of proof,
approaches to problem solving, the application of mathematics in real-life situations, and the relationship between
algebra and geometry. Topics in algebra included linear and
quadratic equations; circles, ellipses and parabolas; poly-
nomials; series and the binomial formula; and the concept of
functions. Graphing was an important component of the program. Geometry units covered polygons and circles, their
transformation and measurement; three-dimensional figures and
their measurement; coordinate geometry; and an introduction
to vectors and trigonometry. The basic texts for the program
were from Scott-Foresman's University of Chicago School
Mathematics Project series. (Mastery of concepts and material suggests a strong B+ performance.)

Lateral Mathematics. Content in this area included the history of mathematics; geometric and arithmetic patterns (such
as the Fibonacci sequence and the golden rectangle); mathematics in art and nature; logic; statistics and probability;
business, economics, consumerism, and the stock market; puzzles; and recreational mathematics.

Applied Mathematics. This was not a course in the traditional sense, but rather an amalgamation of many mathematical
concepts. Activities included learning to use a graphing
calculator, completing 1040 federal tax forms, keeping
financial records on investments and savings, controlling
the financial records of a forty-customer newspaper route,
learning to use computer spreadsheets and databases, applying sequential mathematics to my chemistry and physics
courses (mastery of content in Algebra I, Algebra II, and
Geometry was a prerequisite for taking these courses), and
integrating tempi, rhythms, and time signatures when performing, interpreting, and composing music.

APPENDIX B

The Discovery
Process

The following worksheets are designed to help you mine your memory and search your home for artifacts that are forgotten, hidden, or unnoticed. These lists can be used in several ways.

You might begin by reviewing List A, "Artifacts & Evidence," to discover the enormous variety of items that have portfolio potential. Are there five or ten items that seem connected and could indicate courses, classes, clusters of interest? Remember, a portfolio does not need to fit into a file folder. It may be housed in a box or built into a website, so stay alert for both tangible and virtual objects that you can use.

Alternatively, you can begin with List B, "Memory Archives," brainstorming about your interests and the things you have done during adolescence. For each course, class, trip, or work experience that you can recall, you will use an "Artifact Assessment Worksheet" to record the names of items you think are credible documentation of learning. You will note which supporting artifacts you already have, which you are able to acquire, and which you will need to create especially for your portfolio.

Or, start with List C, "Your Household Archives," checking out all the places and spaces where "stuff" and information are stored in your home. Which items are in plain sight but seen so often that they're overlooked? Which artifacts were stored away? Were they boxed up thematically, chronologically, or in no discernible order? Seeing these artifacts can jog your memory and give you fresh ideas about how you could use them to show the knowledge or skills you have acquired.

The idea is to make the three lists work together, using whatever sequence suits you and your organizational style. Ideally, your family should work together, too! Do this memory-mining project collaboratively so that family members have the opportunity to contribute their memories and ideas. The synergy that results from pooled information and shared recall can create connections and associations which never would have happened had you tried to do this project on your own.

LIST A—ARTIFACTS & EVIDENCE

The following master list is designed to challenge your assumptions of what can be included in a portfolio. It includes a wide variety of artifacts that can document your learning when developing a transcript, too. Some are two-dimensional items, others are three-dimensional and virtual ones. They are organized into the following general categories. Use them as a guide, but be open in your thinking. Could geometric constructions be considered artistic rather than academic?

Might tools used in a specific trade demonstrate competence? Keep the boundaries between categories flexible. You'll discover:

- Academic Evidence
- Art and Crafts (Two-Dimensional, Three-Dimensional, Digital)
- Evidence of Participation, Competency, Mastery
- General Artifacts
- Networking Resources
- Performance Materials
- Personal Interest Artifacts
- Personal Writing
- Trade Products

You also want to give each word on the list the widest definition possible. How broadly can you interpret "diagrams" or "awards"? Some artifacts, such as phone bills, may seem odd inclusions, but they can jog your memory about when you registered for a correspondence course. Or, they might testify that you made contact with a mentor on a weekly basis. Realize that you can be both a *collector* and a *creator* of these items. While you may subscribe to several newsletters, you may also write for one or publish a newsletter of your own.

As you become familiar with archival thinking, you will begin to see patterns in the artifacts you have, suggesting how you have organized and constructed your own learning. You will also begin to note which artifacts you *don't* have but need to acquire or create. When you get to this point, you will be ready to describe your learning in tangible ways that others outside your family can understand. You will be ready to shape the "stuff" of your life into a portfolio or transcript.

ARTIFACTS & EVIDENCE

* three-dimensional artifacts

\+ digital artifacts

† performances

Academic Evidence

annotated teacher's guide

bibliography

book reviews

calendars with academic plans noted

calendars with observational data entered

CD-ROMs bookmarked to specific areas

color photocopies of textbook covers

course catalogs

course descriptions

course outlines

course reading lists

curriculum outlines

data displayed in graphs, charts, tables

demonstration of skill

descriptive narratives

diagrams

experiments (written, diagrammed, or photographed)

field guides

geometric constructions

graded cover sheets from projects, experiments, etc.

graded tests

hand-sketched diagrams

index cards with research notes

Internet bookmark list

labeled science diagrams

list of research materials

math problem sets

music collections

photos of events in a learning process

photos of steps in a project

programmed learning texts

progress charts

project plans

rating sheets

records, cued tapes, and CDs (music, language, spoken word)

rubrics

science equipment

scientific sketches

self-study guides

standardized test results (unofficial copies)

tables of contents

videotapes (instructional, personal, tapes of televised programs and events)

workbooks

Art and Crafts (Two-Dimensional, Three-Dimensional, Digital)

calligraphy

carvings

ceramics

collages

computer animation

computer-assisted drafting and design

computer graphics

creative illustrations

digital art

jewelry

mixed media assemblages

models

observational drawings

paintings

prints

sculptures

thumbnail sketches

Evidence of Participation, Competency, Mastery

athletic scoring or time records

athletic trophies, patches, jackets

awards

badges received as an award

badges showing attendance at an event

celebration artifacts and mementos

certificates (legal, awards, participation, competency)

commendations

congratulatory notes

demonstration of skill

handout sheets from meetings, classes, lectures

invitations to events as member or as guest to provide service, speak, perform

lecture notes

lists mentioning you

membership cards

newspaper or magazine articles about you

pay stubs

photos of you with exhibits and installations

pins

recruiting letters

ribbons

scholarship offers

thank-you notes

General Artifacts

announcements

booklets

brochures

bulletins

diskettes with writing, e-mail, digital photographs, spreadsheets, databases

faxes

flyers

labels

memos

newsletters

pamphlets

questionnaires

schedules

spreadsheets

surveys

webpages

Personal Contacts and Networking Resources

address books and telephone directories

agenda and/or minutes of meetings

autographs

business cards

chat logs

descriptive and public relations brochures

directions for tasks

evaluations from supervisors

guidebooks

handbooks

instruction manuals

instructor feedback

interviews

letters of reference

membership lists

organizational charts

phone bills

phone logs

political campaign artifacts

resume

task lists

timesheets

transcript

Performance Materials

demonstration of skill

scripts

sheet music

text for speech

video- or audiotapes of your spoken or musical performances

Personal-Interest Artifacts

budgets, expenses, financial management information

Christmas letters

concert, film, and drama reviews

edibles

ethnic and religious artifacts

hobby collections: shells, stamps, dolls, jewelry, etc.

Internet bookmark list

itineraries

lyrics

magazines and periodicals that show specialized interest

maps

newspaper or magazine clippings: news, features, editorials, cartoons, ads, photographs

performance programs

photos

postcards

posters

souvenirs (bumper stickers, pencils, miniatures, mugs, T-shirts, caps)

receipts

recipes

ticket stubs

Personal Writing

academic logs

creative writing

diaries

e-mail dialogue and exchange

essays

first through final drafts

letters (personal, business, persuasive)

letters to the editor

outlines

poems

reflective journals (personal, writer's, academic)

sketchbook

travel logs

Trade Products

miniatures

product demonstrations

samples

tools

LIST B—YOUR MEMORY ARCHIVES

This is the place where you start to shape your homeschool experiences into themes for your portfolio and courses for your transcript. These worksheets can be duplicated and kept in a binder or folder to serve as a cumulative reference during your high school years.

Try to list at least a dozen entries for each of the categories below. While this may sound overwhelming at first, it really should be quite simple. You surely will be able to list three entries per category for each of the four years from 9th to 12th grade. Of course, some lists, like Books Read, Performances Attended, and Films Viewed, will probably be much longer. Or, perhaps your family travels a great deal or has gone on an extended trip to a large number of sites. Use whichever worksheets reflect the way you and your family homeschool.

- Academic Courses
- Interest-Driven Instruction
- Home-Designed Academic Courses
- Internships and Apprenticeships
- Cocurricular Activities
- Extracurricular Activities
- Areas of Expertise and Skill
- Areas of Self-Study and Research
- Projects, Performances, Exhibitions, Demonstrations
- Employment
- Volunteerism and Service Projects
- Travel
- Day Trips
- Health, Sports, and Physical Fitness
- Writing Samples
- Books Read
- Performances Attended
- Films Viewed

Once you have made an entry on one of these forms, begin its "Artifact Assessment Worksheet," the place where you will begin listing supporting artifacts that will go into your portfolio.

Patterns will begin to emerge within and across categories as you add to these lists, providing organizational structure for your portfolio and transcript. Dating the entries, especially if you are constructing these lists toward the end of adolescence, can act as a memory aid, calling to mind other activities you did at approximately the same time.

ACADEMIC COURSES

Think of any course or class you have taken in the traditional academic areas (English, Mathematics, Natural Sciences, Social Studies, World Languages, Fine Arts, Business, Technology). These may have been taken in a classroom, through a correspondence school, or via distance learning.

Date: _____

Instructor: _____

School: _____

Course title and description: _____

_____

Date: _____

Instructor: _____

School: _____

Course title and description: _____

_____

Date: _____

Instructor: _____

School: _____

Course title and description: _____

_____

Date: _____

Instructor: _____

School: _____

Course title and description: _____

_____

Date: _____

Instructor: _____

School: _____

Course title and description: _____

_____

ACADEMIC COURSES (cont.)

Date: _____

Instructor: _____

School: _____

Course title and description: _____

_____

Date: _____

Instructor: _____

School: _____

Course title and description: _____

_____

Date: _____

Instructor: _____

School: _____

Course title and description: _____

_____

Date: _____

Instructor: _____

School: _____

Course title and description: _____

_____

Date: _____

Instructor: _____

School: _____

Course title and description: _____

_____

INTEREST-DRIVEN INSTRUCTION

These are areas of intense personal interest where you sought instruction either in a group setting or as a tutorial. They usually do not easily fit into the traditional academic areas, perhaps because they are interdisciplinary and cut across several areas or because they go beyond the scope of traditional school subjects. Even if your instruction did not have a course title, give it one.

Date: _____

Instructor: _____

School: _____

Course title and description: _____

_____

Date: _____

Instructor: _____

School: _____

Course title and description: _____

_____

Date: _____

Instructor: _____

School: _____

Course title and description: _____

_____

Date: _____

Instructor: _____

School: _____

Course title and description: _____

_____

Date: _____

Instructor: _____

School: _____

Course title and description: _____

_____

INTEREST-DRIVEN INSTRUCTION (cont.)

Date: _____

Instructor: _____

School: _____

Course title and description: _____

_____

Date: _____

Instructor: _____

School: _____

Course title and description: _____

_____

Date: _____

Instructor: _____

School: _____

Course title and description: _____

_____

Date: _____

Instructor: _____

School: _____

Course title and description: _____

_____

Date: _____

Instructor: _____

School: _____

Course title and description: _____

_____

HOME-DESIGNED ACADEMIC COURSES

List any subcategory of the traditional academic areas you have explored in depth with a home-constructed curriculum—for example, 20th-Century American Poets (English), The Stock Market (Mathematics and Economics), Coastal Ecology (Natural Sciences), The First Amendment (Social Sciences). These "courses" may have developed over several years or been done during one semester. You should note one backup text or resource for each and give each a title.

Date: _____

Text or resource: _____

Course title and description: _____

_____

Date: _____

Text or resource: _____

Course title and description: _____

_____

Date: _____

Text or resource: _____

Course title and description: _____

_____

Date: _____

Text or resource: _____

Course title and description: _____

_____

Date: _____

Text or resource: _____

Course title and description: _____

_____

Date: _____

Text or resource: _____

Course title and description: _____

_____

HOME-DESIGNED ACADEMIC COURSES (cont.)

Date: _____

Text or resource: _____

Course title and description: _____

_____

Date: _____

Text or resource: _____

Course title and description: _____

_____

Date: _____

Text or resource: _____

Course title and description: _____

_____

Date: _____

Text or resource: _____

Course title and description: _____

_____

Date: _____

Text or resource: _____

Course title and description: _____

_____

Date: _____

Text or resource: _____

Course title and description: _____

_____

APPRENTICESHIPS & INTERNSHIPS

List any opportunity you have had to learn by apprenticeships (close observation of a professional doing his or her job, often with direct instruction in a specialized craft or trade) or by internships (learning about a career through participation in the workplace). Give yourself a job title that extends the term "apprentice" or "intern." Use the list of verbs from the *Department of Labor's Dictionary of Occupational Titles* (see Appendix C) to describe your on-the-job responsibilities.

Date: _____

Supervisor: _____

Skills learned: _____

Job title: _____

Description of duties: _____

_____

Date: _____

Supervisor: _____

Skills learned: _____

Job title: _____

Description of duties: _____

_____

Date: _____

Supervisor: _____

Skills learned: _____

Job title: _____

Description of duties: _____

_____

Date: _____

Supervisor: _____

Skills learned: _____

Job title: _____

Description of duties: _____

_____

APPRENTICESHIPS & INTERNSHIPS (cont.)

Date: _____

Supervisor: _____

Skills learned: _____

Job title: _____

Description of duties: _____

_____

Date: _____

Supervisor: _____

Skills learned: _____

Job title: _____

Description of duties: _____

_____

Date: _____

Supervisor: _____

Skills learned: _____

Job title: _____

Description of duties: _____

_____

Date: _____

Supervisor: _____

Skills learned: _____

Job title: _____

Description of duties: _____

_____

COCURRICULAR ACTIVITIES

These are activities that could be considered aligned with the major academic curriculum areas. List any hobby, club, or interest group that is even marginally connected to English, Mathematics, Natural Sciences, Social Sciences, World Languages, Fine Arts, or Technology.

Date: _____

Contact person: _____

Activity: _____

Knowledge explored or skills practiced: _____

_____

Date: _____

Contact person: _____

Activity: _____

Knowledge explored or skills practiced: _____

_____

Date: _____

Contact person: _____

Activity: _____

Knowledge explored or skills practiced: _____

_____

Date: _____

Contact person: _____

Activity: _____

Knowledge explored or skills practiced: _____

_____

Date: _____

Contact person: _____

Activity: _____

Knowledge explored or skills practiced: _____

_____

COCURRICULAR ACTIVITIES (cont.)

Date: _____

Contact person: _____

Activity: _____

Knowledge explored or skills practiced: _____

_____

Date: _____

Contact person: _____

Activity: _____

Knowledge explored or skills practiced: _____

_____

Date: _____

Contact person: _____

Activity: _____

Knowledge explored or skills practiced: _____

_____

Date: _____

Contact person: _____

Activity: _____

Knowledge explored or skills practiced: _____

_____

Date: _____

Contact person: _____

Activity: _____

Knowledge explored or skills practiced: _____

_____

EXTRACURRICULAR ACTIVITIES

Homeschoolers have the time and flexibility to pursue interests not closely related to the major curriculum areas. They may spend time doing activities as varied as quilting, wedding photography, or landscape design. These activities, which are often at the heart of homeschool learning, make homeschoolers the interesting, complex individuals colleges and employers value.

Date: _____

Contact person: _____

Activity: _____

Knowledge explored or skills practiced: _____

_____

Date: _____

Contact person: _____

Activity: _____

Knowledge explored or skills practiced: _____

_____

Date: _____

Contact person: _____

Activity: _____

Knowledge explored or skills practiced: _____

_____

Date: _____

Contact person: _____

Activity: _____

Knowledge explored or skills practiced: _____

_____

Date: _____

Contact person: _____

Activity: _____

Knowledge explored or skills practiced: _____

_____

EXTRACURRICULAR ACTIVITIES (cont.)

Date: _____

Contact person: _____

Activity: _____

Knowledge explored or skills practiced: _____

_____

Date: _____

Contact person: _____

Activity: _____

Knowledge explored or skills practiced: _____

_____

Date: _____

Contact person: _____

Activity: _____

Knowledge explored or skills practiced: _____

_____

Date: _____

Contact person: _____

Activity: _____

Knowledge explored or skills practiced: _____

_____

Date: _____

Contact person: _____

Activity: _____

Knowledge explored or skills practiced: _____

_____

AREAS OF EXPERTISE & SKILL

Homeschooling frequently allows adolescents to acquire a level of skill mastery usually reserved for adult practitioners. Often, the primary source for information and feedback is an outside mentor. Most areas of expertise and skill have their own specialized terminology that explains concepts, materials, and practices with great precision and can be used when developing transcripts and resumes.

Date: _____

Mentor: _____

Area of mastery: _____

Specialized vocabulary: _____

_____

Date: _____

Mentor: _____

Area of mastery: _____

Specialized vocabulary: _____

_____

Date: _____

Mentor: _____

Area of mastery: _____

Specialized vocabulary: _____

_____

Date: _____

Mentor: _____

Area of mastery: _____

Specialized vocabulary: _____

_____

Date: _____

Mentor: _____

Area of mastery: _____

Specialized vocabulary: _____

_____

AREAS OF EXPERTISE & SKILL (cont.)

Date: _____

Mentor: _____

Area of mastery: _____

Specialized vocabulary: _____

_____

Date: _____

Mentor: _____

Area of mastery: _____

Specialized vocabulary: _____

_____

Date: _____

Mentor: _____

Area of mastery: _____

Specialized vocabulary: _____

_____

Date: _____

Mentor: _____

Area of mastery: _____

Specialized vocabulary: _____

_____

Date: _____

Mentor: _____

Area of mastery: _____

Specialized vocabulary: _____

_____

AREAS OF SELF-STUDY & RESEARCH

Homeschooled adolescents are often *autodidacts,* those who learn by self-study. With time for focused reading, experimentation, or research, they often can achieve high levels of mastery in a subject. Often, they have key resources (people, texts, or organizations) that support their study.

Date: _____

Key resources: _____

Primary area of study: _____

Subtopics: _____

_____

Date: _____

Key resources: _____

Primary area of study: _____

Subtopics: _____

_____

Date: _____

Key resources: _____

Primary area of study: _____

Subtopics: _____

_____

Date: _____

Key resources: _____

Primary area of study: _____

Subtopics: _____

_____

Date: _____

Key resources: _____

Primary area of study: _____

Subtopics: _____

_____

AREAS OF SELF-STUDY & RESEARCH (cont.)

Date: _____

Key resources: _____

Primary area of study: _____

Subtopics: _____

_____

Date: _____

Key resources: _____

Primary area of study: _____

Subtopics: _____

_____

Date: _____

Key resources: _____

Primary area of study: _____

Subtopics: _____

_____

Date: _____

Key resources: _____

Primary area of study: _____

Subtopics: _____

_____

Date: _____

Key resources: _____

Primary area of study: _____

Subtopics: _____

_____

PROJECTS, PERFORMANCES, EXHIBITIONS & DEMONSTRATIONS

Projects, performances, exhibitions, and demonstrations are complex learning tasks that allow students to acquire knowledge and apply it—often in front of an audience. Be sure to include all of the following information.

Date: _____

Collaborators and audience: _____

Subject: _____

Description of the process: _____

_____

Date: _____

Collaborators and audience: _____

Subject: _____

Description of the process: _____

_____

Date: _____

Collaborators and audience: _____

Subject: _____

Description of the process: _____

_____

Date: _____

Collaborators and audience: _____

Subject: _____

Description of the process: _____

_____

Date: _____

Collaborators and audience: _____

Subject: _____

Description of the process: _____

_____

PROJECTS, PERFORMANCES, EXHIBITIONS & DEMONSTRATIONS (cont.)

Date: _____

Collaborators and audience: _____

Subject: _____

Description of the process: _____

_____

Date: _____

Collaborators and audience: _____

Subject: _____

Description of the process: _____

_____

Date: _____

Collaborators and audience: _____

Subject: _____

Description of the process: _____

_____

Date: _____

Collaborators and audience: _____

Subject: _____

Description of the process: _____

_____

Date: _____

Collaborators and audience: _____

Subject: _____

Description of the process: _____

_____

EMPLOYMENT

Employment often has specific starting and ending dates which should be noted. Use the Appendix C listing of the *Department of Labor's Dictionary of Occupational Titles* to discover words that accurately describe your job responsibilities and title.

From: _____ To: _____

Organization: _____

Supervisor: _____

Job responsibilities: _____

Job title: _____

From: _____ To: _____

Organization: _____

Supervisor: _____

Job responsibilities: _____

Job title: _____

From: _____ To: _____

Organization: _____

Supervisor: _____

Job responsibilities: _____

Job title: _____

From: _____ To: _____

Organization: _____

Supervisor: _____

Job responsibilities: _____

Job title: _____

From: _____ To: _____

Organization: _____

Supervisor: _____

Job responsibilities: _____

Job title: _____

EMPLOYMENT (cont.)

From: _____   To: _____

Organization: _____

Supervisor: _____

Job responsibilities: _____

Job title: _____

From: _____   To: _____

Organization: _____

Supervisor: _____

Job responsibilities: _____

Job title: _____

From: _____   To: _____

Organization: _____

Supervisor: _____

Job responsibilities: _____

Job title: _____

From: _____   To: _____

Organization: _____

Supervisor: _____

Job responsibilities: _____

Job title: _____

From: _____   To: _____

Organization: _____

Supervisor: _____

Job responsibilities: _____

Job title: _____

VOLUNTEERISM & SERVICE PROJECTS

Colleges and employers are interested in how homeschoolers move beyond their homes and participate in the community. The areas to which you feel drawn (recycling, fund-raising, elder-care, etc.) may also help shape your career goals. Even if you are not paid for your services, you still should use the Appendix C listing of *Dictionary of Occupational Titles* to describe your responsibilities.

From: _____ To: _____

Organization: _____

Supervisor: _____

Job responsibilities: _____

Who you helped: _____

From: _____ To: _____

Organization: _____

Supervisor: _____

Job responsibilities: _____

Who you helped: _____

From: _____ To: _____

Organization: _____

Supervisor: _____

Job responsibilities: _____

Who you helped: _____

From: _____ To: _____

Organization: _____

Supervisor: _____

Job responsibilities: _____

Who you helped: _____

From: _____ To: _____

Organization: _____

Supervisor: _____

Job responsibilities: _____

Who you helped: _____

VOLUNTEERISM & SERVICE PROJECTS (cont.)

From: _____ To: _____

Organization: _____

Supervisor: _____

Job responsibilities: _____

Who you helped: _____

From: _____ To: _____

Organization: _____

Supervisor: _____

Job responsibilities: _____

Who you helped: _____

From: _____ To: _____

Organization: _____

Supervisor: _____

Job responsibilities: _____

Who you helped: _____

From: _____ To: _____

Organization: _____

Supervisor: _____

Job responsibilities: _____

Who you helped: _____

From: _____ To: _____

Organization: _____

Supervisor: _____

Job responsibilities: _____

Who you helped: _____

TRAVEL

Travel, whether internationally or anywhere outside your local environs, is one way to connect with a variety of people and cultures. Documented travel experiences can help colleges and employers understand the breadth of your homeschool experience. In addition, the maps, brochures, and souvenirs you bring home can help describe your trip not only as a vacation but as an educational event.

Date: _____

Itinerary and destination: _____

_____

Sites visited: _____

_____

Date: _____

Itinerary and destination: _____

_____

Sites visited: _____

_____

Date: _____

Itinerary and destination: _____

_____

Sites visited: _____

_____

Date: _____

Itinerary and destination: _____

_____

Sites visited: _____

_____

Date: _____

Itinerary and destination: _____

_____

Sites visited: _____

_____

TRAVEL (cont.)

Date: _____

Itinerary and destination: _____

_____

Sites visited: _____

_____

Date: _____

Itinerary and destination: _____

_____

Sites visited: _____

_____

Date: _____

Itinerary and destination: _____

_____

Sites visited: _____

_____

Date: _____

Itinerary and destination: _____

_____

Sites visited: _____

_____

Date: _____

Itinerary and destination: _____

_____

Sites visited: _____

_____

DAY TRIPS

Trips close to home are a favorite homeschool resource. Visits to museums, nature conservancies, factories, historic sites, city neighborhoods, rural areas, ethnic restaurants—all add vitality to the learning process. If you go on a day trip with a group, note who your companions were. Sometimes they will have memories, photographs, and artifacts to share.

Date: _____

Destination: _____

Companions: _____

Things seen or done: _____

_____

Date: _____

Destination: _____

Companions: _____

Things seen or done: _____

_____

Date: _____

Destination: _____

Companions: _____

Things seen or done: _____

_____

Date: _____

Destination: _____

Companions: _____

Things seen or done: _____

_____

Date: _____

Destination: _____

Companions: _____

Things seen or done: _____

_____

DAY TRIPS (cont.)

Date: _____

Destination: _____

Companions: _____

Things seen or done: _____

_____

Date: _____

Destination: _____

Companions: _____

Things seen or done: _____

_____

Date: _____

Destination: _____

Companions: _____

Things seen or done: _____

_____

Date: _____

Destination: _____

Companions: _____

Things seen or done: _____

_____

Date: _____

Destination: _____

Companions: _____

Things seen or done: _____

_____

HEALTH, SPORTS & PHYSICAL FITNESS

Homeschoolers are well positioned to excel at individual sports and fitness activities, where achievement demonstrates a high level of self-discipline. If you participate in team sports, note the names of your coaches and teammates. A training log that notes benchmarks of achievement will document both skill development and progress toward personal health and fitness goals.

Date: _____

Activity: _____

Coach and teammates: _____

Extent of progress, level of achievement: _____

_____

Date: _____

Activity: _____

Coach and teammates: _____

Extent of progress, level of achievement: _____

_____

Date: _____

Activity: _____

Coach and teammates: _____

Extent of progress, level of achievement: _____

_____

Date: _____

Activity: _____

Coach and teammates: _____

Extent of progress, level of achievement: _____

_____

Date: _____

Activity: _____

Coach and teammates: _____

Extent of progress, level of achievement: _____

_____

HEALTH, SPORTS & PHYSICAL FITNESS (cont.)

Date: _____

Activity: _____

Coach and teammates: _____

Extent of progress, level of achievement: _____

_____

Date: _____

Activity: _____

Coach and teammates: _____

Extent of progress, level of achievement: _____

_____

Date: _____

Activity: _____

Coach and teammates: _____

Extent of progress, level of achievement: _____

_____

Date: _____

Activity: _____

Coach and teammates: _____

Extent of progress, level of achievement: _____

_____

Date: _____

Activity: _____

Coach and teammates: _____

Extent of progress, level of achievement: _____

_____

WRITING SAMPLES

For each sample chosen, note its literary type (essay, parody, song lyrics, etc.) as well as its length and subject matter. Your goal is what you were hoping to achieve in this particular piece of writing. If you are considering a piece for inclusion in your portfolio, you presumably have reflected on its level of quality and assessed its merits. Briefly note your critique.

Date: _____

Type: _____ Length: _____

Subject: _____

Goal: _____

Assessment: _____

Date: _____

Type: _____ Length: _____

Subject: _____

Goal: _____

Assessment: _____

Date: _____

Type: _____ Length: _____

Subject: _____

Goal: _____

Assessment: _____

Date: _____

Type: _____ Length: _____

Subject: _____

Goal: _____

Assessment: _____

Date: _____

Type: _____ Length: _____

Subject: _____

Goal: _____

Assessment: _____

WRITING SAMPLES (cont.)

Date: _____

Type: _____ Length: _____

Subject: _____

Goal: _____

Assessment: _____

Date: _____

Type: _____ Length: _____

Subject: _____

Goal: _____

Assessment: _____

Date: _____

Type: _____ Length: _____

Subject: _____

Goal: _____

Assessment: _____

Date: _____

Type: _____ Length: _____

Subject: _____

Goal: _____

Assessment: _____

Date: _____

Type: _____ Length: _____

Subject: _____

Goal: _____

Assessment: _____

BOOKS READ

This is a skeletal bibliography to help jog your memory. Note the type of fiction or category of nonfiction. Keywords should bring the book back to you instantly. Mention any detail that is memorable. Your own evaluation, whether instinctive or reflective, should be noted. Your accumulated book lists are a good source of self-discovery as well as sources for building your transcript and portfolios.

Title: _____ Date: _____

Author: _____ Type: _____

Subject: _____

Keywords: _____

Evaluation: _____

Title: _____ Date: _____

Author: _____ Type: _____

Subject: _____

Keywords: _____

Evaluation: _____

Title: _____ Date: _____

Author: _____ Type: _____

Subject: _____

Keywords: _____

Evaluation: _____

Title: _____ Date: _____

Author: _____ Type: _____

Subject: _____

Keywords: _____

Evaluation: _____

Title: _____ Date: _____

Author: _____ Type: _____

Subject: _____

Keywords: _____

Evaluation: _____

BOOKS READ (cont.)

Title: _____ Date: _____

Author: _____ Type: _____

Subject: _____

Keywords: _____

Evaluation: _____

Title: _____ Date: _____

Author: _____ Type: _____

Subject: _____

Keywords: _____

Evaluation: _____

Title: _____ Date: _____

Author: _____ Type: _____

Subject: _____

Keywords: _____

Evaluation: _____

Title: _____ Date: _____

Author: _____ Type: _____

Subject: _____

Keywords: _____

Evaluation: _____

Title: _____ Date: _____

Author: _____ Type: _____

Subject: _____

Keywords: _____

Evaluation: _____

PERFORMANCES ATTENDED

Drama, dance, and musical performances, whether amateur or professional, live or televised, are usually a part of the homeschool experience. Don't forget to include ethnic celebrations, poetry readings, holiday chorales, and informal performances at gatherings of your family and friends. Reflect on how you enjoyed the performance and/or where it might fit in your portfolio.

Date: _____ Place: _____

Type of performance: _____

Author, composer, artist: _____

Keywords: _____

Reflection: _____

Date: _____ Place: _____

Type of performance: _____

Author, composer, artist: _____

Keywords: _____

Reflection: _____

Date: _____ Place: _____

Type of performance: _____

Author, composer, artist: _____

Keywords: _____

Reflection: _____

Date: _____ Place: _____

Type of performance: _____

Author, composer, artist: _____

Keywords: _____

Reflection: _____

Date: _____ Place: _____

Type of performance: _____

Author, composer, artist: _____

Keywords: _____

Reflection: _____

PERFORMANCES ATTENDED (cont.)

Date: _____ Place: _____

Type of performance: _____

Author, composer, artist: _____

Keywords: _____

Reflection: _____

Date: _____ Place: _____

Type of performance: _____

Author, composer, artist: _____

Keywords: _____

Reflection: _____

Date: _____ Place: _____

Type of performance: _____

Author, composer, artist: _____

Keywords: _____

Reflection: _____

Date: _____ Place: _____

Type of performance: _____

Author, composer, artist: _____

Keywords: _____

Reflection: _____

Date: _____ Place: _____

Type of performance: _____

Author, composer, artist: _____

Keywords: _____

Reflection: _____

FILMS VIEWED

Documentaries, Shakespearean plays, political satires, classic screenplays, book adaptations, historical epics, foreign language films . . . you've probably watched all types of films that should have a place in your personal and academic portfolios. Add keywords to help you remember each, and then reflect on where it might fit in your portfolio or transcript.

Title: _____ Date: _____

Actors: _____

Characters, setting: _____

Keywords: _____

Reflection: _____

Title: _____ Date: _____

Actors: _____

Characters, setting: _____

Keywords: _____

Reflection: _____

Title: _____ Date: _____

Actors: _____

Characters, setting: _____

Keywords: _____

Reflection: _____

Title: _____ Date: _____

Actors: _____

Characters, setting: _____

Keywords: _____

Reflection: _____

Title: _____ Date: _____

Actors: _____

Characters, setting: _____

Keywords: _____

Reflection: _____

FILMS VIEWED (cont.)

Title: _____ Date: _____

Actors: _____

Characters, setting: _____

Keywords: _____

Reflection: _____

Title: _____ Date: _____

Actors: _____

Characters, setting: _____

Keywords: _____

Reflection: _____

Title: _____ Date: _____

Actors: _____

Characters, setting: _____

Keywords: _____

Reflection: _____

Title: _____ Date: _____

Actors: _____

Characters, setting: _____

Keywords: _____

Reflection: _____

Title: _____ Date: _____

Actors: _____

Characters, setting: _____

Keywords: _____

Reflection: _____

ARTIFACT ASSESSMENT WORKSHEET

Theme: _____

What artifacts do you: • already have? • need to acquire? • need to create?

On a scale from 1 to 10, rate each artifact's: • credibility • clarity • quality

Use the context section to note how each artifact fits into your portfolio.

Item	Have? Acquire? Create?	Credibility	Clarity	Quality	Context

ARTIFACT ASSESSMENT WORKSHEET (cont.)

Item	Have? Acquire? Create?	Credibility	Clarity	Quality	Context

PORTFOLIO PLANNER

Theme: _____

Type of Portfolio: _____

Your Audience: _____

Their Criteria: _____

Artifacts:

   1.   _____

     Quality: _____ Context: _____

   2.   _____

     Quality: _____ Context: _____

   3.   _____

     Quality: _____ Context: _____

   4.   _____

     Quality: _____ Context: _____

   5.   _____

     Quality: _____ Context: _____

   6.   _____

     Quality: _____ Context: _____

   7.   _____

     Quality: _____ Context: _____

   8.   _____

     Quality: _____ Context: _____

   9.   _____

     Quality: _____ Context: _____

 10.   _____

     Quality: _____ Context: _____

 11.   _____

     Quality: _____ Context: _____

 12.   _____

     Quality: _____ Context: _____

 13.   _____

     Quality: _____ Context: _____

PORTFOLIO PLANNER (cont.)

1. _____

   Quality: _____ Context: _____

2. _____

   Quality: _____ Context: _____

3. _____

   Quality: _____ Context: _____

4. _____

   Quality: _____ Context: _____

5. _____

   Quality: _____ Context: _____

6. _____

   Quality: _____ Context: _____

7. _____

   Quality: _____ Context: _____

8. _____

   Quality: _____ Context: _____

9. _____

   Quality: _____ Context: _____

10. _____

    Quality: _____ Context: _____

11. _____

    Quality: _____ Context: _____

12. _____

    Quality: _____ Context: _____

13. _____

    Quality: _____ Context: _____

14. _____

    Quality: _____ Context: _____

15. _____

    Quality: _____ Context: _____

16. _____

    Quality: _____ Context: _____

LIST C—YOUR HOUSEHOLD ARCHIVES

When you start to develop a portfolio or transcript, you will find it helpful to have a reminder of where you might have stored useful artifacts and information. These worksheets for recording your "Household Archives" will help you discover what you already have.

Because information is less visible than artifacts, it is especially important to know where that information is and how to retrieve it quickly. Information about homeschooling is probably stored in various places around the house such as:

- Personal and Family Calendars
- Homeschool Log or Planbook
- Checkbook or Credit Card Register
- Personal Logs, Journals, and Diaries
- Your Computer's Hard Drive
- Diskettes

Although you probably keep homeschooling documentation in a file cabinet or in manila folders, remember that they hold merely the paper portion of your homeschooling evidence. There are artifacts throughout your home. Look through the following and record what you find:

- Secure Storage
- Map and Travel Brochure Collections
- Photo Albums, Envelopes, and Storage Boxes
- Audio and Videotape Collections
- Boxes and Milk Crates
- File Folders
- Filing Cabinets
- Cupboards, Closets, Cabinets, Shelves, and Drawers
- Bookshelves
- Everyday Evidence

Later, when you start to organize a portfolio around a certain theme, Botany for example, you can use these "Household Archives" lists to recall and locate specific items. When you move your archival information to the "Artifact Assessment Worksheets," which are used to organize information thematically, you will have created the first draft of your portfolio's table of contents. Congratulations!

PERSONAL & FAMILY CALENDARS

A great deal of homeschool information is documented on the refrigerator calendar or in the appointment calendars in our purses or briefcases. Use this sheet to record not only activities that are homeschool-specific but any cultural, athletic, and celebratory event that adds dimension to learning.

Year:	Activity and Date
January	
February	
March	
April	
May	
June	
July	
August	
September	
October	
November	
December	

PERSONAL & FAMILY CALENDARS (cont.)

Year:	Activity and Date
January	
February	
March	
April	
May	
June	
July	
August	
September	
October	
November	
December	

HOMESCHOOL LOG OR PLANBOOK

Some homeschoolers plan beforehand; others log in afterward. Most likely, both parents and students will have information to enter here. While you might organize your planbooks or logs according to traditional subject areas, think in terms of themes and unit studies, too. Note the name of any text or other learning resources you use.

From: To:	Subject, Theme, Unit	Resources Used

HOMESCHOOL LOG OR PLANBOOK (cont.)

From: To:	Subject, Theme, Unit	Resources Used

HOMESCHOOL FINANCES & EXPENSES

Your checkbook register, whether hand-held or computerized, can be used to track down materials and activities for homeschooling expenses. If you use financial management software, code your homeschooling expenses so you can gather them together periodically and print them out. Use this worksheet to organize expenses that appear on your bank or credit card statements.

Date	Cost	Item	Use

HOMESCHOOL FINANCES & EXPENSES (cont.)

Date	Cost	Item	Use

PERSONAL LOGS, JOURNALS & DIARIES

Unless you keep a homeschool journal, it is likely that homeschool-specific entries are hidden in among many other thoughts and comments. When you review your journal, diary, or log, use this worksheet to note not just what you did, but how you felt. Also note any growth you notice.

Date	Subject	Reflection

PERSONAL LOGS, JOURNALS & DIARIES (cont.)

Date	Subject	Reflection

YOUR COMPUTER'S HARD DRIVE

Information is scattered throughout your computer's hard drive. Since each family member probably has his or her own system for labeling and organizing homeschool files, each should fill out one of these sheets. Complete filenames are not as important as being able find the folder where the information is stored.

You might want to take this opportunity to rename any ambiguously titled files, re-sort files into appropriate folders, and make deletions of any unnecessary files.

Folder	File	Contents

YOUR COMPUTER'S HARD DRIVE (cont.)

Folder	File	Contents

DISKETTES

Homeschool information should be backed up and easily accessible. When several family members use the computer, diskettes may be simply stored, not properly filed. Even when properly labeled and filed, information can be difficult to find if a diskette holds several different folders, only one of which is homeschool related. Use the following chart to identify useful diskettes and their locations so that you can retrieve them quickly in the future.

Label	File Box	Contents

DISKETTES (cont.)

Label	File Box	Contents

ITEMS IN SECURE STORAGE

Certain artifacts are central to your portfolio's credibility and duplicate copies are not quickly acquired. Even if you use a safe-deposit box for the originals, it is important to know where you keep copies of the following documents at home.

Item	Location	Comments
Transcripts of courses taken		
Letters of reference, verification, participation		
Test results		
Correspondence with school officials		
Awards and scholarship offers		
Legal documents (passport, birth certificate, etc.)		

ITEMS IN SECURE STORAGE (cont.)

Item	Location	Comments

MAP & TRAVEL BROCHURE BOX

In most families, maps and brochures are rarely sorted and organized when returning from a trip. They are usually put into a catch-all box instead. Sorting through these materials will not only produce good documentation of travel learning, but will remind family members of souvenirs and photographs located elsewhere. Note those items on this worksheet, too.

Date	Destination	Materials Collected	Location

MAP & TRAVEL BROCHURE BOX (cont.)

Date	Destination	Materials Collected	Location

PHOTOGRAPHS

Pictures can provide credible evidence for travel, field trips, and homeschool events. They also can document activities where emphasis is on the learning process. Since it is unlikely that there would be a whole roll of film devoted to an everyday learning event, these pictures may be buried among those taken at seasonal or family celebrations. When you locate them, enter them here.

Date	Site, Occasion, Event, Participants	Location

Date	Site, Occasion, Event, Participants	Location

AUDIO- & VIDEOTAPES

Tapes pertinent to homeschooling may be mixed in with others that the family owns. Include on this worksheet both commercial tapes used for instructional purposes and homemade tapes that chronicle travel, homeschool events, and learning activities in progress. If possible, note where the tape can be cued for easy reference.

Date	Title or Label	Cue	Contents	Location

AUDIO- & VIDEOTAPES (cont.)

Date	Title or Label	Cue	Contents	Location

BOXES & MILK CRATES

Boxes and milk crates are full of papers, books and three-dimensional artifacts that have been stored away once they are no longer in active use. Whether labeled or unlabeled, in the attic, basement, or garage, boxes and milk crates contain an enormous amount of evidence that can be used in developing portfolios or transcripts. P.S.: If the boxes and crates weren't labeled before, label them now!

Date	Label	Contents	Location

BOXES & MILK CRATES (cont.)

Date	Label	Contents	Location

FILE FOLDERS

File folders contain much of the paperwork and two-dimensional artifacts related to home-schooling: magazine articles, newspaper clippings, letters, certificates, and college application materials. However, file folders are not always stored in file cabinets. Once a folder is located, label and record it on this worksheet so the contents can be quickly found when creating a portfolio or transcript.

Date	Label	Contents	Location

FILE FOLDERS (cont.)

Date	Label	Contents	Location

FILING CABINETS

Most families have several filing cabinets or portable file modules, each probably containing a few useful pieces of homeschool information. When you locate something that can be used in developing your portfolio or transcript, you can leave it where it was filed, but note it on this worksheet so you can find it later.

Date	Location	Contents

FILING CABINETS (cont.)

Date	Location	Contents

CUPBOARDS, CLOSETS, CABINETS, SHELVES & DRAWERS

Homeschooling artifacts turn up in the most unlikely places: kitchen cupboards, dresser drawers, and basement storage cabinets. When cleaning or sorting, be alert to items hurriedly stored away and forgotten: booklets, calendars, membership cards, badges, receipts, etc. You might take this opportunity to move more important items to safer locations.

Date	Item	Location

CUPBOARDS, CLOSETS, CABINETS, SHELVES & DRAWERS (cont.)

Date	Item	Location

BOOKSHELVES

Bookshelves hold evidence of personal interests, family values, and homeschool activities. Due to the high number of volumes your family may own, consider looking through several bookcases at a time, perhaps for books on one particular subject or theme. Jot down any remembrances, reflections, or comments, too.

Location	Title	Theme and Comments

BOOKSHELVES (cont.)

Location	Title	Theme and Comments

EVERYDAY EVIDENCE

Much evidence of homeschooling goes unnoticed because it is embedded in daily life. These things, probably not thought of as "educational," reflect a family's unique manner of homeschooling. A favorite nightly news program, vegetables from the family garden, and a souvenir coffee mug can all be part of the homeschool experience and should be noted.

Evidence	Context

EVERYDAY EVIDENCE (cont.)

Evidence	Context

Helpful Words
and Terms

GLOSSARY OF ASSESSMENT TERMS

Accountability: The demand by taxpayers and governmental agencies that state-financed schools be held responsible for student achievement. Because homeschoolers (like private and parochial schools) generally do not receive government funds, the concept of fiscal accountability to the state probably does not apply. However, administrators may make other accountability demands on homeschoolers. All accountability demands should be investigated to determine if they actually are required by state law.

Achievement Test: A standardized test designed to measure the content or skills a student has learned, assumedly through classroom instruction. Using standardized achievement tests can be problematic for homeschoolers because much of their learning has not occured through the direct instruction model used in classrooms. Secondly, since homeschooling parents often develop alternative curricula for their children, the content of a standardized achievement test may not match what has been taught in the homeschool program. Nor may the children have the test-taking skills that are taught by direct classroom instruction. Rather than using *achievement tests,* most homeschooling parents use a variety of assessment tools to *test their children's achievements.*

Achievement tests are different from **Aptitude Tests,** which are purported to measure innate ability. There is debate among educators as to whether certain widely used aptitude tests actually measure innate ability, since test preparation and cultural biases may affect the student's score.

Alternative Assessment: The observation and review of student tasks, performances, products, projects, logs, journals, portfolios, etc., to determine if or how much learning has occurred. All of these are alternatives to traditional paper-and-pencil tests and standardized norm- or criterion-referenced tests.

Analytic Scoring: Breaking down a task into its component parts and scoring each of the sections separately using a set of criteria and a graduated rating scale. For example, an oral presentation may be evaluated using a scale from 1 to 4 on organization, content, the speaker's manner of relating to the audience, qualities of his or her voice, use of gestures, etc.

Assessment Literacy: Professional-level awareness of the wide variety of instruments that can be used to evaluate student work, as well as the ability to discern when it is appropriate to use one assessment tool rather than another. Also, the ability to interpret the results of these assessments so as to come to an understanding of what has been learned. An educator with a high degree of assessment literacy should be comfortable discussing a variety of assessment options with homeschooling parents.

Assessment Task: The specific task done by the student that will be earmarked for assessment. Either the process of performing the task or the product that results from it may be assessed. For homeschoolers, many assessment tasks emerge as projects that are being worked on, and assessment is done informally by the parent. In schools, assessment tasks are usually designed beforehand and teachers assess more formally.

Authentic Assessment: Observing and assessing the student as he or she applies knowledge in tasks that are meaningful, valuable, have a real-world context, and are part of the learning process, not separate from it. Authentic assessment that takes place during the learning process can offer feedback to help improve student performance. Thus, authentic assessment is an ongoing process, not an isolated event. Most homeschoolers routinely use authentic assessment.

Benchmark: An assessment of skill or knowledge at a particular time with the results being used as a reference point to measure subsequent progress. By using benchmarks, personal growth over time can be noticed. Dated work samples in a portfolio can provide benchmarks for homeschooled students.

Competency Test: A test which measures whether the student has the basic information and skills necessary to move to the next level of learning or out into the real world. In schools, competency testing may be done as a precondition for promotion or graduation. Colleges and employers often use competency test results in admissions and hiring. Homeschoolers can use the College Board's CLEP exams as one way of showing academic competency. Employers may ask applicants to demonstrate a desired skill to determine competency.

Content Standards: The list of knowledge and skills that teachers are expected to teach and students are expected to learn. These are *input* standards. Content standards are usually devised by educational organizations such as the National Council of Teachers of Mathematics or by committees at the state level. Homeschoolers who create curricula to meet their children's unique learning needs are creating alternative content standards.

Criterion-Referenced Test: A test that is designed to measure how well a student has mastered the content that was taught. Informal teacher-made tests are usually criterion-referenced, as are most statewide achievement tests, which are designed to measure how well students are mastering the public school curriculum. Because the teacher or the state determines that a certain level of achievement is required to "pass the test" few or many students may do so. See **Norm-Referenced Test.**

Curriculum Alignment: The appropriate match-up between curriculum (content), methodology (instructional practices), and assessment. If a family has made an in-depth study of volcanoes during trips to Mexico and Hawaii, a standardized test designed to assess generic middle school science would be *out of alignment* with the family's homeschool program. Other types of assessments, better aligned to the program should be used. On the other hand, for families who use a textbook-oriented program, standardized tests may be well aligned to the manner in which they homeschool.

Embedded Assessment: Assessment that is fully integrated into a project or task and occurs simultaneously along with it. Embedded assessments may be all but invisible to those who define assessment as something that is separate from the task and done after the fact. Embedded assessments require that the evaluator has the time, the opportunity, and the ability to observe the learning process carefully. For homeschoolers, this is the most used (and most educationally appropriate) model of assessment.

Exemplars: Samples of work that show the highest standard students should strive to achieve. Other work samples usually are made available also so that students can see the range of quality from exemplary through poor. Students can begin to understand what quality looks like and how their work compares. This strategy, which is well suited to projects, experiments, and written work, also helps students become more sophisticated self-evaluators.

Exhibition: A comprehensive interdisciplinary project with considerable student input in the selection and treatment of the topic. The student presents his or her Exhibition publicly and responds to questions about it. An **Exit Exhibition** is a culminating exhibition that demonstrates conclusively to one's community that the student is ready for a new, more advanced level of education and/or work.

Formative Assessment: Assessment during the learning process that identifies what the student needs to learn so that changes can be made in order to improve learning. Most homeschoolers routinely engage in formative assessments.

High-Stakes Testing: Tests that have important consequences for students, their teachers, and their schools. At the high school level, high-stakes testing is related to promotion, graduation, and college admission. For homeschoolers, a high-stakes assessment is *any* assessment that threatens their ability to homeschool with minimal governmental oversight.

Holistic Scoring: Assessing the overall quality of a performance or product rather than analyzing and scoring each of its criteria separately. The opposite of **Analytic Scoring.** Homeschoolers might use analytic techniques during the learning process to teach or fine tune a particular skill, and holistic assessment after the project is completed.

Norm-Referenced Tests: A test in which a student or group's performance is compared to that of a group of students chosen by the test developer. The results of this select group of students are used to create scores and set standards. Because the test developer looks at the norm, or midpoint, of the scores, half the test-takers will score above the norm and half will fall below it. When students take a norm-referenced test, this is the group to which their results are compared. Students in the norm group can be divided into sub-groups (e.g., gender, race, ethnicity, private and parochial schools, etc.) so that comparisons for these groups can be established. When considering a particular norm-referenced test, ask if it has been normed for homeschoolers.

Objective Test: Often mistakenly thought to mean that the *content* of the test is factual and therefore not open to question or speculation, the term "objective test" actually refers to the *scoring* system. Objective tests are used when there are multiple scorers, so that personal interpretations will not be a factor in correcting and grading the tests. Machine-scored tests also need to be "objective." As an alternative to using objectively scored standardized tests to verify parent assessments, homeschoolers might ask an outside reviewer to use a **Rubric** and **Analytic Scoring** to grade student work.

On-Demand Assessment: An assessment scheduled outside the normal routine, usually after learning is thought to have occurred. The opposite of **Embedded Assessment.**

Performance-Based Assessment: Observation and evaluation of a student's applying his or her knowledge in performing an assessment task. This can be either ongoing or scheduled, but interaction between teacher and student for feedback and reflection usually occurs. The student should be aware of the assessment criteria on which he or she is being evaluated.

Performance Standards: The level of learning that students are expected to display in order to be considered proficient in a subject. These are *output* standards. Decisions regarding performance standards are often made at the state level and are tied to **Accountability** issues. Requiring higher performance standards is sometimes termed "raising the bar." Homeschoolers can use portfolios and other alternative assessment tasks to demonstrate that they have met high performance standards. These standards, of course, may differ from those of the public schools.

Portfolio: A thoughtful selection of artifacts that provides clear and credible evidence of learning. It may be assessed only for completeness, or its quality may evaluated by either **Analytic** or **Holistic Scoring.**

Process: A series of steps in which a student engages when performing a task. Many homeschooling activities are process-oriented and do not result in tangible products such as a piece of written work. Evaluating growth by observing process is a familiar homeschool assessment strategy.

Product: A tangible result of a performance task. Because they *are* tangible, work products can be archived, then retrieved for inclusion in the student's portfolios.

Problem: A situation where there is no easily discernable route to a solution. Following a set formula (mathematical or otherwise) to come up with an answer is not problem-solving.

Project: A multifaceted set of tasks or activities focused on a common theme. Projects may be done either individually or collaboratively and usually result in some sort of product that can be archived for the student's portfolio.

Rubric: A scoring system composed of two parts: criteria, and a rating scale that explicitly describes a range of quality from exemplary to poor for each criterion.

Self-Assessment: A student's ability to evaluate his or her work by using criteria, exemplars, rubrics, past work, and other assessment tools. When we ask our children to participate in the assessment process, we encourage self-reflection and judgment.

Standardized Test: Any test that is administered in a uniform manner and then scored objectively. It does not necessarily reflect high **Performance Standards** or contain questions related to the **Content Standards** of the curriculum.

Subjective Test: A test in which the assessor uses his or her professional judgment in the scoring or evaluating of student work. Because subjective tests often use open-ended questions or tasks, there may be a variety of correct responses. Homeschoolers are well positioned to use informal subjective tests that encourage complex and reflective responses

Summative Assessment: Assessment made after the learning process in order to determine whether knowledge or skills were learned. Summative assessments may be used as a culminating activity at the end of a unit, semester, or year. Homeschoolers may find that summative assessments are useful in creating **Benchmarks** to help chart future growth.

Transcript: Traditionally, a cumulative list of courses taken or subjects learned with a numerical or letter grade for each. Alternative transcript formats are suitable for homeschoolers whose learning program differs from that of the public school.

YOUR LEARNING SELF: BLOOM'S TAXONOMY

Learning is an internal process. If you want to discuss it, whether within your family or with those outside your home, you need words that help you communicate effectively. The following list, a personal one derived from many sources, is based on "Bloom's Taxonomy of Learning," a sequence of learning that goes from simple to sophisticated. Notice that the levels are not age-related, but describe how a learner of any age moves from novice to expert. By and large, these verbs are clear, commonplace, and jargon-free. This list is an excellent resource to turn to when reflecting and writing about learning.

Knowledge: The ability to recall facts and information previously learned.

cites	matches	repeats
defines	memorizes	reproduces
identifies	names	retells
indicates	quotes	selects
knows	recalls	states
labels	recites	underlines
lists	records	

Comprehension: The ability to grasp principles, concepts, and theories and then restate and explain them in your own words.

classifies	interprets	restates
describes	locates	reviews
discusses	paraphrases	substitutes
explains	recognizes	summarizes
expresses	rephrases	tells
illustrates	reports	translates

Application: The ability to utilize established methods and procedures when applying the information you learned in new situations.

applies	exhibits	prepares
computes	illustrates	presents
demonstrates	interprets	schedules
displays	operates	shows
dramatizes	organizes	uses
edits	practices	utilizes
employs	predicts	

Analysis: The ability to break down the whole into its component parts, comprehending its structure, and understanding the relationships among the parts.

analyzes	diagrams	inventories
categorizes	differentiates	investigates
classifies	discovers	outlines
compares	dissects	questions
contrasts	distinguishes	revises
debates	examines	reworks
detects	experiments	rewrites
determines	inquires	solves
diagnoses	inspects	surveys

Synthesis: The ability see new relationships among elements and then put them together to form a new whole.

arranges	develops	performs
assembles	devises	plans
associates	extends	predicts
collects	formulates	prepares
combines	generalizes	produces
compiles	hypothesizes	projects
composes	integrates	proposes
connects	invents	synthesizes
constructs	modifies	tests
creates	organizes	theorizes
designs	originates	writes

Evaluation: The ability to use a variety of criteria in order to make judgments about the quality of data, methods, materials, and learning.

appraises	deduces	measures
arranges	defends	rates
assesses	estimates	reflects
concludes	evaluates	scores
considers	grades	selects
criticizes	infers	values
critiques	judges	weighs
decides	justifies	

YOUR WORKING SELF: DICTIONARY OF OCCUPATIONAL TITLES

If you want to describe your work experience and aspirations to an employer, it helps to use a vocabulary that is familiar and precise. The U.S. Department of Labor has a coding system that describes occupations by assigning a numerical value for the skill required when interacting with data, people, and things. The levels move from simple to more complex, but note that the ratings go in inverse order, with jobs requiring higher-order thinking skills having *lower* numbers.

Data	People	Things
0–Synthesizing	0–Mentoring	0–Setting Up
1–Coordinating	1–Negotiating	1–Precision–Working
2–Analyzing	2–Instructing	2–Operating-Controlling
3–Compiling	3–Supervising	3–Driving–Operating
4–Computing	4–Diverting	4–Manipulating
5–Copying	5–Persuading	5–Tending
6–Comparing	6–Speaking-Signaling	6–Feeding-Offbearing
	7–Serving	7–Handling
	8–Taking Instructions-Helping	

Each of the categories has its own set of verbs that can be used when communicating about your work experience and career goals.

Data: **Dealing with intangibles such as words, numbers, symbols, ideas, information, concepts, and knowledge.**

analyzes	creates	formats
arranges	critiques	formulates
calculates	decides	gathers
classifies	designs	integrates
collates	develops	interprets
collects	discovers	investigates
compares	draws	orders
compiles	enters data	organizes
composes	estimates	plans
computes	evaluates	publishes
coordinates	examines	purchases
copies	files	recommends

records	selects	tabulates
reports	sorts	transcribes
researches	studies	translates
reviews	summarizes	writes
schedules	surveys	

(0) Synthesizing: Integrating data to develop knowledge and concepts.

(1) Coordinating: Determining action to be taken; taking action or reporting on events.

(2) Analyzing: Examining and evaluating data; presenting alternative actions.

(3) Compiling: Gathering, collating, or classifying information; reporting or carrying out an action relative to it.

(4) Computing: Performing mathematical operations; reporting or carrying out an action relative to them.

(5) Copying: Transcribing, entering, or posting data.

(6) Comparing: Observing similarities or differences of data, people, or things.

People: Dealing with human beings (or with animals) on an individual basis.

advises	demonstrates	plans
amuses	directs	plays
assesses	entertains	presents
assists	evaluates	sells
attends to	guides	serves
cares for	instructs	supervises
coaches	leads	supports
collaborates	manages	teaches
communicates	mediates	trains
coordinates	motivates	treats
counsels	negotiates	tutors
debates	performs	visits
decides	persuades	

(0) Mentoring: Dealing with individuals in terms of their total personality to advise, counsel, and/or guide them using professional principles.

(1) Negotiating: Exchanging ideas, information, and opinions; formulating policies and programs; arriving jointly at decisions, conclusions, or solutions.

(2) Instructing: Teaching or training by explanation, demonstration, supervised practice; making recommendations based on technical disciplines.

(3) Supervising: Determining or interpreting work procedures, assigning specific duties, maintaining harmonious relations, promoting efficiency.

(4) Diverting: Amusing others, usually through stage, screen, television, or radio.

(5) Persuading: Influencing others in favor of a product, service, or point of view.

(6) Speaking-Signaling: Talking with and/or signaling people to convey or exchange information; giving assignments and/or directions.

(7) Serving: Attending to the needs, requests, and wishes of people or animals. Immediate response involved.

(8) Taking Instructions-Helping: Attending to instructions or orders of a supervisor.

Things: Dealing with tangible and inanimate objects, substances, materials, machines, tools, equipment, and products. Vocabulary specific to a particular trade should also be used in describing your accomplishments.

adjusts	guides	observes
arranges	handles	operates
assembles	inserts	package
carries	installs	places
cleans	lifts	refinishes
constructs	loads	removes
controls	maintains	repairs
cuts	manufactures	restores
delivers	measures	shapes
disassembles	models	tends
drives	molds	turns
fills	monitors	
fixes	moves	

(0) Setting Up: Preparing and operating a variety of machines; planning the order of operations; installing and adjusting components; setting controls; verifying quality of machines, materials, and practices; using precision instruments.

(1) Precision Working: Using body members or tools to work, move, guide, or place objects or materials. Task requires exercise of considerable judgment.

(2) Operating-Controlling: Starting, stopping, controlling, or adjusting machines or equipment; observing gauges, dials, etc.; turning valves and other devices to regulate factors such as temperature, pressure, flow of liquids, speed of pumps, and reactions of materials.

(3) Driving-Operating: Starting, stopping, and controlling machines such as cranes, conveyor systems, tractors, and paving and hoisting machines for which a course must be steered or guided; observing gauges and dials; estimating distances; determining speed and direction; turning cranks and wheels; pushing or pulling gear lifts or levers.

(4) Manipulating: Using body members, tools, or special devices to work, move, guide, or place objects or materials. Involves some latitude for judgment.

(5) Tending: Starting, stopping, and observing machines; adjusting controls, timers, and gauges; turning valves; flipping switches. Little judgment involved.

(6) Feeding-Offbearing: Inserting, throwing, dumping, or placing materials in or removing them from automatic machines or those operated by others.

(7) Handling: Using body members, hand tools, or special devices to work, move, or carry objects or materials. Involves little or no latitude for judgment.

One final note on writing resumes. Books on resumes written several years ago stressed using verbs to describe your experience. Nowadays, however, if you are submitting a digital resume the rules have changed. The concept of "key word resumes" is transforming the way resumes are written. When creating a keyword resume the emphasis is on using nouns instead of verbs. This allows the computer to scan for job descriptions that the employer has deemed relevant in order to select the resumes with the most matches. Most homeschoolers do not need to format their digital resumes with such sophistication during adolescence. However, they eventually will, which is why it is important to keep informed about current workplace phenomena and employment strategies. Still, the verb list above can act as a guide in developing vivid and accurate descriptions of your homeschool activities in order to communicate effectively with a prospective employer.

Excerpted and adapted from the *Dictionary of Occupational Titles,* Fourth Edition, Revised 1991.

YOUR PERSONAL TRAITS

These are adjectives and phrases that might describe you. Although they are organized into categories that employers find desirable, they can be used for college applications, self-reflection, goal setting, and personal growth.

Dependability	Common Sense	Interpersonal Skills
accurate	adaptable	accommodating
attentive to detail	decisive	agreeable
deliberate	flexible	assertive
dependable	mature	considerate
disciplined	reflective	enthusiastic
industrious	resourceful	outgoing
logical	sensible	patient
methodical	takes initiative	polite
neat	displays problem-solving skills	positive
organized		sensitive
punctual		sincere
reliable		tolerant
responsible		displays leadership
steady		displays teamwork
thorough		
follows through		
meets deadlines		

Manageablilty	Communication Skills	Personality Traits
attentive	articulate	confident
cooperative	persuasive	creative
loyal	poised	determined
open-minded	diplomatic	energetic
respectful	tactful	imaginative
willing	presentation skills	independent
follows instructions	public speaking skills	
	written communication skills	

Print and Internet
Resources

BOOKS

ALTERNATIVE EDUCATION DURING ADOLESCENCE

Colfax, David and Micki. *Homeschooling for Excellence.* Warner Books, Inc.: New York, 1988. ISBN: 0446389862

> The story of how a California couple homeschooled their four sons, priming them for success in college and adult life. The Colfaxes give support to parents who are attempting to blend the flexibility of unschooling with the seemingly rigorous demands of the college admissions process.

Hailey, Kendall. *The Day I Became an Autodidact.* Dell Publishing: New York, 1989. ISBN: 0440550130

> How do you construct a life as an autodidact, a person who learns on your own? This book chronicles how Kendall eschewed both college attendance and full-time employment while designing a scholarly alternative unique in our culture.

Llewellyn, Grace. *The Teenage Liberation Handbook: How to Quit School and Get a Real Life and Education.* Lowry House: Eugene, OR, 1998. ISBN: 0962959170

> The classic reference guide that belongs on every homeschooler's bookshelf. It is addressed to the adolescent rather than the parent, but I borrowed my son's copy so often that I finally bought a copy for myself! It is truly comprehensive, addressing all the academic disciplines from a fresh perspective. In addition, the chapter "College Without High School" raises such a host of reflective questions that alone are worth the price of the book.

Llewellyn, Grace, ed. *Real Lives: Eleven Teenagers Who Don't Go to School.* Lowry House: Eugene, OR, 1993. ISBN: 0962959138

> First-person narratives by eleven teenagers, the oldest of whom was sixteen when the book was written. *Real Lives* gives homeschooling families a window on what can be done when adolescents discover they have unlimited potential. A truly extraordinary book.

MODELS OF SCHOOLING

Each of these authors proposes an alternative to the way American education is configured today. These working models for school reform are being used in selected schools throughout the United States. Because of this, colleges and universities are familiar with their philosophies and vocabulary. Even if you disagree with an author's overall perspective, note which of his emphases could be useful in communicating your homeschool experience to outside reviewers.

Adler, Mortimer. *The Paideia Program: An Education Syllabus.* Macmillan Publishing Company: New York, NY, 1984. ISBN: 0020130406

> Paideia Schools are based on "columns" of knowledge, skills, and values. They recognize and encourage a variety of instructional styles including coaching and Socratic dialogue, both of which are familiar homeschool "teaching" practices.

Hirsch, E. D., Jr. *The Schools We Need: And Why We Don't Have Them.* Random House, Inc.: New York, NY, 1999. ISBN: 0385495242

> Written by the author of *Cultural Literacy,* this book proposes a content-rich curriculum. If your homeschooling philosophy leans toward the classical approach, Hirsch will encourage you and explain why colleges and employers might find this type of curriculum important.

Sizer, Theodore. *Horace's School: Redesigning the American High School.* Houghton Mifflin Company: Boston, MA, 1993. ISBN: 0395659736

> This book was our family's valued and trusty resource as we attempted to translate homeschooling into a vocabulary and format that school officials and college admissions personnel would understand. Sizer's "Exhibitions" and "less is more" philosophy are powerful concepts that homeschoolers will find familiar.

CAREER AND COLLEGE COACHING

Barkley, Nella. *How to Help Your Child Land the Right Job (Without Being a Pain in the Neck).* Workman Publishing: New York, NY, 1993. ISBN: 1563051524

> Nella Barkley's concept of parent-as-coach is refreshing, and well suited to the interdependent relationships that homeschooled adolescents tend to have with their parents. Her three-step model for support helps young adults and their parents work together to explore issues of identity and work. This book, written with the parent as the intended audience, is encouraging, empowering, sensible, and down-to-earth.

Boldt, Lawrence G. *Zen and the Art of Making a Living: A Practical Guide to Creative Career Design.* Penguin USA: New York, NY, 1999. ISBN: 0140195998

> A book designed to help both adolescents and adults explore their values, talents, skills, and career options. Its worksheets, exercises, and activities dovetail nicely with the self-discovery aspect of the portfolio process.

Bolles, Richard Nelson. *What Color is Your Parachute? 2000.* Ten Speed Press: Berkeley, CA, 1999. ISBN: 1580081231

> Revised annually for over twenty-five years this is a classic resource. Although aimed at job-hunters and career-changers, its charts, checklists, and exercises are useful for adults and adolescents—those entering the workplace and those selecting a college. Homeschoolers who use portfolios for self-assessment will enjoy the book's emphasis on finding work that is personally fulfilling.

Cohen, Cafi, et al. *And What About College?: How Homeschooling Can Lead to Admissions to the Best Colleges & Universities.* Holt Associates: Cambridge, MA, 1997. ISBN: 0913677116

> A comprehensive book full of useful ideas for homeschoolers, whether schooled-at-home or unschooled, who are approaching the college admissions process. The Appendix includes many samples and examples of high school documentation.

Estell, Doug, et al. *Reading Lists for College Bound Students.* ARCO: New York, NY, 1993. ISBN: 0671847120

> An excellent resource for building a literary background, *Reading Lists* also provides a unique window through which to view a school's mission and values. It also offers home-schoolers a wealth of ideas for organizing the literature component of their transcripts.

Kohl, Herbert. *The Question Is College: On Finding and Doing Work You Love.* Heinemann: Portsmouth, NH, 1998. ISBN 0867094346

> In this challenging and thought-provoking book, Kohl helps students and their parents move away from the question of *which* college in order to ask *why* college at all. In the second half of the book, he uses a profile template to help students explore career options, discover their vocations, and then determine whether attending college is the best route to achieve their goals.

PERIODICALS AND ARTICLES

ALTERNATIVE EDUCATION PUBLICATIONS

AERO
417 Roslyn Road
Roslyn Hts., NY 11577
800-769-4171
516-621-2195
e-mail: JerryAERO@aol.com
Internet: www.edrev.org

Holt Associates/*Growing Without Schooling*
2380 Massachusetts Avenue
Suite 104
Cambridge, MA 02140-1226
617-864-3100
e-mail: info@HoltGWS.com
Internet: www.holtgws.com

Home Education Magazine

P.O. Box 1083
Tonasket, WA 98855
800-236-3278
509-486-1351
e-mail: HEM@home-ed-magazine.com
Internet: www.home-ed-magazine.com/

Homeschooling Today

P.O. Box 1608
Ft. Collins, CO 80522-1608
954-962-1930
e-mail: MMCAFF@aol.com
Internet: www.homeschooltoday.com/home.htm

The Moore Foundation

Box 1
Camas, WA 98607
800-891-5255
360-835-5500
e-mail: moorefnd@pacifier.com
Internet: www.moorefoundation.com

The Teaching Home

Box 20219
Portland OR 97294-0219
503-253-9633
e-mail: tth@TeachingHome.com
Internet: www.teachinghome.com/

MAINSTREAM EDUCATION PUBLICATIONS

Education Week/Teacher Magazine

6935 Arlington Road
Suite 100
Bethesda, MD 20814
800-728-2790 (*Education Week*)
e-mail: ew@epe.org
800-728-2753 (*Teacher Magazine*)
e-mail: tm@epe.org
Internet: www.edweek.org/edsearch.cfm

Educational Leadership

1703 N. Beauregard Street
Alexandria, VA 22311-1714
800-933-2723
e-mail: info@ascd.org
Internet: www.ascd.org/pubs/el/intro.html

Phi Delta Kappan
Phi Delta Kappa International
408 N. Union St.
P.O. Box 789
Bloomington, IN 47402-0789
800/766-1156
e-mail: headquarters@pdkintl.org
Internet: www.pdkintl.org/kappan/kappan.htm

PRINT ARTICLES ONLINE

Home Education Magazine

Older homeschoolers article list:

www.home-ed-magazine.com/INF/oh_index.html

Cohen, Cafi. "The Changing Face of College Admissions." *Home Education Magazine*, January–February 1998.

www.home-ed-magazine.com/INF/OH/oh_cc.clgadmin.html

Cohen, Cafi. "How Do We Know When We're Done?" *Home Education Magazine*, July–August 1998.

www.home-ed-magazine.com/HEM/HEM154.98/154.98_clmn_ok.html

Henry, Barb. "Helping Homeschoolers Go to College." *Home Education Magazine*, May–June 1999.

www.home-ed-magazine.com/HEM/163.00/mj_art_cllg.html

Kaseman, Larry and Susan. "Don't Let Credentials Get You Down." *Home Education Magazine*, March–April 1998.

www.home-ed-magazine.com/HEM/HEM152.98/152.98_clmn_tkch.html

Kaseman, Larry and Susan. "Responding to Requests from Officials for Our Homeschooling Records." *Home Education Magazine*, November–December 1998.

www.home-ed-magazine.com/HEM/HEM156.98/156.98_clmn_tch.html

Kaseman, Larry and Susan. "User Friendly Homeschooling Records." *Home Education Magazine*, September–October 1998.

www.home-ed-magazine.com/HEM/HEM155.98/155.98_clmn_tkch.html

McKee, Alison. "Fly-Fishing to College: The Value of Uniqueness vs. Orthodoxy." *Home Education Magazine*, March–April 1998.

www.home-ed-magazine.com/HEM/HEM152.98/152.98_art_fly.clg.html

Stevens, Earl Gary. "The Door is Open." *Home Education Magazine*, July–August 1997.

www.home-ed-magazine.com/INF/OH/oh_tal.opdr.html

Educational Leadership

McTighe, Jay. "What Happens Between Assessments?" *Educational Leadership*, V. 54 No. 4, December 1996.

www.ascd.org/pubs/el/dec96/mctighe.html

Meisels, Samuel J. "Using Work Sampling in Authentic Assessments." *Educational Leadership*, V. 54 No. 4, December 1996.

www.ascd.org/pubs/el/dec96/meisels.html

HOMESCHOOL/HIGH SCHOOL

GENERAL HOMESCHOOL INFORMATION WEBSITES

ERIC Overview and Resource List

www.accesseric.org:81/resources/parent/homesch.html

www.accesseric.org/resources/parent/hmoesc2.html

Homeschooling Unitarian Universalists, Humanists

www.dsport.com/jdowling/HUUHarchives.html

Karl Bunday's Website

http://learninfreedom.org/

Kidnews Homeschool Page

www.kidnews.com/Edusource2.html#part1

McGraw Hill

http://familyeducation.com/topic/front/0,1156,4-2618,00.html

COMPREHENSIVE HIGH SCHOOL HOMESCHOOL WEBSITES

A to Z Home's Cool

www.gomilpitas.com/homeschooling/index.html

Cafi Cohen's Homeschool-High School Website

www.concentric.net/~Ctcohen

Karl Bunday's Homeschool-High School Webpage

> http://leraninfreedom.org/colleges_4_hmsc.html

HIGH SCHOOL HOMESCHOOL MESSAGE BOARDS

Kaleidoscopes Message Board

> www.kaleidoscapes.com/colleges/

Independent Study High School Message Board

> www.paradise-web.com/plus/plus.mirage?who=jlg

VegSource Homeschool High School Message Board

> www.vegsource.com/wwwboard/hischool/wwwboard.html

SECONDARY EDUCATION FOR HOMESCHOOLERS

MODELS OF SCHOOLING

Coalition of Essential Schools

> www.essentialschools.org/
>
> www.essentialschools.org/aboutus/aboutus.html
>
> www.essentialschools.org/pubs/exhib_schdes/3pic.html

Core Knowledge

> www.coreknowledge.org/

DIPLOMA- AND CREDIT-GRANTING INSTITUTIONS

Note: These institutions are mentioned as samples of what is available. This list should not be construed as a recommendation or endorsement of any specific program.

List of Diploma-Granting Institutions

> www.concentric.net/~Ctcohen/diploma.htm

Individualized, Custom-Designed Learning Model

Alger Learning Center
121 Alder Drive
Sedro-Woolley, WA 98284
800-595-2630
e-mail: orion@nas.com
Internet: www.independent-learning.com/

Clonlara School and Compuhigh
1289 Jewett Street
Ann Arbor, MI 48104
734-769-4511
e-mail: clonlara@wash.k12.mi.us
Internet: www.clonlara.org/index78.html#anchor1679372
www.clonlara.org/index81.html#anchor3027882

Royal Academy (individualized, custom-designed learning model)
P.O. Box 1056
Gray, ME 04039
207-657-2800
e-mail: info@HomeEducator.com
Internet: www.homeeducator.com/HEFS/royalacademy.htm

Proficiency Documentation Model

North Atlantic Regional Schools
116 Third Avenue
Auburn, ME 04210
800-882-2828 Ext 16
e-mail: narsinfo@homeschoolassociates.com
Internet: www.homeschoolassociates.com/NARS/HSServices.mv

Correspondence Course Model

American School
2200 East 170th Street
Lansing, IL 60438
708-418-2800
e-mail: american@www.iit.edu
Internet: www.iit.edu/~american/

Keystone
School House Station
420 W. 5th Street
Bloomsburg, PA 17815-1564
800-255-4937
Internet: www.keystonehighschool.com/

Oakmeadow School(alternative curriculum)
P.O. Box 740
Putney, VT 05346
802-387-2021
e-mail: oms@oakmeadow.com
Internet: www.oakmeadow.com/

North Dakota Division of Independent Study (public)
1510 12th Avenue North
State University Station
P.O. Box 5036
Fargo, ND 58105-5036
701-231-6000
e-mail: ensrud@sendit.nodak.edu
Internet: www.dis.dpi.state.nd.us

University of Nebraska-Lincoln Independent Study High School (web-based courses available)
Division of Continuing Studies
P.O. Box 839100
Lincoln, NE 68583-9100
402-472-2175
e-mail: dcsreg@unl.edu or unldde@unl.edu
Internet: www.unl.edu/conted/disted/ishs.html
http://class.unl.edu/final_web/index.html

Switched-On Schoolhouse
300 North McKemy Avenue
Chandler, AZ 85226-2618
877-688-2652
e-mail: bola@switched-onschoolhouse.com
Internet: www.switched-onschoolhouse.com/bola/procedures_a.htm

Non-Diploma Model, Individual Courses (Correspondence and Web-Based)

Indiana University
Division of Extended Studies
Owen Hall
Bloomington, IN 47405
800-334-1011
e-mail: extend@indiana.edu
Internet: www.extend.indiana.edu/

University of Missouri
Center for Distance and Independent Study
136 Clark Hall
Columbia, MO 65211-4200
800-609-3727
e-mail: cdis@missouri.edu
Internet: http://cdis.missouri.edu/

University of Oklahoma
College of Continuing Education
1700 Asp Avenue
Norman, Oklahoma 73072-6400
800-942-5702
Internet: www.occe.ou.edu/isd/high_sch.html

Alternative Colleges

Charter Oak State College
(public, credit through portfolio review, Associate's and Bachelor's degrees)
55 Paul Manafort Drive
New Britain, CT 06053
860-832-3800
e-mail: info@mail.cosc.edu
Internet: www.cosc.edu/

Regents College
(private, virtual university, credits by exam, Associate's and Bachelor's degrees)
7 Columbia Circle
Albany, NY 12203-5159
888-647-2388
e-mail: rcinfo@regents.edu
Internet: http://regents.edu/
http://regents.edu/077.htm

Homeschoolers Accrediting Homeschoolers

Pennsylvania Homeschoolers Accrediting Agency

http://pahomeschoolers.com/diplorgs.html

http://home-school.com/Articles/HomeschoolDiplomas.html

http://pahomeschoolers.com/diplomas.html

http://pahomeschoolers.com/phaa.html

COLLEGE ADMISSIONS FOR HOMESCHOOLERS

COLLEGES ADMITTING HOMESCHOOLERS

Colleges Admitting Homeschoolers

http://learninfreedom.org/colleges_4_hmsc.html

Colleges' Homeschool Policies

www.eho.org/collrev.hrm

www/gomilpitas.com/homeschooling/extras/CollegeHSpages.htm

Homeschool-Friendly Colleges

http://rsts.net/college/index.html

www.homeschooltoday.com/college/default.htm

COLLEGE ADMISSIONS PROCEDURES

Cafi Cohen: *And What About College?* Chapter One

www.concentric.net/~ctcohen/chapter.htm

Cafi Cohen's Procedures Webpage

www.concentric.net/~ctcohen/policies.htm

College Board Homeschool Webpage

www.collegeboard.org/features/home/html/intro.html

Edsource: Stanford Admissions Office Interview

www.kidnews.com/Edusource2.html

Public College Admissions Issues

www.heir.org/borbrf01.htm

www.thedaily.washington.edu/archives/1996_Spring/May231996/
homeschool1052396.html

"So how do homeschoolers apply?" *Christian Science Monitor*

www.csmonitor.com/durable/1997/10/06/feat/learning.4.html

Study: American Association of Collegiate Registrars and Admissions Officers

www.aacrao.com/datadisp.htm#NE

HOMESCHOOLED STUDENTS' ESSAYS AND WEBSITES

Homeschoolers' College Essays

www.concentric.net/~Ctcohen/essays/htm

Homeschooler's Websites

www.gomilpitas.com/homeschooling/explore/teensites.htm

www.gomilpitas.com/hoemschooling/extras/CollegeStories.htm

www.cis.upenn.edu/%7ebrada/homeschooling.html

EDUCATIONAL RESEARCH

Education Index

www.educationindex.com/index/html

ERIC Database

http://ericir.syr.edu/Eric/

ERIC Digests

    http://www.ed.gov/databases/ERIC_Digests/index/

Ask ERIC

    http://ericir.syr.edu/About/

Michigan State University Educational Links Website

    www.lib.msu.edu/corby/education/index.htm

San Antonio College Educational Links Website

    www.accd.edu/SAC/LRC/susan/educatio.htm

State Government Links

    www.ehnr.state.nc.us/EHNR/files/usa.htm

Thomas B. Fordham Foundation

    www.edexcellence.net/surfing/surfing.htm

U.S. Department of Education

    http://search.ed.gov

Index

NOTES

NOTES

NOTES